Lessons and Recipes from the School of Contemporary Cooking

Lessons and Recipes
from the School of

Contemporary
Cooking

Sherri Zitron
with Charles G. Powell

Houghton Mifflin Company   Boston   1982

Library of Congress Cataloging in Publication Data

Zitron, Sherri.
  Lessons and recipes from the School of Contemporary Cooking.

  Includes index.
    1. Cookery, International.   I. Powell, Charles G.
II. School of Contemporary Cooking (New York, N.Y.)
III. Title.
TX725.A1Z54   641.5'14   81-13261
ISBN 0-395-31843-2   AACR2

Printed in the United States of America

V 10 9 8 7 6 5 4 3 2 1

Design / Edith Allard, Designworks

To our mothers, who gave us a love of cooking,
and our loved ones, who made it worthwhile.
S.Z. and C.P.

Contents

Introduction

In a family where I was the youngest of five children, and always the first one home from school, my regular job was to help my mother prepare the evening meal. With all of us and at least a friend or two, there were never fewer than eight for dinner. Each day, with what appeared to be the greatest of ease, my mother prepared (from scratch) an interesting variety of dishes. Somehow, everything always came together at the right moment and was presented attractively and on time.

When I once asked her how she managed to do this — as easily for company as for family — she replied, "If you like to eat, it's easy to cook." It was obvious to me then that I satisfied the condition of that adage. And I am sure that it was my early kitchen experience that led me to pursue a food-related career, especially the one of teaching others how to cook with pleasure and with ease.

For more than ten years, I have been giving classes at my School of Contemporary Cooking in New York City, and although food trends have changed through the years, the basic principles that I teach have not. These are: a menu properly balanced for tastes, colors, and textures; the simplification of tedious classic techniques; and the organization of activities to lessen last-minute tasks.

The first principle is easy, once you've learned self-control and understand that it isn't necessary to cook everything in your repertoire for one meal to impress your guests. Also, food preparation has become much less complicated with the advent of the electric mixer, the blender, and the food processor, and with the availability of restaurant-quality knives and cookware in retail stores.

But the proper organization of an entire menu is the area I stress most in my classes because I believe it to be the most important. Today, entertaining at home has taken on new dimensions in our way of living. But, ironically, while our interest in sophisticated foods has grown enormously, the availability of time to prepare these dishes is at a premium. Certainly, most of the students in my classes work full or part time or are otherwise involved in activities outside the home. What they ask me for are interesting recipes that incorporate new ideas in foods from many cuisines — but most of all they want to know how to produce a meal for company in the most efficient manner and the shortest possible time.

This book is a capsulation of my school. It is divided into twelve monthly chapters and contains a menu for each week of the year, designed to fit the seasons. For each menu I have tried to give as much procedural information as I would normally cover in a class period. The fact that the recipes look long does not mean that they necessarily will take long to prepare — often, quite the contrary. The instructions are lengthy and detailed because I've tried to anticipate and answer whatever questions may arise when you are in your kitchen preparing the dish.

After you have worked with a recipe several times and are confident of the result, try experimenting. You will notice that I suggest substitutes for various ingredients, but you may want to find your own. Use the recipe as a guideline and create a dish that is truly your own.

I believe cooking is an art form in which you, the creator, should feel free to express your own individual taste, style, and interpretation. I try to impart this message to my students, and since I consider anyone using this book to be one of my students, I pass it along to you.

Sherri Zitron

Editor's Note

This symbol, used throughout the book, indicates that a recipe may (or, in some cases, *should*) be prepared in advance up to the point at which the symbol appears. ◀

January

LESSON 1

Celeriac Rémoulade
Navarin of Lamb
Pears Poached in Red Wine

LESSON 2

Baked Clams Oreganata
Veal Shanks with Gremolata
Raspberry Tortoni

LESSON 3

Escargots in Mushroom Caps
Chicken in Tarragon Cream
Tarte Tatin

LESSON 4

Coquilles St. Jacques
Roast Duckling Montmorency
Wild Rice au Chinois
Chocolate Cream Roulade

LESSON 5

Chicken Livers Bourguignonne
Coulibiac of Salmon
Orange Bavarian Cream

2

1

Celeriac Rémoulade

Navarin of Lamb

Pears Poached in Red Wine

This French country menu works very well as a buffet, since the crunchy celeriac and the tender lamb chunks in rich sauce fit nicely onto a single plate, and there is no need to serve an additional salad.

Celeriac Rémoulade

2 large, 3 medium, or 4 small
  pieces celeriac
2 carrots (optional)
Juice of 1 lemon
2 large egg yolks
1 tablespoon Dijon mustard
2 tablespoons freshly squeezed
  lemon juice
A dash each of salt, white
  pepper, and cayenne pepper
1 cup oil (olive, safflower, corn,
  or vegetable oil, or a mixture of
  any of these)
2 tablespoons finely chopped
  fresh parsley
Boston lettuce leaves

Celeriac, also known as celery root or knob celery, has all the good taste of celery with none of the strings or the watery texture. Shredded, it is really a sort of French cole slaw, but with a much more delicate flavor. The *sauce rémoulade* is nothing more than a very mustardy homemade mayonnaise. It will keep for a week or two in the refrigerator. The celeriac will keep for several days if it is well coated with the dressing.

Peel the celeriac with a sharp knife, taking care to remove all the brown outer covering. Slice it crosswise into very thin slices. Then stack the slices and slice them lengthwise as thinly as you can, to create julienne strips. This can also be done in a food processor using the julienne, or thin-shredding, disk. If you use the carrots, slice or shred them in the same manner. Immediately after cutting the celeriac, add the juice of a lemon and combine; this keeps it from discoloring. Set aside while you make the *sauce rémoulade*.

  Put the egg yolks, mustard, 2 tablespoons lemon juice, salt, and peppers into the container of an electric blender or a food processor fitted with the steel blade. Blend for a few seconds and then begin adding the oil, a drop at a time, until the mixture starts to thicken. Increase the addition of the oil to a slow, steady stream until it is all incorporated. Never add the oil too fast, or the mixture will separate.

  When the *sauce rémoulade* is done, taste it for additional salt, peppers, lemon juice, or mustard. Be sure it is very spicy. Add it to the shredded vegetables and combine well. Add the chopped parsley and mix through. Chill for at least 1 hour.

  To serve, spoon portions of the shredded salad on Boston lettuce leaves. It may be garnished or served plain. An attractive presentation is a circle of thinly sliced halves of red onion around the shredded vegetables surrounded by a circle of well-drained shoestring beets; place cherry tomatoes and black olives next to the beets.

Navarin of Lamb

Every cuisine has a lamb stew, but only the French have a *navarin*. At the late lamented Le Pavillon in New York City, the *navarin* was presented in a *cocotte* with an arrangement of beautifully cut and turned vegetables. The secret of a *navarin* is the little bit of sugar, which, when cooked into a caramel, helps to darken and enrich the sauce.

Trim the meat of all fat and gristle and cut it into 1-inch cubes. Season well with salt and pepper. Dredge lightly in flour and shake off the excess.

Heat the oil and butter in a large, deep Dutch oven with a tight-fitting lid, or an oven-proof casserole. Add the meat and sauté until golden brown on all sides. If all of the meat does not fit in the pot at one time, dredge it as you need it, add oil and butter as you go, and sauté the meat in small batches until all has been cooked. Put all the pieces back in the pot, sprinkle the sugar over the meat, and stir well. Cook over high heat a few more minutes, until the sugar melts and begins to caramelize.

Put the tomatoes into boiling water for a minute or two, then drain and rinse with cold water. Gently cut out the stem of each one and slip off the skins. Chop the pulp and set it aside.

Preheat the oven to 350°. Add the stock, tomatoes, tomato paste, garlic, rosemary, thyme, bay leaves, and additional salt and pepper to the pot and mix well. Cover and put into the preheated oven. Braise for about 30 minutes.

Add the potatoes, turnips, and carrots. Cover the pot and continue to braise another 30 minutes. The dish can be made a day ahead up to this point.

Drop the pearl onions into boiling water and blanch for 3 minutes. Drain and gently cut off the root ends. Slip off the skins. Add the peeled onions to the pot. Cover and braise another 15 minutes.

Remove the bay leaves and discard. Scatter the peas and beans on top of the stew, but do not mix them in. Leave them on top, re-cover the pot, and braise an additional 15 minutes or until the peas and beans are tender.

4 pounds lamb stew meat (either boneless shoulder or neck meat on the bone)
Salt and black pepper to taste
1 cup flour
4 tablespoons olive oil
4 tablespoons butter
2 tablespoons sugar
3 ripe tomatoes, peeled and chopped (or 1 cup canned tomatoes, drained and chopped)
3 cups beef stock (homemade or canned)
2 tablespoons tomato paste
2 cloves garlic, minced or mashed
1 teaspoon dried rosemary
1 teaspoon dried thyme
2 bay leaves
20 small red-skinned new potatoes, peeled
6 medium-sized white turnips, peeled and cut into quarters
6 carrots, peeled and cut into 1-inch chunks
20 small white pearl onions
1 pound fresh peas, shelled (or 1 package frozen peas, defrosted)
1 pound fresh green beans, ends removed and cut into 1-inch pieces

Pears Poached in Red Wine

January is the perfect month for pears. Comice are the best for this recipe, but Anjou and Bosc also work well. Just remember to choose firm but ripe pears and start the recipe the day before, because overnight marinating in the wine mixture is just as important as the poaching, and gives the pears their beautiful claret color.

If you like, marinate the pears for several days. When ready to serve, you can add other fresh fruit, such as grapefruit, tangerine, or orange segments, or sliced bananas.

The *crème fraîche* recipe given here is your answer to the seldom seen and prohibitively expensive real article that's occasionally flown in from France. Sour cream is the secret.

1 teaspoon lemon juice
4 fresh pears
The rinds of 1 lemon and 1 orange removed in long strips
The juice from the lemon and orange
1 bottle red table wine
2 cups sugar
4 sticks cinnamon
6 whole cloves
6 cups cold water

Fill a large bowl with cold water and add the teaspoon of lemon juice. Peel the pears with a vegetable peeler, cut them in half lengthwise, and carefully scoop out the core and stem. As they are peeled and cored, drop them into the acidulated water to prevent them from darkening.

When all the pears have been prepared, put the lemon and orange juices, rind strips, wine, sugar, cinnamon sticks, cloves, and fresh cold water into a deep kettle. Bring this mixture to a rapid boil. Reduce the heat to simmer and gently drop the prepared pears into the wine syrup. Cover the pot, reduce the heat to very low, and poach the pears in the barely simmering liquid about 10 minutes or until they seem tender when stabbed with a toothpick. Do not overcook them; they should have some resistance.

Cool the pears in the pot and then refrigerate them. The longer the pears chill in the wine syrup, the better.

Crème Fraîche

1 cup heavy cream
2 teaspoons sugar
1 teaspoon vanilla extract
½ teaspoon ground cinnamon
1 cup sour cream

When ready to serve the pears, prepare the *crème fraîche*. Whip the heavy cream with the sugar, vanilla, and cinnamon until it is thick and stiff. Gently fold in the sour cream.

Put a pear half into a small dessert bowl. Spoon some of the wine syrup over the pear, place a dollop of the *crème fraîche* on top, and serve at once.

2

Baked Clams Oreganata

Veal Shanks with Gremolata

Raspberry Tortoni

This menu's entrée is the kind of veal dish — often called *osso buco* — you would be likely to get in a regional Italian restaurant that specializes in hearty peasant fare. The *gremolata* gives this recipe its authentic Milanese identity.

Baked Clams Oreganata

When you consider that there's more cheese, garlic, parsley, and basil in this dish than oregano, the name certainly speaks for the taste power of this characteristically Italian herb — a little goes a long way. If you use clams larger than littlenecks, you might want to chop them before topping with the bread-crumb mixture. That way you'll ensure tenderness.

48 littleneck clams on the half shell
½ cup chopped fresh parsley
2 tablespoons chopped fresh basil (or 1 tablespoon dried basil)
1 tablespoon dried oregano
½ cup freshly grated Parmesan cheese
3 cloves fresh garlic, well minced or mashed
Salt and freshly ground black pepper to taste
⅓ cup finely grated unseasoned bread crumbs
¼ cup olive oil

Ask your fishmonger for clams on the half shell. Most will do this for you while you wait. Be sure the clams are loosened from the bottom shell.

Mix all the remaining ingredients in a small bowl until the mixture is moist enough to hold together. If you need more oil, add another tablespoon. If the mixture is too oily, add another tablespoon of bread crumbs.

Place the clams on the half shell in one layer on a cooky sheet. Preheat the oven to 450°. Distribute the crumb mixture evenly over all the clams, but do not pack it down too tightly. Bake the clams in the preheated oven for about 15 minutes or until the top crumbs seem crisp and toasted. Serve at once with lemon wedges.

Veal Shanks with Gremolata

When you buy the meat, tell the butcher what you're making so he can saw the veal shanks for you. Because of the bone, you'd never be able to do it at home.

This dish improves with reheating, so make it two or three days ahead if you like — or make twice as much and freeze half. Keep the *gremolata* separate. It should be stirred in just before serving to retain its crisp, fresh flavor.

Season the pieces of veal with salt and pepper. Heat the butter and oil in a Dutch oven or an oven-proof casserole with a tight-fitting lid. Dredge the pieces of meat in the flour, shaking off the excess, and sauté them in the hot butter and oil. Turn each piece until it is golden brown on all sides. As the pieces of meat are done, remove them and set aside.

Add a bit more butter and oil to the pot if necessary, and stir in the diced carrots, onion, and celery. Gently sauté them until they are soft and golden, about 5 minutes. Stir in the garlic and spread this vegetable mixture evenly over the bottom of the pot. Place the pieces of meat on top of the vegetables, standing each piece upright so the marrow will not fall out.

Preheat the oven to 350°.

Drop the tomatoes into boiling water for 1 minute, then rinse with cold water. Gently cut out the stems and slip off the skins. Chop the pulp. Add the wine, stock, tomato pulp, tomato paste, and dried herbs to the pot. Cover it and bring the liquid to a boil on top of the stove. Transfer the pot to the preheated oven. Braise for 1½ to 2 hours or until the meat around the bone is very tender and the sauce has thickened slightly.

While the meat is braising, prepare the *gremolata*. Mix the grated lemon rind with the parsley, garlic, and anchovies to form a paste. Set aside.

Just before serving, place the pieces of meat on a large serving platter and stir the *gremolata* into the sauce in the pot. Mix well and spoon the sauce over the meat.

Serve with Risotto Milanese, page 87.

4 large veal shanks (about 2 pounds each), sawed into 2-inch pieces
Salt and pepper to taste
3 tablespoons butter
3 tablespoons olive oil
½ cup flour
2 carrots, finely diced
2 medium-sized onions, finely diced
2 stalks celery, finely diced
3 cloves garlic, minced or mashed
4 fresh, ripe tomatoes (or 1½ cups canned tomatoes, drained and chopped)
1 cup dry white wine
1 cup beef stock (homemade or canned)
2 tablespoons tomato paste
1 teaspoon dried rosemary
1 teaspoon dried basil
½ teaspoon dried thyme
Grated rind of 1 lemon
2 tablespoons finely chopped fresh parsley
1 clove garlic, minced or mashed
4 anchovy fillets, drained of oil and minced

Raspberry Tortoni

2 packages (10 ounces each)
  frozen raspberries
2 egg whites
2 cups heavy cream
½ cup sugar
6 *amaretti*

An imperious chef I once knew said, "I have seen frozen strawberries, but I haven't found a use for them yet." Well, thankfully, that doesn't go for frozen raspberries, because here is an extra-simple recipe for an extra-fancy dessert in which frozen raspberries are the star. Make sure you use the Italian macaroons, *amaretti*, not only for taste but because most others are too soft to crush.

Defrost the raspberries and drain them thoroughly in a fine sieve. Set the juice aside for future use (it is delicious in gelatin desserts or cold fruit punches). Purée the raspberry pulp in a food processor or blender, and then press the pulp through a fine sieve to remove the seeds. Set aside.

Put the egg whites in one bowl, the cream in another. Whip the cream until it is thick and stiff. Whip the egg whites until soft peaks form, gradually add the sugar, and continue beating until stiff and firm.

Put the cookies into a food processor or a blender and chop them until you have semifine crumbs. Or place the cookies in a paper bag and crush them with a rolling pin.

To assemble, fold the whipped cream, whipped egg whites, and cooky crumbs gently into the raspberry purée, combining well until the mixture is pale pink. Pile the mixture into a 3-quart soufflé dish or line twelve muffin tins with paper cups and spoon the mixture into them. Freeze until firm.

3

Escargots in Mushroom Caps

Chicken in Tarragon Cream

Tarte Tatin

For a family meal, you might want to use a whole chicken in this entrée, but boneless, skinless breasts of chicken make the dish fit for the most elegant dinner party, and there is no need to carve at the table.

Escargots, a by-product of the Burgundy vineyards, and an apple tart, baked upside-down and flipped, complete this very French menu.

Escargots in Mushroom Caps

By serving escargots in mushrooms, you don't have to give your guests a lesson on working those awkward reverse tweezers and poking around in shells. The compound butter used in this dish can be made in large quantities (freeze some of it), because it also goes very well with fresh steamed vegetables and broiled chicken, fish, or steak.

8 tablespoons salted butter, very soft
4 shallots, finely minced
2 cloves garlic, finely minced or mashed
2 tablespoons chopped fresh parsley
½ teaspoon salt
Freshly ground black pepper to taste
4 tablespoons finely grated unseasoned bread crumbs
24 medium-sized fresh white mushrooms
24 canned escargots

Combine 6 tablespoons of the butter with the shallots, garlic, parsley, salt, and pepper until you have a smooth paste.

Put the remaining 2 tablespoons of butter in a small skillet and heat until hot and foamy. Stir in the bread crumbs and sauté them over medium heat until golden brown. Set aside.

Drain off all the liquid from the escargots. Rinse them with cold water and pat dry with paper towels.

Snap the stems out of the mushrooms and wipe the caps clean with a damp paper towel. The stems may be saved to use in soups or stews.

Preheat the oven to 375°.

Place a small amount of the butter mixture in the bottom of each mushroom cap and top with an escargot. Distribute the remaining butter evenly over them and sprinkle bread crumbs on each one.

Place the stuffed mushrooms on a lightly buttered shallow baking dish. Bake them for about 20 minutes or until the butter is hot and bubbly and the crumbs are lightly toasted. Serve at once.

Chicken in Tarragon Cream

This is my version of the *poulet estragon* that was served at one of the most perfect meals I ever had, at the three-star L'Oustau de Baumanière in Les Baux de Provence. Though simple in its elements, their dish was served in a terra cotta crock sealed with pastry. In this easier recipe, *sans* pastry and crock, you'll still get all those wonderful heady aromas.

Heat the butter and oil in a deep saucepan and gently sauté the minced vegetables for about 5 minutes until they are soft and golden. Pour in the cognac and allow it to boil and reduce by half. Add the peppercorns, cloves, parsley, tarragon, tomato paste, chopped tomatoes, and wine. Bring this mixture to a rolling boil, cover, reduce the heat to simmer, and cook for about 20 minutes. While this mixture is simmering, prepare the chicken and mushrooms.

Cut each breast in half, forming sixteen *suprêmes* of chicken. Trim any excess fat and tendon or cartilage from each piece. Wipe the mushrooms clean with a damp paper towel, and slice the stems off flush with the caps. Thinly slice the mushrooms.

Heat 4 of the 6 tablespoons butter in a large skillet and gently sauté the pieces of chicken, over low heat, so they cook but do not color. They should remain very pale. As they are done, remove them from the skillet to a platter and set aside.

When all the chicken is done, add the remaining 2 tablespoons of butter to the skillet and gently sauté the sliced mushrooms until they are pale golden but not brown. Sprinkle the lemon juice over them to keep them white, and remove them with a slotted spoon to the platter with the chicken.

Take the vegetable sauce that has been cooking and carefully strain out the liquid, through a fine sieve, pressing with the back of a wooden spoon to extract all juices. Discard the solids. Return the juices to the saucepan and stir in the heavy cream. Bring to a boil. Mix the soft butter with the flour to form a soft paste called a *beurre manié*. While the sauce is gently boiling, whisk in small bits of the flour-butter paste and allow the sauce to continue to boil, whisking constantly, for another minute until it thickens. Return the chicken and mushrooms to the skillet and pour the sauce over them. Cover and heat through. If fresh tarragon is available, stir it through the sauce just before serving. Serve with steamed rice.

---

2 tablespoons butter
2 tablespoons olive oil
2 carrots, finely minced
1 medium-sized onion, finely minced
2 stalks celery, finely minced
6 shallots, finely minced
2 cloves garlic, minced or mashed
¼ cup cognac or Calvados
½ teaspoon whole black peppercorns
4 whole cloves
4 sprigs of fresh parsley
1 teaspoon dried tarragon
¼ cup tomato paste
4 ripe tomatoes, chopped
1 cup dry white wine
8 whole boneless and skinless breasts of chicken
1 pound fresh white mushrooms
6 tablespoons butter
1 tablespoon freshly squeezed lemon juice
1 cup heavy cream
2 tablespoons soft butter
2 tablespoons flour
1 tablespoon chopped fresh tarragon (optional)

Tarte Tatin

Here's the first appearance of pastry crust, which I hope will become an easy first step to a lot of delicious French tarts, American pies, and other pastry specialties that you'll find in future lessons.

In selecting apples for this recipe, look for kinds without red skins: Golden Delicious, Granny Smith, or Greening. They have more flavor and provide greater taste and texture contrasts. The caramelized top is classic, and the heavy cream whipped with apple brandy is almost gilding the lily, but what a combination! Flaky pastry, soft apples, a crunchy caramel top, and airy whipped cream.

¾ cup flour, sifted with ¼ teaspoon salt and 1 teaspoon sugar
4 tablespoons cold sweet butter, cut up into small bits
1 to 2 tablespoons ice water
1 cup sugar
½ cup water
2 tablespoons light Karo syrup
8 medium-sized green or yellow apples
Several tablespoons sweet butter
Several tablespoons sugar
1 teaspoon vanilla extract
1 cup heavy cream
1 tablespoon sugar
1 tablespoon Calvados

Put the flour-salt-sugar mixture into a bowl for the electric mixer and add the butter. Begin mixing on low speed until the mixture forms a granular consistency. Add the ice water slowly, and continue to mix until the dough forms a soft ball, adhering to the beaters and leaving the sides of the bowl clean. Gather the dough together and wrap it in wax paper. Chill for 30 minutes.

While the dough is chilling, put the sugar, water, and Karo syrup into a small heavy-duty saucepan and bring it to a boil over medium heat. Continue to cook until the mixture gets syrupy and turns amber. Pour this mixture into the bottom of a 9-inch heavy cake pan or copper dish and swirl it around to completely coat the bottom. Set it aside to cool.

Carefully peel, core, and thinly slice the apples. Melt several tablespoons of sweet butter in a large skillet and sauté the apples until they are slightly golden and soft. Don't overcook them; they should keep their shape and retain some texture. Sprinkle them with several tablespoons of sugar and continue to cook until the sugar carmelizes slightly. Sprinkle the vanilla over them and set them aside to cool. When they are cool enough to handle, spread them attractively in a spiral over the hardened caramel in the cake pan, mounding them slightly in the middle. Set aside.

Preheat the oven to 400°.

On a lightly floured pastry cloth or board, roll out the pastry to a size that fits just inside the pan, and gently transfer the pastry onto the top of the apples. Make sure the pastry is not sealed to the sides of the pan. You must allow steam to escape while the tart is baking.

Bake the tart for 1 hour or until the caramel syrup in the bottom of the pan is dark brown, thick, and sticky-looking. It shouldn't be too runny. You can check this by tipping the pan slightly to the side. If it needs more baking time, leave it in the oven another 10 to 15 minutes. If the top pastry crust is getting too brown, cover it lightly with aluminum foil, but do not seal the edges.

After removing the tart from the oven, let it cool to room temperature. Then invert it onto a serving platter and allow it to cool completely.

To glaze the top of the tart, cook another batch of the caramel, using half the amount this time — ½ cup sugar, ¼ cup water, and 1 tablespoon Karo syrup. When it has caramelized and is syrupy, use a pastry brush to brush it lightly over the top of the cooled tart. Glaze the top completely and cool again to room temperature. As the caramel cools, it will harden like candy.

Whip the heavy cream with the sugar and Calvados until it is soft but not too thick. Serve the tart cut into wedges and pass the cream on the side.

Coquilles St. Jacques

Roast Duckling Montmorency

Wild Rice au Chinois

Chocolate Cream Roulade

This menu is Parisian to the core. It's designed for an elegant dinner party. The roast duckling, with a sauce of Bing cherries, julienne of orange, piquant ginger marmalade, and port wine, is a far cry from the more usual sweet duck *à l'orange*. The recipe for wild rice given here goes equally well with other duck or poultry dishes.

Coquilles St. Jacques

Although bay scallops are called for, you can economize a bit by using sea scallops cut in quarters. Or you can use cut-up baby shrimp or any boneless fleshy white fish — but of course then you can't really call the dish Coquilles St. Jacques.

The sauce is a variation on hollandaise; the egg yolks make the tops puff as they expand under the browning Parmesan cheese.

Combine the scallops, parsley, bay leaves, salt, peppercorn-thyme bag, water, and wine in a medium-sized saucepan and bring to a boil on top of the stove. As soon as the liquid is boiling, cover and remove the pot from the heat. Allow it to stand for 2 minutes. Immediately drain off the liquid and reserve 1½ cups. Discard the parsley, bay leaves, and peppercorn-thyme bag. Let the scallops continue to drain while you make the sauce.

Strain the reserved scallop liquid through fine cheesecloth. Melt 2 tablespoons butter in a small saucepan and, when it is hot and foamy, whisk in the flour, stirring to form a *roux*. Pour in the reserved scallop liquid and whisk until the mixture comes to a boil and thickens and smooths. Cook for another minute, whisking constantly; then remove the pan from the heat and transfer the contents to a bowl. Using either an electric mixer or a whisk, add the remaining 5 tablespoons butter, a small bit at a time, beating well after each addition, until it is all incorporated. Beat in the egg yolks, one at a time, and add the lemon juice and cayenne. Taste the sauce for additional salt, pepper, or lemon juice. Set aside.

Wipe the mushroom caps clean with a damp paper towel and slice off the stems flush with the caps. Slice the mushrooms thinly. Heat the 2 tablespoons butter in a small skillet and gently sauté the mushroom slices for a few minutes, until they are pale golden but not too brown. Sprinkle a bit of fresh lemon juice over them to keep them white, and remove them from the skillet. Drain them through a fine sieve to remove excess liquid.

To prepare the coquilles, divide half the sauce evenly over the bottom of eight small scallop shells (available in cookware shops or departments). Combine the drained scallops

2 pounds fresh bay scallops
2 sprigs fresh parsley
2 bay leaves
1 teaspoon salt
½ teaspoon whole black peppercorns and ½ teaspoon dried thyme tied together in cheesecloth for easy removal
½ cup water
½ cup dry white wine
7 tablespoons butter
3 tablespoons flour
2 egg yolks
1 tablespoon freshly squeezed lemon juice
A dash of cayenne pepper
½ pound small white mushrooms
2 tablespoons butter
Freshly grated Parmesan cheese

and the mushrooms and place the mixture on top of the sauce in the shells. Divide the remaining sauce evenly over the scallops and sprinkle the tops with grated Parmesan cheese. At this point, the shells may be refrigerated for several hours or overnight. Bring them to room temperature before baking. ◄

To bake, preheat the oven to 450° and bake the shells on a cooky sheet for 15 minutes or until the tops are bubbly. Turn the oven to high-broil and slide them under the broiler for a minute or two to brown the tops. Serve at once.

Roast Duckling Montmorency

SERVES 8

Roasting the ducks in pieces saves you the trouble of carving at the table, but the best advantage is the chance to remove much of the fat before roasting. With the hot water below the roasting rack, the meat will remain moist and any remaining fat will not smoke or splatter in the oven.

2 ducklings, 4 to 5 pounds each, cut into quarters (the butcher will do this)
Salt and freshly ground black pepper to taste
1 navel orange
1 lemon
A 1-pound can of pitted black Bing cherries
2 tablespoons cornstarch or arrowroot
¼ cup dark brown sugar
¼ cup port wine
¼ cup ginger marmalade

Preheat the oven to 450°. Lay out the pieces of duck on a board and trim off all the excess fat you can see. Season each piece of duck with salt and pepper and place the pieces of duck, skin side down, on a rack fitted over a large, shallow roasting pan. Pour about ½ cup hot water into the bottom of the pan.

Roast the duck for 30 minutes. Turn the pieces over, and roast them another 30 minutes.

While the duck is roasting, prepare the sauce. Peel the skin from the orange and lemon in long strips, using a very sharp knife. Try to take just the zest, not the white pith. Lay the strips of peel flat on a board, and slice them into very thin julienne strips. Juice the orange and lemon and put the juice into a small saucepan. Add the julienne strips of peel.

Drain the cherries and set them aside, reserving the juice. Put the cornstarch into a small bowl and add 2 tablespoons of the drained cherry juice, stirring to form a smooth, thin paste. Put the cornstarch mixture and remaining cherry juice into the saucepan along with the brown sugar, port, and ginger marmalade. Bring this mixture to a boil and stir until the sauce is very thick and shiny. Remove from the heat and stir in the reserved cherries.

When the second 30 minutes of roasting are up, remove the pan from the oven and reduce the heat to 400°. Remove the pieces of duck from the rack and set them aside. Lift the rack from the pan and pour off all the fat that has accumulated in the bottom. Wipe out the pan with a paper towel and return the rack to the pan. Replace the pieces of duck on the rack, skin side down.

Spoon half the sauce over the pieces of duck, return the duck to the oven, and roast for another 30 minutes. Turn the pieces of duck skin side up, pour the remainder of the sauce over them, and roast for a final 30 minutes (2 hours roasting time in all).

Place the pieces of duck on a platter and spoon over them any excess sauce from the bottom of the roasting pan. Surround the duckling with wild rice.

Wild Rice au Chinois

SERVES 8

This is an elegant and traditional accompaniment to the rich, mahogany-colored pieces of duck.

Rinse the wild rice in a colander and drain. Put it into a medium-sized pot and add water to cover the top of the rice by 1 inch. Add a dash of salt and bring to a boil. Reduce the heat to simmer and cook for about 20 minutes, stirring occasionally, until all of the water has been absorbed by the rice. When the rice seems tender, remove it from the heat and pour it back into the colander to remove any water that may be at the bottom. Set aside.

While the rice is cooking, drain the water chestnuts and slice them into thin rounds. Mince the shallots. Wipe the mushrooms with a damp paper towel and slice off the stems flush with the caps. Thinly slice the mushrooms. Chop the parsley and set it aside.

Heat the butter in a large skillet and sauté the shallots, mushrooms, and water chestnuts for about 3 minutes or until golden brown. Stir in the drained rice and salt and pepper to taste. Mix well. If the rice seems too dry, add another tablespoon or two of butter. Heat through and stir in the chopped parsley.

8 ounces wild rice
An 8-ounce can of peeled water
  chestnuts
3 shallots
½ pound mushrooms
Several sprigs fresh parsley
4 tablespoons butter
Salt and pepper to taste

Chocolate Cream Roulade

6 eggs
10 tablespoons sugar
6 tablespoons unsweetened
  cocoa
2 teaspoons vanilla extract
1 teaspoon almond extract
1 teaspoon ground cinnamon
1 teaspoon ground star anise
2 cups heavy cream
4 tablespoons unsweetened
  cocoa
½ cup sugar
1 teaspoon vanilla extract
Shaved chocolate or finely
  chopped pistachio nuts

Do try to find the star anise; it's available in Oriental groceries and many specialty food shops. If you buy it whole, you can grind it yourself in a mortar, blender, or coffee grinder. Although you can make this cake roll without it, star anise does add an unusual and distinctive flavor.

Butter an 11-by-16-inch jelly-roll pan and line it with wax paper. Butter the wax paper and trim excess paper from the edges. Set aside.

Separate the eggs, putting the whites into one clean, dry bowl, the yolks into another. Beat the egg yolks with an electric mixer on high speed and gradually pour in the 10 tablespoons sugar. Continue to beat until the mixture is thick, creamy, vanilla-colored, and "spins a ribbon." Turn off the mixer and add the 6 tablespoons cocoa, vanilla and almond extracts, cinnamon, and star anise. Turn the machine on to low and mix in these ingredients. Set the mixture aside.

Preheat the oven to 350°.

Whip the egg whites on high speed until firm peaks form. Carefully fold the beaten egg whites into the cocoa mixture and combine until the egg whites are completely incorporated. Pour this mixture into the prepared pan, smoothing the top and spreading the batter evenly into the corners.

Bake the cake for 25 minutes or until the sides shrink away slightly from the pan and the top of the cake springs back when pressed lightly. Remove the cake from the oven and immediately loosen it from the sides of the pan all the way around, using the tip of a knife. Cover it with a slightly dampened kitchen or linen hand towel and invert the cake onto the towel. Peel off the wax paper and gently roll up the cake in the towel, rolling from the *wide* side. The moisture created by the damp towel on the warm cake allows the cake to roll without cracking. Set it aside to come to room temperature. This can be done early in the day.

While the cake is baking, put the heavy cream, 4 tablespoons cocoa, sugar, and vanilla into a bowl for the electric mixer. Put it, along with the beaters, in the refrigerator to chill.

To fill the cake, whip the heavy-cream mixture until it is

very thick and stiff. Unroll the cake from the towel. Put about ½ cup of the whipped-cream mixture into a pastry bag fitted with a rosette nozzle and set this aside. Spread the inside of the cake with half the remaining cream. Reroll the cake carefully and transfer it to a serving tray. Spread the remaining cream over the top and sides of the cake. Using the cream in the pastry bag, pipe out rosettes along the top of the cake. Sprinkle the top with shaved chocolate or chopped pistachio nuts and refrigerate the cake until serving. The cake can be filled and held in the refrigerator for several hours.

5

Chicken Livers Bourguignonne

Coulibiac of Salmon

Orange Bavarian Cream

Coulibiac of salmon is an ambitious undertaking, but it can be prepared in stages with the work spread over several days. Basically a hot fish pie, it is one of Russia's most elegant entrées.

Chicken Livers Bourguignonne

Sliced water chestnuts add texture to this dish and the hearty Burgundy gives it a distinctive flavor.

This chicken liver dish is versatile. Serve it for lunch with scrambled eggs or for supper on a bed of fresh buttered noodles. Be careful not to overcook chicken livers. They should be firm, but still pink inside.

Pat the livers dry with a paper towel and season them with salt and pepper. Put the livers in a colander fitted over a bowl and sprinkle the flour over them. Toss well, letting the excess flour fall through the colander.

Heat the butter in a skillet and sauté the livers, turning often, until they are golden brown on all sides. When they are firm but still pink in the middle, remove them from the skillet and set aside.

Add more butter to the skillet if necessary and sauté the mushrooms, water chestnuts, and shallots for a few minutes until pale golden. Return the livers to the skillet and stir in the Sauce Espagnole and the wine. Bring the mixture to a boil, reduce the heat, and simmer it for a few minutes to heat through.

Serve the livers in individual ramekins or on plates. Garnish with the chopped parsley.

2 pounds fresh chicken livers
Salt and pepper to taste
½ cup flour
4 tablespoons sweet butter
½ pound fresh mushrooms, thinly sliced
An 8-ounce can of peeled water chestnuts, drained and thinly sliced
4 shallots, finely minced
½ cup Sauce Espagnole (page 120)
¼ cup Burgundy wine
¼ cup chopped fresh parsley

Coulibiac of Salmon

The brioche dough in this recipe can be made a day ahead, or even well ahead and frozen. Making it in a food processor is a 5-minute exercise, followed by a 5-hour rising. The yeast-based brioche has been chosen over the more frequently used pie crust because of its rich and flaky texture, its browning qualities, and its slicing ease.

Brioche Dough

1 envelope active dry yeast
1 tablespoon sugar
¼ cup lukewarm milk (110°)
6 tablespoons soft sweet butter
2 large eggs
2 cups flour, sifted with ½
  teaspoon salt

Dissolve the yeast and sugar in the warm milk. Set aside in a warm place and allow the mixture to activate and bubble up until it doubles in size. This takes about 10 minutes. When the yeast has activated, put the butter and eggs in a food processor fitted with the steel blade and blend. Add the yeast mixture and blend a few seconds more. Add the sifted flour mixture and blend until the mixture forms a soft ball of dough and leaves the sides of the bowl clean. (This process also can be done in an electric mixer, or by hand.)

When the dough has been well formed, it should be slightly sticky but not sticking to your hand. Lightly butter a large bowl and roll the ball of dough around in the bowl to coat it with butter. Place the ball in the bowl and cut a small X in the top of the dough to allow for greater expansion. Cover the bowl with a towel and place it in a warm, draft-free place for at least 3 hours to allow the dough to rise and double in bulk. After this first rising, punch the dough down with your hands to remove air, re-form it into a ball, and place it back in the bowl. Cut another X in the top, and allow the dough to rise again for another 1½ to 2 hours. At this point, the dough can be punched down and wrapped tightly in a plastic bag. It can be refrigerated for several days or frozen for several months.

Poached Salmon

2 tablespoons sweet butter
1 carrot, sliced
1 stalk celery, sliced
1 onion, sliced
Several sprigs fresh parsley
2 bay leaves
1 teaspoon whole black
  peppercorns
1 teaspoon salt
2 cups dry white wine
6 cups cold water
Several pounds of fish
  trimmings, such as bones and
  heads
A 2-pound piece of fresh salmon

Melt the butter in a deep kettle or fish poacher and add the sliced vegetables and parsley. Stir the vegetables in the butter over medium heat for about 2 minutes to soften them. Then add the bay leaves, peppercorns, salt, wine, water, and fish trimmings. Cover the kettle and bring this mixture to a boil. Reduce the heat to simmer and allow it to cook for about 5 minutes.

Meanwhile, wrap the piece of salmon in cheesecloth. When the stock has simmered for 5 minutes, gently lower the piece of salmon into it, bring the liquid back to a boil, reduce the heat to very low, and cover the pot. Poach the salmon about 10 minutes (5 minutes per pound).

When the salmon is done, lift it out of the stock and set it on a rack over a pan to drain and cool. Strain the stock through fine cheesecloth, discard the solids, and set aside 2 cups stock. The remaining stock can be frozen in 1-cup containers for future use in fish soups and sauces.

Velouté de Poisson (Creamy Fish Sauce)

Melt the butter in a small saucepan and when it is hot and foamy, whisk in the flour, stirring to form a *roux*. Pour in the fish stock, whisking constantly to prevent lumping. Bring to a rolling boil and cook for a minute or two. Remove from the heat and stir a small amount of this hot sauce into the beaten egg yolks to warm them. Then return the egg yolk mixture to the remaining sauce and mix well. Stir in the lemon juice, salt, and cayenne.

2 tablespoons sweet butter
3 tablespoons flour
1 cup strained fish stock (see page 24)
2 egg yolks, lightly beaten
1 tablespoon fresh lemon juice
Salt and a dash of cayenne pepper to taste

Salmon and Rice Filling

Melt 2 tablespoons butter in a medium-sized skillet and sauté the mushrooms for a few minutes until they are golden but still firm. Transfer them to a large bowl and toss them with the salt, pepper, and lemon juice. Set aside.

Melt 4 tablespoons butter in the skillet and add the chopped onions. Sauté for a few minutes until golden and soft. Transfer to the bowl with the mushrooms.

Melt the remaining 2 tablespoons of butter in the skillet and add the rice, stirring to coat it well with the butter. Reduce the heat to very low, pour in the stock, cover the skillet, and cook for about 10 minutes or until the rice is tender and has absorbed all the liquid. If more stock is needed, add it and continue cooking until the rice is tender. Stir the cooked rice into the bowl with the mushrooms and onions. Add the dill and hard-boiled eggs and combine.

Unwrap the cooked salmon from its cheesecloth and flake the meat of the fish away from the skin and bones. Do this carefully to be sure to remove all bones. Add the flaked fish to the bowl with the other ingredients and discard the bones and skin.

Stir the *velouté de poisson* through the mixture to bind it. Set the mixture aside.

To assemble the *coulibiac* for baking, place the chilled ball of brioche dough on a lightly floured pastry board or cloth. Roll it out into a rectangle about 12 inches wide and 18 inches long. Trim off a 2-inch piece from one end and set it aside.

Lightly beat an egg with 1 tablespoon cold water. Brush this egg wash over the entire surface of the rectangle of dough. Spread the salmon filling down the center of the dough, mounding it high and leaving at least 4 inches of dough exposed on each long side and a 2-inch piece on each end. Pull one of the long sides up and over the loaf and then do

8 tablespoons sweet butter
½ pound fresh mushrooms, thinly sliced
Salt and pepper to taste
2 tablespoons fresh lemon juice
3 onions, finely chopped
½ cup raw rice
1 cup strained fish stock (see page 24)
½ cup chopped fresh dill
3 hard-boiled eggs, finely chopped
1 cup *velouté de poisson* (see above)

25

the same with the other side, pressing firmly so the dough sticks together and forms a seam down the center.

Brush the short ends with some of the egg wash and pull them up and over the loaf, pressing the dough together. Lightly butter a shallow cooky sheet and turn the loaf over onto the sheet, seam side down. Cut a small hole in the exact center of the loaf to allow steam to escape while the loaf is baking.

Using the reserved piece of dough, cut out decorative flowers, leaves, and stems and attach them to the top of the loaf, using the egg wash to hold them in place.

Preheat the oven to 400°.

Cut a long piece of aluminum foil to fit around the entire loaf and fold it in half. Butter one side and attach it around the loaf, buttered side in, affixing it with string. This acts as a collar while the loaf is baking and holds it firmly in place so the dough will not break. Brush the entire surface of the loaf with egg wash.

Bake the prepared loaf for 30 minutes, carefully remove the collar, and continue baking for another 10 minutes or until the loaf is golden brown all over. Remove it from the oven and allow it to stand for 10 minutes before slicing.

Orange Bavarian Cream

Despite the name, Bavarian creams are classic French molded desserts. The chopped glazed fruits called for in this recipe are a departure from tradition. They add color and texture and a bit more flavor.

Put the chopped glazed fruits in a small bowl and pour the Grand Marnier over them. Toss well and set aside to macerate.

Lightly oil an 8-cup metal mold and wipe out the excess with a paper towel. Chill the prepared mold.

Sprinkle the gelatin over the orange juice and let it soften. Separate the eggs and put the whites in a clean, dry bowl. Set them aside. Put the yolks in the top of a double boiler and stir in 1 cup of sugar and the cornstarch. Beat with a wire whisk until well mixed. Heat the milk in a small saucepan just to the boiling point; then stir it into the egg yolk mixture. Set the top of the double boiler over barely simmering water and cook the custard, stirring constantly, until it coats the back of a wooden spoon. Remove it from the heat and stir in the softened gelatin mixture. Keep stirring until the gelatin is dissolved; then transfer the mixture to a bowl. Cover it tightly with plastic wrap and chill until the mixture begins to thicken and mounds slightly when dropped from a spoon. This will take about 2 hours.

When the custard is chilled enough, beat the egg whites with 3 tablespoons of sugar and the salt until stiff and thick peaks form. Beat the heavy cream until thick and stiff. Gently fold both into the chilled custard. Drain the juice from the chopped glazed fruits and stir the fruit through the custard.

Pour the mixture into the prepared mold, smoothing the top. Chill for at least 6 hours, or overnight.

To serve, run a small knife around the edge of the mold. Dip the mold in hot water for about 20 seconds; then invert it onto a serving platter. Serve with Raspberry Sauce, page 127.

½ cup chopped mixed glazed
  fruits
2 tablespoons Grand Marnier
2 tablespoons unflavored gelatin
¼ cup fresh orange juice
8 eggs
1 cup sugar
1 tablespoon cornstarch
1½ cups milk
3 tablespoons sugar
A dash of salt
1 cup heavy cream

27

February

LESSON 6

Mushrooms Stuffed with Crab Meat
Turban of Sole with Nantua Sauce
Chocolate Delice

LESSON 7

Baked Oysters Vert
Chicken Pavillon
Coeur à la Crème

LESSON 8

Cold Eggplant Salad
Cornish Hens à la Diable
Black Forest Cake

LESSON 9

Vegetable Terrine
Carbonnade of Beef
Linzertorte

6

Mushrooms Stuffed with Crab Meat

Turban of Sole with Nantua Sauce

Chocolate Delice

This entire menu is a lesson in construction, because each recipe is created by layering or composing a variety of ingredients to create the structured appetizer, entrée, and dessert.

There are many do-ahead steps. The dessert can be done up to two days ahead and the sole dish can be assembled for baking and refrigerated the day before. Because the accompanying Nantua sauce is made independently, it can also be made a day ahead. The entrée would go well with a simple green vegetable and it is designed so that the center of the turban can be filled with white rice.

If you wish, serve the stuffed mushrooms as an hors d'oeuvre with cocktails and start the meal at the table with a tossed salad. Select small mushroom caps for eating out of hand.

Mushrooms Stuffed with Crab Meat

The Madeira in the sauce adds a touch of sweetness that heightens the flavor of the crab meat. It can also improve the taste of other shellfish, such as lobster or shrimp. As a matter of fact, either of these could be substituted for the crab meat in the recipe. Prepare the crab meat mixture and stuff the mushroom caps early in the day. Refrigerate until ready to bake.

32 large mushrooms
6 strips bacon
1 pound fresh or frozen crab
  meat
2 tablespoons butter
2 tablespoons flour
1 cup milk
Salt, white pepper, and a dash
  of nutmeg
4 tablespoons Madeira wine
1 heaping teaspoon Dijon
  mustard
3 tablespoons butter
¼ cup finely grated bread
  crumbs
1 clove garlic, mashed

Snap the stems out of the mushroom caps, trim the bottom of the stems, and chop the stems fine. Wipe the caps clean with a damp paper towel and set them aside. Dice the bacon. Pick the crab meat over carefully to remove any cartilage and chop it fine.

Heat a small skillet and add the diced bacon, sautéing it until crisp. Tip the skillet and drain off all but 2 tablespoons of the bacon fat. Add the crab meat and the chopped mushroom stems to the skillet and sauté for a minute or two. Set this mixture aside.

Melt the 2 tablespoons butter in a saucepan and when it is hot and foamy, whisk in the flour, stirring to form a *roux*. Add the milk and bring the mixture to a boil, whisking constantly to remove lumps. Stir in the salt, white pepper, nutmeg, and Madeira. Add the mustard, mix well, and cook a few minutes longer. Remove from heat and stir in the crab meat mixture. Set this aside to cool.

Melt the 3 tablespoons butter and stir in the bread crumbs and mashed garlic. Mix well. Fill the mushroom caps with the cooled crab meat mixture and sprinkle the crumb mixture evenly over the tops.

Place the stuffed mushroom caps on a shallow cooky sheet and bake them in a preheated 400° oven for about 20 minutes or until the mushroom caps are softened. Do not overcook them or they will collapse.

Turban of Sole with Nantua Sauce

Imagine the headdress that might be worn by the sultan of Baghdad and you will realize why this is called a turban.

Any ring mold — glass, pottery, or metal — will do to create this distinctive shape. When unmolding, do so over the sink so you can tip the serving platter slightly and pour off the excess juices. Then nap the turban with some of the Nantua sauce, fill the center with white rice, sprinkle with chopped parsley, and serve the remainder of the sauce separately.

Cut the salmon into small cubes and put them into a food processor fitted with the steel blade or into the jar of an electric blender. Purée the fish until smooth. Add the egg whites, one at a time, and then add the chilled cream, a tablespoon at a time, blending constantly until the cream has been completely incorporated. Add salt, peppers, and nutmeg to taste and transfer the purée to a small bowl. Cover tightly and refrigerate while you prepare the mold.

Select an 8-cup ring mold and butter it all over with the soft butter. Cut a ring of wax paper to fit over the top of the mold and butter it on one side. Set aside.

Lay out the slices of sole on a board with the skin side facing you. Sprinkle each slice with salt and white pepper. Place the slices in the mold, white side down, slightly overlapping, and press them down into the curve of the mold. Allow the ends of the fish to hang over the edge of the mold.

Preheat the oven to 375°.

Spoon and pack the chilled salmon mixture into the mold and lift the ends of sole up and over the salmon mixture, tucking them in to completely enclose the salmon. Place the wax paper, buttered side down, on top of the mold and cover it tightly with aluminum foil. (The dish may be prepared in advance up to this point. Refrigerate, and return to room temperature before proceeding.) Place the prepared mold in a larger pan filled with several inches of hot water.

Put the mold in its water bath into the oven. Bake it for 1 hour, remove it from the oven, and lift it out of the water bath. Remove the aluminum foil and wax paper and place a serving platter over the mold. Holding the mold and the platter over the sink, invert the mold onto the platter. Tip the platter slightly and allow the juices to run off.

1 pound fresh salmon, skinned and boned
2 egg whites
1 cup chilled heavy cream
Salt, white pepper, cayenne pepper, and a dash of nutmeg
2 tablespoons soft sweet butter
8 slices boneless fillet of sole
Salt and white pepper to taste

33

½ pound raw shrimp in the shell
3 tablespoons butter
4 shallots, finely minced
1 clove garlic, mashed
2 tablespoons cognac
¾ cup dry white wine
1 tablespoon tomato paste
4 tablespoons butter
4 tablespoons flour
2 cups Fish Stock (page 110)
1 cup heavy cream
Salt, white pepper, and a dash of cayenne pepper to taste

SERVES 8

5 egg whites
¼ teaspoon cream of tartar
¾ cup granulated sugar
1¾ cups confectioners' sugar
⅓ cup unsweetened Dutch cocoa

Nantua Sauce

Peel and devein the shrimp. Reserve the shells. Chop the shrimp and set them aside. Melt the 3 tablespoons butter in a saucepan and stir in the shrimp shells, shallots, and garlic. Sauté over medium heat for a few minutes until the shells turn bright pink. Pour in the cognac and allow the mixture to come to a boil; reduce the cognac to a bare glaze. Add the wine and tomato paste, reduce the heat to low, cover the pan, and cook for about 10 minutes.

Melt the 4 tablespoons butter in a small saucepan and when it is hot and foamy, whisk in the flour, stirring to form a *roux*. Pour in the Fish Stock, mix well, and allow the mixture to come to a rolling boil. Cook for a few minutes; then remove from heat.

Strain the shrimp-shell mixture through a fine sieve, pressing hard on the solids to extract all juices. Stir the sieved juices into the white sauce and add the heavy cream and seasonings. Bring the entire mixture to a boil over medium heat and stir in the chopped shrimp. Cook for another minute or two, remove from the heat, and serve. The sauce can be made a day ahead and reheated for serving.

Chocolate Delice

The best way to make this dessert symmetrical is to use the bottom of a 9-inch cake pan to mark the diameter of the meringues on wax paper before baking. Use two cake pans to mold the ice cream layers. Then, when layering the dessert, everything will be the same size and it will be easier to frost.

Select any two ice-cream flavors, but be sure they contrast in flavor and color to make for a more interesting combination when the dessert is sliced.

Put the egg whites in a clean, dry bowl for the electric mixer and begin to beat on high speed. Add the cream of tartar and continue to beat until they hold soft peaks. Gradually pour in the ¾ cup granulated sugar and continue beating until you have a stiff and shiny meringue.

Sift the confectioners' sugar and ⅓ cup cocoa together. With the mixer on low speed, slowly add the sifted mixture to the meringue. Beat until well mixed.

Preheat the oven to 275°.

Lightly butter three cooky sheets and line them with wax paper. Using a 9-inch cake pan as your guide, draw three circles on the wax paper. Divide the meringue mixture evenly over the three circles, and spread it to a thickness of about ¼ inch. Bake the sheets of meringue in the preheated oven for about 40 minutes or until they are dry and crisp to the touch.

Remove the cooky sheets from the oven and invert the meringues onto cake racks. Carefully peel off the wax paper and let the sheets of meringue cool and continue to dry and crisp. They can be baked as early as two days before serving, covered lightly with aluminum foil, and held at room temperature.

To make the ice-cream layers, line two 9-inch cake pans with plastic wrap. Soften two flavors of ice cream until they are malleable, then press each into the lined cake pans, smoothing and flattening them. Cover the tops of the ice-cream layers with more plastic wrap and return them to the freezer to resolidify. This step can also be done several days ahead.

To assemble the dessert, pour the heavy cream into a chilled bowl and beat until soft peaks form. Slowly add the cocoa and sugar and continue to beat until the mixture is thick and stiff.

Place a meringue layer on a serving platter. Pull off the covering of plastic wrap from one of the ice-cream layers and lift it out of the cake pan, using the plastic-wrap lining to lift it out easily. Turn the ice-cream layer over onto the meringue layer and peel off the plastic wrap. Place another layer of meringue on top of this and do the same thing with the other layer of ice cream. Place the third meringue layer on top and frost the entire top and sides with the whipped cream mixture. Swirl the whipped cream on the top decoratively and sprinkle shaved chocolate over all for garnish. Return to the freezer until ready to slice and serve.

It is advisable to remove the dessert from the freezer about 10 minutes before serving. This facilitates slicing.

2 quarts ice cream (two different flavors)
2 cups heavy cream
6 tablespoons unsweetened Dutch cocoa
½ cup granulated sugar
Shaved chocolate

7

Baked Oysters Vert

Chicken Pavillon

Coeur à la Crème

Although it is good for any occasion, this menu is a natural for a Valentine's Day dinner, what with the supposedly aphrodisiac quality of oysters, the romance of a champagne sauce for the delicate chicken breasts, and a heart-shaped *coeur à la crème*. For an intimate dinner for two, quarter each recipe.

The dessert must be prepared the day before and the oyster topping may be, leaving a quick assembly and bake for the appetizer and a 30-minute preparation for the entrée as the only cooking chores for the evening's meal.

Baked Oysters Vert

The watercress and Italian parsley in the spinach topping add new flavor nuances to a basic Oysters Rockefeller recipe. The topping holds well in the refrigerator for several days. On another occasion, use this topping to stuff mushroom caps.

Setting the oysters on a layer of coarse or kosher salt for baking serves two purposes. The uneven shells will not tip during baking and lose their juices, and the salt retains heat to help keep the oysters hot during service.

Have the fishmonger open the oysters for you. Spread them out on a shallow cooky sheet or roasting pan covered with a thick layer of coarse or kosher salt.

Pull off the thick stems from the spinach leaves and thoroughly wash the leaves in cold water. When they are free of sand, spread them on paper towels to drain. Cut off the thick stems of the watercress and chop the leaves. Chop the parsley leaves. When the spinach has dried slightly, chop the leaves fine. (Alternatively, the spinach, watercress, and parsley can be chopped together in a food processor fitted with the steel blade.)

Heat the butter in a small skillet and add the chopped greens, the shallots, and the garlic. Sauté over high heat about 2 minutes, until the liquid has evaporated and the mixture seems dry. Pour in the cream and allow it to come to a boil and reduce. Add the seasonings, Worcestershire sauce, Tabasco, and Pernod, and continue to cook over high heat until all the liquid is gone. Remove from the heat and stir in the combined grated cheeses and the bread crumbs. Mix well and allow to cool slightly.

Distribute the cooled green topping mixture evenly over the oysters and sprinkle additional grated Parmesan cheese over the tops. Preheat the oven to 450° and bake the oysters for about 20 minutes. Then slide them under a hot broiler for a minute or two to glaze the tops.

Serve at once with lemon wedges.

32 fresh oysters on the half shell
1 pound fresh spinach
1 bunch fresh watercress
1 cup parsley leaves, preferably the flat Italian variety
4 tablespoons sweet butter
6 shallots, finely minced
2 cloves garlic, mashed
¼ cup heavy cream
Salt, white pepper, and a dash of nutmeg to taste
1 teaspoon Worcestershire sauce
A dash of Tabasco
1 tablespoon Pernod
½ cup combined grated Swiss and Parmesan cheeses
2 tablespoons dried fine bread crumbs
Additional grated Parmesan cheese
Lemon wedges

37

Chicken Pavillon

The 1939 World's Fair brought classic French cooking to America. Henri Soulé, who managed the French Pavillon restaurant, stayed on to found Le Pavillon in New York City. Long after his death and the demise of the restaurant, the Pavillon remains a symbol of the ultimate in classic French cuisine. This is one of its many notable dishes.

Champagne is the ideal wine for this dinner. It goes with all three courses. However, if you only need the champagne for the sauce, buy a split, which will give you 1 cup for the recipe with a sip or two left over.

8 skinless and boneless whole breasts of chicken
Salt and white pepper to taste
1 ounce dried French morels
4 tablespoons sweet butter, or more if necessary
½ cup flour
6 shallots, finely minced
1 cup champagne
1 cup heavy cream

Cut each breast of chicken in half, giving you sixteen pieces in all. Season them lightly with salt and pepper and set aside.

Cover the dried mushrooms with hot water in a small bowl and let them soak and reconstitute for about 10 minutes. When they are soft, drain off the liquid and squeeze them. Cut the larger ones in half to achieve even pieces. Open the champagne bottle and set aside 1 cup.

Heat the butter in a large skillet that has a tight-fitting lid. Dredge the pieces of seasoned chicken in the flour and shake off the excess. Sauté the chicken in the hot butter, over medium heat, taking care not to get the pieces too brown. They should remain pale golden. As they are done, remove them from the skillet and set them aside. Add more butter to the skillet if needed and sauté the shallots and morels for about 2 minutes, stirring well. Pour in the champagne and bring the mixture to a rolling boil. Let it boil for a minute or two to burn off the alcohol. Pour in the cream and cook the mixture over high heat, uncovered, for about 5 minutes, until it reduces slightly and begins to thicken.

Return the chicken pieces to the skillet, spoon some of the sauce over them, cover the skillet, and cook over very low heat for about 20 minutes or until the chicken is quite tender.

Serve this dish with parslied white rice and a crisp green vegetable.

Coeur à la Crème

This custardy dessert is basically a sweetened combination of cottage cheese and cream cheese, bound with whipped cream. It is traditionally prepared in a heart-shaped mold with a sieved bottom to drain off the moisture of the cottage cheese. The heart is unmolded by inverting, so it is necessary to line the mold with damp cheesecloth to maintain the shape and facilitate removing the dessert from the mold. The cheesecloth makes an interesting woven pattern on the top of the unmolded cheese heart. (*Coeur à la crème* molds are available in specialty cookware shops and departments.)

In France, *fraises des bois* are served with this dessert. These wild strawberries are virtually unobtainable in America, but you can make do with fresh strawberries macerated in a currant-jelly-and-port-wine bath as described in the recipe. Or you can omit this step and serve plain berries in a basket.

1 pound cottage cheese
8 ounces cream cheese
½ cup confectioners' sugar
2 teaspoons vanilla extract
2 cups heavy cream
1 cup currant jelly
½ cup port wine
1 quart fresh strawberries

Put the cottage cheese and cream cheese in a bowl for the electric mixer or a food processor fitted with the steel blade and blend well to reduce the size of the cottage cheese curds. Add the sugar and vanilla and continue to beat until smooth. Remove to a large bowl. Whip the cream in a clean, chilled bowl until thick and stiff. Fold it into the cheese mixture.

Line an 8-cup heart-shaped mold that has a sieved bottom, or an 8-cup heart-shaped basket, with a piece of dampened cheesecloth large enough to fit inside the mold with an overhang. Pack the cheese mixture into the mold, pressing down to shape the cheese into the corners. Lift the overhanging cheesecloth up and over the mold, pressing down on it further. Put the prepared mold on a rack fitted over a shallow pan and refrigerate overnight. The extra moisture will drain through the cheesecloth and sieved bottom.

Several hours before serving, melt the currant jelly in a small saucepan until smooth. Stir in the port and mix well. Wash and hull most of the strawberries and put them into a bowl. (Reserve a few for the garnish.) Pour the wine mixture over them, combine, and chill.

To serve, lift the cheese heart out of the mold, using the cheesecloth to pull it up. Invert it onto a platter and pull the cheesecloth away. Garnish the heart with the reserved berries and serve it with a bowl of the macerated berries.

Cold Eggplant Salad

Cornish Hens à la Diable

Black Forest Cake

Cornish game hens are great examples of the popularization of gourmet food, yet they are simple to prepare, invariably roasted and served whole, and the diner gets to do the carving. This recipe allows for the stuffing to be made ahead and cooled, and the birds to be stuffed and marinated, ready for the oven, the day before. They will taste the better for it.

The first course combines chilled baked eggplant with a zesty fresh tomato sauce. Both, too, are day-ahead projects to allow for proper chilling time. The salad should be composed, however, just before serving.

The chocolate cake layers can be baked ahead, but they should be well wrapped in foil. Build the cake on the day of service with the chilled cherry filling, butter cream, and whipped cream frosting.

Cold Eggplant Salad

Baby eggplants, about 3 inches long, make the best appearance because they can be halved lengthwise for baking. Larger varieties are just as tasty, and if they are all you can find, slice them lengthwise in ovals about ½ inch thick.

The sauce is simple, a fresh tomato and herb blend, and needs fast, open cooking to evaporate the liquid. The result, in French culinary jargon, is a *coulis de tomates*. It freezes well and can be served with other cold cooked vegetables. (When cooking with fresh tomatoes in wintertime, it's advisable to purchase them a few days before you plan to use them; let them ripen at room temperature in a brown paper bag.)

This dish can become a serve-yourself cocktail spread for crackers or black bread; simply chop the baked eggplant and mix it with the sauce.

Preheat the oven to 400°. Trim the stem ends of the eggplants, but do not peel them. Cut small eggplants in half lengthwise or larger ones into ½-inch slices. Using the tip of a small paring knife, slash the flesh side of each slice; brush olive oil liberally over each one. The slashes allow the oil to penetrate the eggplant. Spread out the slices (flesh side up) on a shallow cooky sheet, in one layer. Do not stack the slices; use two cooky sheets if necessary. Bake the slices in the preheated oven for 20 to 30 minutes or until the slices are browned and the pulp is soft. Remove them from the oven, cool to room temperature, cover, and refrigerate for several hours or overnight.

Drop the tomatoes into a large pot of boiling water and leave them for a few minutes. Drain and run cold water over them to refresh. When they are cool enough to handle, cut the stems out with the tip of a small knife and gently slide off the skins. Chop the skinned tomatoes into fine dice and set aside.

Heat 2 tablespoons olive oil in a large skillet and sauté the onion and garlic for a few minutes until the onion softens and turns golden. Add the chopped tomatoes, oregano, and basil, stir, and allow the mixture to cook, uncovered, over medium heat, for about 20 minutes or until all the excess liquid has evaporated and the mixture cooks down to a thick sauce. Stir occasionally.

4 baby eggplants or 2 larger ones
1 cup olive oil
4 pounds very ripe fresh tomatoes
1 large onion, finely chopped
2 cloves garlic, mashed
1 teaspoon dried oregano
1 teaspoon dried basil
¼ cup capers
1 tablespoon chopped fresh parsley
Salt and freshly ground black pepper to taste

When the sauce is done, remove it from the heat and stir in the capers, parsley, salt, and pepper. Transfer it to a bowl, cover tightly, and chill for several hours or overnight.

To serve, lay a slice of chilled eggplant on a salad plate and spoon some chilled sauce over it. Garnish with additional chopped parsley and a lemon wedge.

Cornish Hens à la Diable

Though any — or even no — stuffing will do, the chicken livers add a pâté-like flavor and texture and the herbs permeate the birds from the stuffing inside and the marinade outside.

The mustard piquancy of the sauce is enhanced by green and pink peppercorns, and is in no way too overpowering for the game flavor of the roasted birds. Note the Sauce Espagnole required for the Diable sauce. It can be made several days ahead or even frozen, if desired. Or perhaps you already have some frozen and available.

SERVES 8

4 tablespoons butter
4 fresh chicken livers
4 shallots, finely minced
1 clove garlic, mashed
4 mushrooms, minced
¼ teaspoon each dried thyme, marjoram, basil, and rosemary
1 teaspoon chopped fresh parsley
Salt and freshly ground black pepper to taste
8 Cornish game hens, ready for stuffing
½ cup olive oil
¼ teaspoon each dried thyme, marjoram, basil, and rosemary
Salt and freshly ground black pepper to taste
¼ cup dry white wine
¼ cup dry red wine
¼ cup cognac
4 shallots, finely minced
2 cups Sauce Espagnole (page 120)

Melt 2 tablespoons of the butter in a skillet and sauté the chicken livers until they are firm but still pink inside. Remove them from the skillet and set aside to cool.

Add the remaining 2 tablespoons butter to the same skillet and sauté the shallots, garlic, mushrooms, dried herbs, parsley, salt, and pepper. Finely dice the cooled livers and add them to the skillet. Sauté this mixture for about 3 minutes, until well mixed. Remove it from the skillet and set aside to cool.

When the stuffing is cool enough to handle, stuff a small amount into each hen and close the hens with skewers or string. Put the hens in a deep glass or stainless steel bowl and pour in the combined oil, herbs, salt, and pepper. Turn the hens to coat them completely. Allow the hens to marinate for several hours or overnight.

To roast the hens, place them in a shallow roasting pan and spoon the marinade over them. Roast in a preheated 400° oven for 30 minutes; then turn them over gently and roast for another 30 minutes or until they are golden brown and crisp all over.

Remove the hens from the oven when they are done, turn off the oven, and transfer the hens to a serving platter. Put the hens in the turned-off oven to keep warm while you make the Diable sauce. Put the roasting pan across two burners on top of the stove and add the wines, cognac, and shallots. Cook over high heat, scraping the bottom of the roasting pan to incorporate all browned bits, and allow the mixture to come to a rolling boil to burn off the alcohol. Reduce the liquid by half. Add the Sauce Espagnole, crushed peppercorns, cayenne pepper, mustard, and cream. Cook a few minutes more, strain through a fine sieve, and pour into a sauceboat. A few whole green and pink peppercorns may be stirred through the finished and strained sauce, for garnish.

Serve the hens with a small amount of the sauce napped on the top and chopped parsley sprinkled over them. Be sure to remove the skewers or string before serving. Pass extra sauce in a separate sauceboat.

1 teaspoon green peppercorns, crushed
1 teaspoon pink peppercorns, crushed
A dash of cayenne pepper
1 heaping tablespoon Dijon mustard
2 tablespoons heavy cream
Chopped parsley (for garnish)

Black Forest Cake

This popular German dessert is typified by kirsch-flavored Bing cherries. You can make the chocolate cake layers and the cherry filling a day ahead, but the whipped cream frosting and the butter cream should be prepared just before you assemble the cake.

Butter two 9-inch cake pans and line each with wax paper. Butter the wax paper and set the pans aside.

Preheat the oven to 350°.

Cream the butter, sugar, eggs, and vanilla in an electric mixer until light and fluffy. Melt the unsweetened chocolate in the top of a double boiler and cool it slightly. Stir it into the butter mixture. Sift the flour, soda, and salt together and add it, alternately with the ice water, to the chocolate mixture, starting and ending with the dry ingredients. Mix well and pour the batter into the prepared pans. Bake in the preheated oven for 30 minutes or until the cake springs back lightly when you touch it. Let the cake cool in the pans for 5 minutes and then invert the layers onto racks, peel off the wax paper, and cool the layers completely.

Drain the cherries and reserve ¾ cup of the juice. Put the cherries into a small bowl and pour the kirsch over them. Put

⅔ cup sweet butter, softened to room temperature
1¾ cups sugar
2 eggs
1 teaspoon vanilla extract
2½ ounces unsweetened baking chocolate
2½ cups flour
1¼ teaspoons baking soda
½ teaspoon salt
1¼ cups ice water
A 1-pound can of pitted black Bing cherries
2 tablespoons kirsch
1½ tablespoons cornstarch
8 tablespoons sweet butter, softened to room temperature

2 cups sifted confectioners'
   sugar
2 egg yolks
1 teaspoon vanilla extract
2 cups heavy cream
2 tablespoons sugar
2 tablespoons kirsch
2 squares semisweet chocolate
Long curls of semisweet chocolate
Glazed red cherries (for garnish)
Crystallized mint leaves (for
   garnish)

the cornstarch into a small saucepan and add 1 tablespoon of the reserved juice to dilute it. Then add the remaining juice and the macerated cherries. Cook this mixture over low heat until it comes to a boil and thickens. Remove it from the heat, transfer to a small bowl, cover tightly with plastic wrap, and chill thoroughly.

When you are ready to assemble the cake, put the softened butter, confectioners' sugar, and egg yolks into a bowl for the electric mixer and beat thoroughly until light and fluffy. Add the vanilla, mix, and set aside.

Put the heavy cream into a chilled bowl for the electric mixer and beat it until soft peaks form. Add the sugar and kirsch and continue to beat until very thick and stiff. Transfer ½ cup of this cream to a pastry bag fitted with a rosette nozzle.

Grate the semisweet chocolate squares. Have the chocolate curls, the cherries, and the mint leaves ready.

Put one cake layer onto a serving platter and spread a ring of the butter cream about 1 inch wide around the outside edge of the cake. Fill the center of this ring with the chilled cherries. Place the second cake layer on top of this and frost the entire top and sides of the cake with the whipped cream. Pipe out a decorative border of whipped cream around the edges of the cake at the bottom and the top. Pipe out several rosettes of cream on the top. Gently pat the finely grated chocolate around the sides of the cake and scatter the long curls of chocolate over the top. Place a glazed cherry and mint leaf in the center of each rosette on top of the cake to resemble a flower. Refrigerate the cake until serving time.

LESSON

9

Vegetable Terrine

Carbonnade of Beef

Linzertorte

A *carbonnade* of beef is practically Belgium's national dish. It is similar to beef *bourguignon,* with beer taking the place of wine as the braising liquid. Since the *carbonnade* is cooked slowly and improves with reheating, it can be made several days in advance.

The Linzertorte should be baked the same day it is served. That way the crust will be properly crisp. A time-saving step, if needed, is to make the dough in advance and keep it chilled for up to three days, or frozen for a longer period.

The *carbonnade* makes a fine buffet dish, as does the vegetable terrine.

Vegetable Terrine

There is more than a little coincidence between the sweeping popularity of the food processor and the development of *nouvelle cuisine*. Julienne garnishes, vegetable purées as thickeners for sauces, airy textured mousses, and this terrine would all be difficult to prepare without the aid of a processor.

Instead of the tangy watercress sauce, you could substitute the piquant Sauce Andalouse, page 163.

½ pound very thin young green beans
1 pound fresh shelled peas or 1 package frozen peas
4 carrots
6 shallots, finely minced
2 tablespoons sweet butter
2 pounds cooked ham or raw boneless and skinless chicken breasts
The juice of 1 lemon
2 tablespoons Madeira wine
1 teaspoon salt
White pepper and a dash of cayenne pepper to taste
A dash of nutmeg
2 teaspoons tomato paste
2 egg whites
1 cup chilled heavy cream
1 small bunch fresh watercress
2 scallions, trimmed
Several sprigs of fresh dill
1 cup mayonnaise
½ cup sour cream

Snap the ends off the beans, shell the peas, peel the carrots, and cut them into sticks approximately the same length as the beans. Cook each vegetable in 1 inch of lightly salted boiling water for about 3 minutes, just to soften. Drain immediately and rinse each with cold water to refresh. Drain them and chill while making the mousse.

Sauté the minced shallots in the butter for 2 minutes until softened. Scrape them into a food processor fitted with the steel blade or into the jar of an electric blender. Cut the ham or chicken into small pieces and add them to the processor. Add the lemon juice, Madeira, salt, peppers, nutmeg, and tomato paste. Blend for a few seconds until the mixture is smooth. Add the egg whites, one at a time, continuing to blend. Add the chilled cream, beginning with a tablespoon at a time, blending constantly until all the cream has been incorporated. Transfer this mixture to a bowl, cover tightly, and chill for several hours.

Butter the bottom and sides of an 8-cup rectangular terrine mold. Or a bread pan will do. Cut a piece of wax paper to exactly fit the bottom of the mold and place it in the mold. Butter it. Cut a piece of wax paper to exactly fit over the inside top of the mold, butter it on one side, and put it aside.

To assemble the terrine, dry the beans, peas, and carrots with a paper towel. Spread a thin layer of the mousse over the bottom of the mold and place a layer of beans lengthwise over the mousse. Add another layer of mousse. Place the carrots over this in the same manner as the beans. Cover with another thin layer of the mousse. Scatter on the peas and spread the remaining mousse mixture over them. Press the buttered wax paper down over the top and cover the mold tightly with aluminum foil. Place it in a larger pan filled with several inches of hot water.

Preheat the oven to 325° and bake the terrine in its water bath for 1 hour or until it seems firm when pressed on the top. Remove it from the oven and lift it out of the water bath. Allow the terrine to cool to room temperature; then refrigerate it overnight or for several days.

To prepare the watercress sauce, trim the thick stems off the watercress and place the leaves into a food processor fitted with the steel blade or into the jar of an electric blender. Cut up the scallions and add them along with the dill, mayonnaise, and sour cream. Blend this combination until the greens are finely minced and the mixture is pale green.

Remove the aluminum foil and the top piece of wax paper from the terrine and run a knife around the sides to loosen it. Invert it onto a rectangular serving platter and scatter chopped fresh parsley over the top. If you wish, garnish the platter with sprigs of parsley and lemon wedges. Slice the mold and serve the watercress sauce in a sauceboat.

Carbonnade of Beef

SERVES 8

Economical cuts of meat, such as trimmed, boneless chuck or top round, are good choices for this recipe. These cuts have a hearty flavor and the long simmering tenderizes them.

The peeled orange garnish beautifies the dish for presentation. The orange zest adds the merest hint of flavor.

Trim the meat of fat and cut it into 1-inch cubes. Season with salt and pepper. Place the meat cubes in a colander over a bowl and sprinkle the flour over them. Toss the pieces, allowing the excess flour to fall away through the colander.

Heat the oil in a deep oven-proof casserole or Dutch oven with a tight-fitting lid. Sauté the pieces of meat in the hot oil, taking care not to overcrowd them, and remove each piece as it is done. Add the butter to the pot and stir in the onions and garlic. Sauté a few minutes until the onions are golden and soft. Pour in the cognac and bring the liquid to a rolling boil. Reduce it by half; then pour in the beer and stock. Return the meat to the pot and add the bouquet garni, vinegar, and brown sugar. Stir well, cover, and cook over low heat until the liquid comes to a boil.

While the *carbonnade* is cooking on top of the stove, pour hot water over the dried mushrooms and let them soften.

4 pounds boneless chuck or top round
Salt and freshly ground black pepper to taste
½ cup flour
½ cup vegetable oil
4 tablespoons butter
4 large onions, thinly sliced
4 cloves garlic, mashed
¼ cup cognac
2 cans (12 ounces each) light beer
1 cup beef stock (homemade or canned)
A bouquet garni consisting of 1 leek, 2 sprigs parsley, 2 bay leaves, 2 stalks celery, and

47

¼ teaspoon whole black
peppercorns tied together in
cheesecloth for easy removal
2 tablespoons red wine vinegar
2 tablespoons dark brown sugar
2 ounces dried Italian *porcini*
mushrooms (optional)
Fresh orange peel and chopped
parsley (for garnish)

SERVES 8

1½ cups flour
⅛ teaspoon ground cloves
¼ teaspoon ground cinnamon
½ cup sugar
1 cup finely ground whole
unblanched almonds
1 teaspoon grated lemon peel
2 hard-boiled egg yolks,
chopped
1 cup (2 sticks) sweet butter,
cut into small bits
2 egg yolks
1 teaspoon vanilla extract
2 cups thick raspberry preserves
1 egg
1 tablespoon cream
½ cup sifted confectioners'
sugar

Drain off the water and squeeze the liquid out of the mushrooms. Chop them and add to the pot.

Transfer the pot to a preheated 350° oven and braise the
carbonnade for about 2 hours or until the meat is fork-tender.
Remove the bouquet garni and discard it. Peel the rind from a
large navel orange in a long spiral if possible and curl it over
the top of the *carbonnade*. Sprinkle chopped parsley over all
and serve with buttered noodles.

Linzertorte

Most Austrian desserts that aren't served *mit Schlag* (with
whipped cream) often get a thorough confectioners'-sugar
dusting, like this Linzertorte.

The spices in the dough add a great flavor to the crunchy
crust and the raspberry jam makes it classic Linzer. The simple substitution of apricot preserves will give a different, but
equally delicious, result. If you like, serve the sliced torte with
a scoop of vanilla ice cream.

Sift the flour, cloves, cinnamon, and sugar together into a
bowl for the electric mixer. Add the almonds, lemon peel, and
chopped egg yolks. Add the bits of butter, the raw egg yolks,
and the vanilla. Mix until the dough forms a soft ball. Gather
the dough together, wrap it in wax paper, and chill at least 1
hour to firm it up.

Have ready a 9-inch cake or torte pan with a removable
bottom. Lightly butter the pan. Cut off a quarter of the ball of
dough and return it to the refrigerator. Put the remaining
dough in the center of a lightly floured pastry cloth and roll it
out to fit the bottom and sides of the pan. Fit the dough into
the pan, using your fingers to press it out to the edge and up
the sides of the pan to the top. Trim off excess dough.

Preheat the oven to 350°.

Spread the preserves evenly over the bottom of the lined
pan. Place the remaining piece of dough on the pastry cloth
and roll it out to a 10-inch square. Cut ten 1-inch-wide strips
from this dough. Arrange five of these strips vertically across
the jam in the bottom of the pan and trim excess dough.
Rotate the pan about one quarter turn away from you,
clockwise, and arrange the remaining five strips of dough

across the others, creating a crisscross or diamond-shaped pattern with the strips. Use a knife to loosen the dough that extends up the sides of the pan beyond the strips and fold this down to create a border around the inside of the pan. Press to seal.

Lightly beat the egg with the cream and brush this egg wash over the top strips and border of dough. Bake the torte in the preheated oven for 1 hour or until the top is very crisp and brown. Remove it from the oven and set the pan on a cake rack to cool completely.

To remove the torte from the pan after it is cool, run a knife between the crust and the sides of the pan. Place the pan on a coffee can and allow the sides to drop away. Slide a spatula between the bottom of the pan and the cake and gently lift it onto a serving platter. Dust the entire top with sifted confectioners' sugar before slicing and serving.

March

LESSON 10

Pasta Primavera
Rollatini of Veal
Florentine Tomatoes
Sacher Torte

LESSON 11

Asparagus Maltaise
Leg of Lamb au Bretagne
Fruit Compote

LESSON 12

Smoked Salmon Cornucopias
Chicken with Lemon Sauce
Coffee Charlotte

LESSON 13

Cheese Toasts with Anchovy Sauce
Shrimp Gratinée
Lime Chiffon Pie

LESSON 14

Orange and Fennel Salad
Cannelloni
Melon with Raspberry Cream

10

Pasta Primavera

Rollatini of Veal

Florentine Tomatoes

Sacher Torte

Only the pasta and its sauce require last-minute cooking, but you can prepare the ingredients for the sauce ahead of time. If you prefer to start the meal with a simple salad, the pasta is a good accompaniment to the veal.

Pasta Primavera

Although most of the vegetables in this recipe are now available year-round, the dish, as the name implies, is really an Italian springtime specialty. Be sure to time the sauce and the pasta, which should be served *al dente*, so they finish at the same moment. If you follow the directions carefully, the timing will work out just right.

Remember, the cutting and blanching of the four green vegetables can be done as much as a day ahead.

1 bunch broccoli
2 medium-sized zucchini
1 pound fresh asparagus
½ pound fresh green peas or 1 package frozen peas, defrosted
½ pound fresh white mushrooms
2 cloves garlic
4 fresh tomatoes
1 tablespoon chopped fresh basil or 1 teaspoon dried basil
1 tablespoon chopped fresh parsley
6 tablespoons sweet butter
2 cups heavy cream
4 tablespoons safflower oil
2 tablespoons tomato paste
Salt and freshly ground black pepper to taste
1 pound thin spaghetti
¼ cup grated Parmesan cheese
¼ cup pine nuts (optional)
Additional grated Parmesan cheese

Trim off the top florets from the broccoli. Cut them into small pieces. Cut the bottom third off each stem and discard. Slice the remaining stems on the diagonal, into about ¼-inch-thick slices. Trim the ends from the zucchini but do not peel them. Dice the zucchini. Cut off the bottom third of the asparagus stems and discard. Cut off the tips evenly and set them aside. Slice the remaining stems on the diagonal, about ¼ inch thick. Shell the peas. (If you use frozen peas, it isn't necessary to cook them.) Cook each prepared vegetable separately in an inch of salted water for about 2 minutes. As soon as each is done, drain and immediately refresh with cold water. Put all the vegetables into a colander to drain and cool.

When you are ready to begin the sauce, thinly slice the mushrooms, mash the garlic, cut the tomatoes into thin wedges, and chop the herbs. Begin heating water for the spaghetti. Put the butter in a small saucepan to melt and put the cream in another small pan to heat. Have all the ingredients for the sauce ready at the stove.

Heat 2 tablespoons of safflower oil in a large deep skillet and add the mushrooms. Sauté for a minute or two; then remove them from the skillet with a slotted spoon and put them into the colander with the green vegetables. Add the remaining 2 tablespoons of oil and stir in the garlic, tomatoes, herbs, and tomato paste. Add the salt and pepper and cook for a few minutes, stirring carefully so as not to break apart the tomato wedges. When this mixture is heated through, it will be time to add the spaghetti to its pot.

Cook the spaghetti 6 to 8 minutes for dry, 3 to 4 minutes for fresh. While the spaghetti is cooking, add the green vegetables and mushrooms to the skillet, pour in the hot cream, and add the grated Parmesan cheese. Allow the mixture to heat through.

The spaghetti will be ready at this time, so drain it, do not rinse, then return it to its pot and toss with the melted butter.

Serve the spaghetti with the hot sauce spooned over. Pass separate bowls of grated Parmesan cheese and pine nuts.

Rollatini of Veal

SERVES 8

2 tablespoons butter
3 shallots, finely minced
1 clove garlic, mashed
¼ pound sweet Italian sausage meat, crumbled
4 slices prosciutto, shredded
1 teaspoon dried rosemary
1 teaspoon dried basil
1 tablespoon chopped fresh parsley
½ ounce dried Italian *porcini* mushrooms
¼ cup chicken stock
½ cup finely grated bread crumbs
2 tablespoons grated Parmesan cheese
½ cup grated mozzarella cheese
2 egg yolks, lightly beaten
16 veal scallops, pounded thin
Salt and freshly ground black pepper to taste
4 tablespoons butter (approximately)
½ cup flour
½ cup dry white wine
2 cups Sauce Espagnole (page 120)

The rollatini shape is an interesting and extending way to treat veal scallops. The stuffing is a savory mixture, equally at home rolled inside a flattened chicken breast. The same cooking procedure applies.

If you are cooking ahead, make the stuffing, stuff and roll the scallops, sauté, and cover with sauce the day before. Refrigerate overnight and bring to room temperature before the 20-minute braising.

Heat the 2 tablespoons butter in a skillet and sauté the shallots, garlic, sausage meat, prosciutto, and herbs for a few minutes until the sausage cooks through. While the meat is sautéing, cover the dried mushrooms with hot water, soak them for a few minutes, then squeeze the liquid out and chop. Add them to the skillet along with the chicken stock and allow the mixture to come to a rolling boil. Reduce the liquid completely. Stir in the bread crumbs. Remove the pan from the heat and stir in the grated Parmesan and mozzarella cheeses and the egg yolks. Mix well to bind and create a stuffing consistency. Cool to room temperature, or refrigerate overnight, before stuffing the veal.

Lay out the pieces of veal on a board and sprinkle each lightly with salt and pepper. Place a spoonful of the cooled stuffing mixture at the bottom end of each scallop and roll up tightly, securing it with a toothpick. Try to encase the stuffing completely by folding the sides over as you roll. Set the rolls aside as you go.

To fry the meat, melt the 4 tablespoons butter in a skillet. Dredge each roll in the flour, shaking off the excess, and place the rolls side by side in the skillet, taking care that they do not touch. Sauté for a few minutes on one side, turn over gently, and sauté on the other side until pale golden. When all the rolls have been sautéed, pour the white wine and the Sauce Espagnole into the skillet and cover.

Over low heat, braise for 20 minutes or until the meat is fork-tender. (Or the braising can be done in an oven-proof casserole at a temperature of 350° for the same 20 minutes.)

To serve, place the rolls on a platter and pull out the toothpicks. Strain the pan juices through a sieve and serve with the meat.

Florentine Tomatoes

SERVES 8

These spinach-topped tomatoes are an attractive and tasty vegetable dish to serve with the veal rolls. Indeed, they are good with most meat entrées, and have a particular affinity for lamb.

½ pound fresh spinach
2 tablespoons olive oil
1 clove garlic, mashed
4 anchovy fillets, drained of oil and chopped
½ teaspoon dried basil
½ teaspoon dried oregano
½ teaspoon dried marjoram
½ teaspoon dried thyme
¼ cup pitted black olives, chopped
1 teaspoon capers
1 tablespoon chopped fresh parsley
¼ cup finely grated bread crumbs
¼ cup grated Parmesan cheese
8 medium-sized tomatoes

Wash and dry the spinach. Pull the thick stems off the leaves and chop the leaves fine. This should yield about ½ cup chopped spinach. (Or substitute one 7-ounce package of chopped frozen spinach, defrosted, with the juice squeezed out.) Heat the olive oil in a small skillet and sauté the spinach, garlic, anchovies, herbs, olives, capers, and parsley until slightly crisp, about 3 minutes. Stir in the bread crumbs and Parmesan cheese and mix well. Remove from the heat.

Preheat the oven to 400°.

Slice the tomatoes in half and lay them out on a cooky sheet. Distribute the spinach mixture evenly among the tomato halves, spreading it flat over the surface. Sprinkle a bit more grated Parmesan over the tops and bake the tomatoes for 15 to 20 minutes, until they are soft but not too mushy. (They will collapse if cooked too long.) If you like, you can run the tomatoes under a hot broiler for a minute just before serving to crisp the tops.

Sacher Torte

SERVES 8 TO 10

Chocolate cakes abound, but the Viennese have probably made the most of them, and made more of them than anyone else. This recipe is the signature dessert of Vienna's famed Sacher Hotel and it is true to form, even to service "mit Schlag"!

Lightly butter two 9-inch cake pans and line the bottoms with wax paper. Butter the wax paper and set the pans aside.

Combine the 3 ounces chocolate, ⅔ cup sugar, ½ cup milk, and one egg in a small saucepan. Mix well and cook over medium heat, stirring constantly, until the chocolate is melted and the mixture is smooth. Do not bring to a boil. Remove the pan from the heat as soon as the chocolate is completely melted. Set it aside to cool slightly.

Preheat the oven to 350°.

Put the stick of butter into a bowl for the electric mixer and beat until soft. Add the 1 cup sugar gradually and continue to beat until the mixture is light and fluffy. Add the vanilla and the two eggs and mix well. Sift the dry ingredients together and add them, alternately with the ⅔ cup milk, to the butter-and-egg mixture, starting and ending with dry ingredients. Mix well. Pour in the cooled chocolate mixture, mix again, and pour the batter into the prepared pans.

Bake in the preheated oven for 20 to 30 minutes or until the cake springs back lightly when you touch it. Remove it from the oven, allow it to sit in the pans for 5 minutes, and then invert it onto cake racks. Peel off the wax paper and allow the layers to cool completely.

To finish the cake, put the 6 ounces of chocolate and the ½ cup butter into the top of a double boiler. Melt over simmering water until smooth. Remove from heat and transfer the mixture to a bowl for the electric mixer. Beat in the confectioners' sugar, salt, vanilla, and enough boiling water to make a smooth and shiny glaze consistency.

Purée the apricot jam through a fine sieve into a small bowl and set aside. Cut each layer of cake horizontally into two layers, giving you four layers in all. Put a layer of cake onto a serving platter and spread it with one third of the apricot purée. Cover with some of the glaze. Place another layer on top and do the same thing. Add a third layer of cake, the remaining apricot purée, and more chocolate glaze in the same manner. Put the fourth layer in place on top and frost the entire top and sides of the cake with the remaining chocolate glaze, creating a smooth and shiny finish.

Whip the heavy cream with the sugar and vanilla until it is soft and thick. Serve a dollop of whipped cream on top of each slice of cake.

The cake tastes and slices best if it is chilled before serving.

3 ounces unsweetened baking chocolate
⅔ cup sugar
½ cup milk
1 egg
½ cup (1 stick) sweet butter
1 cup sugar
1 teaspoon vanilla extract
2 eggs
2 cups flour
1 teaspoon baking soda
¼ teaspoon salt
⅔ cup milk
6 ounces unsweetened baking chocolate
½ cup (1 stick) sweet butter
2 cups confectioners' sugar
A dash of salt
2 teaspoons vanilla extract
3 to 4 tablespoons boiling water
1 cup apricot jam
1 cup heavy cream
1 teaspoon sugar
1 tablespoon vanilla extract

11

Asparagus Maltaise

Leg of Lamb au Bretagne

Fruit Compote

Almost every province of France has its own hearty peasant-type fare. This roast leg of lamb, accompanied by a well-flavored bean casserole, is one of Brittany's best examples. The beans can be prepared over a two- or three-day period, thus splitting the work into manageable segments.

Asparagus Maltaise

Choose asparagus spears with equal diameters for even cooking. They can be cut short to eliminate strings, but peeling achieves the same result and a lot more asparagus, with long and beautiful stalks.

Cut off about 1 inch from the bottom of each asparagus spear and discard. Using a vegetable peeler, peel the remaining stalk, up to about 1 inch from the tip, removing its stringy outside covering. Put the peeled asparagus in cold water to soak and rid themselves of sand. Set them aside to drain after soaking.

Heat the butter in a small saucepan until it is hot and foamy. Transfer the butter to a glass measuring cup with a pouring spout. Put the egg yolks, lemon juice, and orange juice into the container of a blender or a food processor fitted with the steel blade. Blend for a few seconds. Add the salt and peppers and, while the machine is running, begin adding the hot butter, a drop at a time. As the mixture begins to thicken, increase the butter to a slow, steady stream, until it has all been incorporated. Don't add the butter too fast, or the mixture will separate. When all the butter has been added, transfer the mixture to a small glass or stainless steel bowl and stir in the orange rind to taste. If you have used an electric blender, leave the mixture in the blender jar. To keep the sauce warm until serving, place the bowl or glass jar into a larger container filled with hot water. Change the hot water periodically to hold the sauce at its proper consistency and temperature.

When ready to serve, place the asparagus in a pot with 1 inch of boiling salted water. Cover and steam for about 5 minutes, until tender but still firm. (A special asparagus steamer is ideal for this.) There should be six spears per person. Divide the asparagus among the serving plates and spoon a small amount of sauce over the center of the asparagus. Serve at once, with additional sauce passed on the side.

2 pounds or 48 spears fresh asparagus
1 cup (2 sticks) sweet butter
4 egg yolks
1 tablespoon fresh lemon juice
1 tablespoon fresh orange juice
¼ teaspoon salt
¼ teaspoon white pepper
A dash of cayenne pepper
Freshly grated orange rind

Leg of Lamb au Bretagne

Since the bean casserole in this recipe is prepared separately from the roast lamb, you could serve it another time with just a simple broiled lamb chop.

Bean Casserole

2 cups dried baby lima, navy, or Great Northern beans

1 large onion, studded with four whole cloves

A ¼-pound piece of bacon (optional)

1 large carrot, peeled and cut into chunks

½ teaspoon dried thyme

2 bay leaves

1 teaspoon salt

4 large onions

6 shallots

2 cloves garlic

4 tablespoons butter

2 Idaho potatoes

¼ teaspoon dried basil

½ teaspoon dried oregano

½ teaspoon dried thyme

Salt and freshly ground black pepper to taste

A 2-pound can of Italian plum tomatoes packed in tomato paste

½ cup beef stock (homemade or canned)

4 tablespoons butter

1 cup finely grated bread crumbs

2 tablespoons chopped fresh parsley

Put the beans in a deep bowl or kettle and cover them with cold water. Soak overnight to plump them. If possible, use French baby lima beans called *flageolets*. (These beans are available both dried and canned. Do not use the canned variety.)

The next day, drain off the water from the beans and return them to the kettle. Cover them with fresh cold water and add the clove-studded onion, the piece of bacon, and the carrot, thyme, and bay leaves. Stir in the salt, cover the pot, and bring it to a boil. Reduce the heat to simmer and cook the beans for about 1 hour or until they are tender but still firm. Remove them from the heat and lift out the bacon. Set it aside to cool. Discard the onion, the carrot pieces, and the bay leaves. Drain the beans and allow them to continue to drain in a colander.

When the bacon is cool, dice it into small cubes. Chop the onions and shallots, and mash the garlic. Melt 4 tablespoons butter in a skillet and sauté the cubes of bacon with the onions, shallots, and garlic for about 5 minutes or until the onions are golden and the bacon begins to crisp. Thinly slice the potatoes in their skins and add them to the skillet, along with the herbs, salt, pepper, tomatoes, and beef stock. Break up the tomatoes with the back of a spoon into smaller pieces. Bring this mixture to a boil and let it cook for about 15 minutes, until slightly thickened. Remove it from the heat and cool.

To assemble the casserole, spoon a small amount of the tomato mixture over the bottom of a 3-quart oven-proof casserole or Dutch oven. Spread a layer of beans over this, then more tomato mixture. Continue layering in this fashion until all of the beans and sauce are in the casserole. Bake in a 400° oven for 30 minutes, uncovered.

While the casserole is baking, melt 4 tablespoons butter in

a small skillet and toss the bread crumbs in the butter until they begin to toast and crisp. Stir the chopped parsley through the crumbs. After the casserole has baked for 30 minutes, spread the crumbs evenly over the entire top, creating a crust. Continue to bake another 15 to 20 minutes or until the crumbs are quite brown and crisp.

The casserole can be baked for the initial 30 minutes and refrigerated overnight. To finish, bring it to room temperature before proceeding with the crumbs and final baking.

Roast Leg of Lamb

Roll and tie the lamb so it keeps its shape while roasting. Season the leg of lamb well with salt and pepper. Spread the chopped vegetables and the herbs over the bottom of a shallow roasting pan and place the lamb on a rack over the vegetables. Combine the wine and stock and pour half of the mixture into the bottom of the pan.

Put the lamb into a preheated 400° oven and roast for 40 minutes, turning it once during this time and basting occasionally with the pan juices. After the first 40 minutes, add the remaining liquid and continue to roast another 40 minutes for rare, 50 minutes for medium, and 60 minutes for well-done. If the pan juices reduce, add a bit more wine and stock.

When the meat has reached the desired doneness, remove it from the oven and allow it to rest for about 10 minutes before slicing. Serve the sliced meat with the bean casserole. Strain the pan juices and pass separately.

Note: If you use a meat thermometer, it should be placed into the heaviest part of the meat. It should register 140° for rare, 155° for medium, and 175° for well-done.

A 5-pound boneless leg of lamb
Salt and freshly ground black
 pepper to taste
1 carrot, chopped
1 onion, chopped
1 stalk celery, chopped
¼ cup chopped fresh parsley
1 teaspoon dried rosemary
1 teaspoon dried thyme
1 cup dry white wine
1 cup chicken stock

Fruit Compote

The fruits selected for this compote are just that, a selection. Feel free to add, substitute, or eliminate, based on availability and preference. However, do try for a mix of dried, fresh, and canned. Then you will achieve a balance in texture and flavor. The last-minute additions of uncooked fresh fruit are a beautiful garnish that adds more flavor and zest.

½ pound dried prunes
½ cup port wine
4 ripe pears, peeled, cored, and cut into large pieces
2 ripe baking apples, peeled, cored, and cut into large pieces
A 1-pound can of apricot halves
A 1-pound can of pitted black Bing cherries
A 1-pound can of purple plums
1 lemon
½ cup brown sugar
3 cinnamon sticks
¼ teaspoon allspice
¼ teaspoon nutmeg
½ cup combined syrup from the canned fruits
1 large navel orange
1 large pink grapefruit
1 banana
2 tablespoons dark rum (optional)
½ pound fresh seedless green grapes (optional)
1 cup heavy cream
2 teaspoons confectioners' sugar
¼ teaspoon ground cinnamon
½ teaspoon vanilla extract
1 cup sour cream
A sprinkling of slivered almonds (for garnish)

Pour the port over the prunes and allow them to soak for about an hour until they plump. Drain and reserve the wine juices. Prepare the pears and apples and put them into a deep bowl. Add the prunes to the apples and pears. Drain all the canned fruits, reserving ½ cup of the combined syrup. Remove the stones from the plums and stir the fruits into the bowl.

Carefully remove the rind from the lemon in long strips. Stack these strips on a board and cut them into very thin julienne. Cut the lemon in half and juice it. Add the lemon rind and juice, brown sugar, spices, reserved port wine juices, and canned fruit syrup to the fruits in the bowl and mix well.

Turn the fruits into a 3-quart casserole or oven-proof bowl and bake in a 350° oven, uncovered, for 1 hour, until the fruit is quite soft. Cool to room temperature; then chill the compote overnight.

Before serving, peel and segment the orange and grapefruit. Slice the banana and soak the slices in the rum, if you wish. Cut the grapes in half. Whip the heavy cream in a chilled bowl with an electric mixer until soft peaks form. Then add the sugar, cinnamon, and vanilla and continue beating until thick and stiff. Fold in the sour cream by hand. Stir the orange, grapefruit, banana slices, and grapes through the chilled compote and serve it in glass bowls with a scattering of sliced nuts on top. Pass a sauceboat of the whipped cream mixture separately.

Smoked Salmon Cornucopias

Chicken with Lemon Sauce

Coffee Charlotte

Planning is needed for this menu because the gelatin dessert must chill and set overnight. The chicken also benefits from an extra day of marinating, and as a matter of fact, the cornucopias can be assembled a day ahead. This leaves only the quick chicken sauté and sauce finish for the last minute.

Smoked Salmon Cornucopias

Smoked salmon is an elegant dish whenever and however it is served. In this recipe, the addition of a compound butter incorporating tuna and lemon juice introduces a subtle new flavor to the lightly salted salmon.

The vegetable salad, with a variety of ingredients for color and crunch, is referred to as *à la Russe* in French cuisine. It makes an excellent accompaniment to any cold meat or fish entrée.

A 7-ounce can of tuna, drained
4 tablespoons soft sweet butter
1 tablespoon fresh lemon juice
Freshly ground black pepper to taste
8 slices Nova Scotia salmon
½ cup diced carrots
½ cup diced potatoes
½ cup diced white turnips
½ pound fresh peas, shelled
½ pound fresh green beans, diced
½ cup mayonnaise
2 scallions, finely chopped
2 shallots, finely chopped
1 teaspoon chopped fresh tarragon (optional)
1 tablespoon chopped fresh parsley
1 teaspoon snipped fresh chives (optional)
Salt and freshly ground black pepper to taste

Mash the tuna and mix it with the butter, lemon juice, and pepper until the texture is smooth. Lay out the slices of salmon on a board and make sure they are of the same length and width. Spread the tuna mixture evenly and thinly over the slices and roll them up, making cornucopias. Transfer the rolls to a platter and chill.

In a small covered pot, cook the diced carrots, potatoes, and turnips in an inch or two of boiling salted water for about 5 minutes or until tender when pierced with a fork. Drain and immediately run cold water over them. Drain again. Cook the peas and diced beans in another inch of boiling salted water for about 3 minutes. Drain and refresh. Put all the vegetables into a bowl and add the mayonnaise, scallions, shallots, herbs, salt, and pepper. Mix well. Cover and chill.

To present the dish, spread the chilled vegetable mixture into a flat circle on a round platter. Place the rolls of salmon on top of the vegetables like spokes of a wheel. Put an attractively carved lemon half in the center and garnish the platter with sprigs of parsley or watercress.

Chicken with Lemon Sauce

This recipe has more than a nodding acquaintance with the famous Chinese lemon chicken. Both start with marinated chicken and both have a sweet and sour lemon-flavored sauce, but there the recipes part company. In this version, the chicken is stir-fried instead of dipped in batter and deep-fried, and the sauce is garnished with raisins and toasted almonds.

The gin in the marinade is used for its sweetly perfumed juniper berry flavor, which offsets the salt in the soy sauce.

Cut each breast of chicken in half and then into long strips, about ½ inch wide. Mix the soy sauce, sesame oil, gin, and salt in a glass or metal bowl and add the chicken pieces. Toss to coat well, cover the bowl, and allow the chicken to marinate for several hours or overnight.

Spread the nuts out on a cooky sheet and put them in a preheated 350° oven. Toast the nuts for about 15 minutes or until golden brown. Remove them from the oven and set aside.

Put the sugar and vinegar into a saucepan. Dilute the cornstarch in a tablespoon or two of the chicken broth and add it and the remaining broth to the pot. Remove the rind from the lemons in long, thin strips and cut the strips into thin julienne. Juice the lemons. Add the rind and juice to the pot. Cook this over medium heat until the mixture comes to a boil and thickens. Stir in the lemon extract and raisins and cook a few minutes longer. Keep warm while the chicken is being prepared.

Heat the oil in a large skillet. Dip the pieces of chicken in the flour, shake off the excess, and drop them in the hot oil. Stir-fry the chicken pieces over high heat for about 5 minutes, until they become firm and brown on all sides. Remove the chicken from the skillet with a slotted spoon as it is finished, adding more chicken if all doesn't fit into the skillet in one batch. Place the finished chicken on a heated serving platter.

Serve the chicken with the sauce spooned over and the toasted nuts sprinkled on top. White rice and lightly steamed snow peas go well with this dish.

**8 boneless and skinless whole
  breasts of chicken**
¼ cup soy sauce
A few drops of sesame oil
2 tablespoons gin
A dash of salt
½ cup blanched whole almonds
1 cup sugar
½ cup distilled white vinegar
**2 cups chicken broth
  (homemade or canned)**
4 tablespoons cornstarch
2 lemons
1 teaspoon lemon extract
½ cup raisins
¼ cup safflower or peanut oil
½ cup flour

Coffee Charlotte

SERVES 8 TO 10

A charlotte is a molded, custardlike dessert encased in a cake crust. This recipe calls for an exterior lining of ladyfingers, which produces an attractive pattern on the top and sides of the dessert when it is unmolded. Because it is filled with a gelatin-based cream, it slices well.

16 ladyfingers, split in half
8 egg yolks
1 cup sugar
2 tablespoons instant powdered
  coffee, preferably espresso
2 cups milk
2 teaspoons vanilla extract
¼ cup cognac
2 tablespoons unflavored gelatin
¼ cup cold water
2 cups heavy cream
Shaved chocolate or
  chocolate-covered coffee beans
  (for garnish)

Special charlotte molds can be purchased. They have handles to help invert the dish. A springform will do nicely if you don't have a charlotte mold.

Line the sides of a 9-inch charlotte mold or springform with ladyfinger halves, flat sides facing in. Trim any pieces that extend above the top rim of the mold, so when inverted onto a serving platter the mold will be flat to the surface of the platter. Arrange a daisylike pattern of ladyfinger halves on the bottom of the mold, flat side up. Cut a small round of ladyfinger to fit in the center of the petals. Chill the prepared mold while you are cooking the filling.

Put the egg yolks, sugar, and coffee into the top of a double boiler and beat well with a hand-held mixer or wire whisk. Heat the milk in a small saucepan to scalding and slowly pour it into the beaten egg mixture, whisking constantly. Set this mixture over slowly simmering water and cook the custard, stirring constantly with a wooden spoon, until it thickens and coats the back of the spoon.

Remove it from the heat and stir in the vanilla and cognac. Let the custard cool slightly.

Sprinkle the gelatin over the cold water in a small glass bowl and put the bowl into a saucepan. Add 1 inch of water to the saucepan and bring it to a boil on top of the stove. Allow the gelatin mixture to dissolve, remove it from the pan, and set it aside to cool. Stir it into the cooled custard, transfer the custard to a small bowl, and cover tightly with plastic wrap. Chill this mixture until it begins to thicken and mounds slightly when dropped from a spoon.

Whip the heavy cream in a chilled bowl until it is thick. Fold it gently into the chilled custard and pour the mixture into the prepared mold. Chill for at least 6 hours or overnight.

To serve, run a knife around the sides of the mold to loosen. If you are using a springform, remove the sides and gently invert the mold onto a platter. If you are using a charlotte mold, invert it onto the platter and lift it off. In either case, the daisy pattern will now be on the top of the mold. Garnish the outline of the daisy with extra whipped cream piped through a pastry bag fitted with a rosette nozzle. Sprinkle shaved chocolate or chocolate-covered coffee beans over the top.

Cheese Toasts with Anchovy Sauce

Shrimp Gratinée

Lime Chiffon Pie

The cheese toasts and the shrimp are last-minute projects, but portions of each can be prepared ahead. The topping for the shrimp may be prepared as much as two days ahead, since it does not contain any seafood itself.

Cheese Toasts with Anchovy Sauce

Deep-frying food traps heat, thereby cooking the interior while the outside develops a crunchy, browned crust. This dish can be deep-fried in any kettle or deep skillet, as long as the cooking oil is at least 2 inches deep. The warm anchovy sauce is best passed separately, so anchovy lovers can be as generous as they like and those without the taste for anchovies can pass it by.

2 pounds mozzarella cheese
2 loaves unsliced firm white bread
Solid vegetable shortening or cooking oil (for deep-frying)
1 cup milk
4 eggs
2 cups flour
2 tablespoons olive oil
2 cloves garlic, mashed
A 2-ounce tin of anchovy fillets, drained of oil
1 cup dry white wine
½ cup Sauce Espagnole (page 120)
1 tablespoon tomato paste
1 tablespoon finely minced fresh parsley

Slice the mozzarella cheese about ½ inch thick and cut the slices into 2-inch rounds, using a cooky cutter. Slice the bread ½ inch thick, then into 2-inch rounds, again using the cooky cutter. Make sixteen sandwiches of the bread and cheese, pressing firmly so they adhere. The sandwiches may be wrapped tightly in plastic wrap (to prevent them from drying out) and refrigerated.

To fry, heat solid vegetable shortening or cooking oil in a pot or skillet to a depth of 2 to 3 inches. The fat should be at 375°. If you don't have an electric deep-fryer, use a deep-fry thermometer. Dip each sandwich in the milk to moisten. Beat the eggs in a bowl with a pinch of salt and a tablespoon or two of cold water. Dip the sandwiches in the flour, then in the egg, and then in the flour again, creating a thick coating. Drop them into the hot fat as they are dipped and ready. Allow the sandwiches to fry on one side until golden, about 3 minutes; then flip them over and fry on the other side until golden brown and crisp all over. Remove with a slotted spoon and drain on paper towels for a few minutes.

To prepare the anchovy sauce, heat the olive oil in a small saucepan and add the garlic. Cook for a minute or two. Mince the anchovies finely. Add them to the saucepan and stir. Pour in the wine and bring to a boil over high heat. Reduce the liquid to about ½ cup. Stir in the remaining ingredients and cook for about 5 minutes.

Serve two toasts to each guest and pass the hot anchovy sauce separately. Garnish the plates with sprigs of parsley, if you wish.

Shrimp Gratinée

To fantail shrimp, leave the last shell joint and tail on. As the shrimp cook, the tails will crisp, brown, and spread out like a fan. To butterfly shrimp, just imagine a butterfly with its wings spread, and you have the picture. Start cutting from the outside curve, deveining as you go, and cut to — but not through — the inside curve. Then pound the shrimp slightly to open and flatten them. The occasional miscut will be hidden by the topping.

Melt the 3 tablespoons butter in a skillet and sauté the onion, mushrooms, garlic, thyme, and tarragon for a few minutes until soft and golden. Stir in the sieved egg yolk and pour in the heavy cream. Let the cream come to a boil and cook down, thickening the mixture. Add the bread crumbs, mix, and remove from heat. Stir in the raw egg yolk and the chopped parsley. Mix well and set aside to cool. This mixture can be made ahead and refrigerated for several days.

▶ Shell, fantail, devein, and butterfly the shrimp. Flatten them slightly and set them side by side in a shallow gratin dish or put six shrimp in each of eight individual gratin dishes. Spread the cooled topping mixture evenly down the center of each shrimp and season with salt and pepper. Sprinkle the grated cheese on top and drizzle the melted butter over all.

Preheat the broiler to high and put the rack on the second level down from the broiler. This is so the shrimp tails won't burn as they firm up. Slide the prepared dish under the broiler and cook for about 5 minutes or until the shrimp are bright red and cooked through. Serve at once. Buttered carrots and crisp green beans or broccoli would be suitable vegetables to serve with this dish.

3 tablespoons butter
1 small onion, finely minced
¼ pound fresh mushrooms, finely minced
1 clove garlic, mashed
½ teaspoon dried thyme
½ teaspoon dried tarragon
1 hard-boiled egg yolk, sieved
½ cup heavy cream
½ cup finely grated bread crumbs
1 raw egg yolk
1 tablespoon chopped fresh parsley
48 large raw shrimp (scampi size, if available)
Salt and freshly ground black pepper to taste
¼ cup grated Parmesan cheese
3 tablespoons melted butter
Lemon wedges and parsley sprigs (for garnish)

Lime Chiffon Pie

1½ cups flour
1 teaspoon sugar
½ teaspoon salt
8 tablespoons cold sweet butter,
 cut into small bits
1 egg
2 teaspoons milk
2 medium-sized limes
1 tablespoon unflavored gelatin
½ cup sugar
A dash of salt
¼ cup cold water
4 eggs
½ cup sugar
1 cup heavy cream
1 cup shredded coconut
1 cup heavy cream
1 tablespoon sugar
1 teaspoon vanilla extract

This pie is made with a fully baked pie shell, a basic short crust recipe. Your favorite graham cracker crust could be substituted, eliminating the baking step completely.

The filling may also be served as a lime mousse garnished with fresh whipped cream and crisply toasted shredded coconut.

Sift the flour, sugar, and salt together and set aside. Put the butter, egg, and milk into a bowl for the electric mixer and blend. Add the dry ingredients and, using the lowest speed, mix until a soft ball of dough is formed that leaves the sides of the bowl clean. Gather the dough together and wrap it in wax paper. Chill for 30 minutes.

Preheat the oven to 400°.

Lightly flour a pastry cloth or board and put the ball of dough in the center. Roll it out to fit a 9-inch glass pie plate and transfer it to the plate. Fit the dough firmly to the bottom and sides of the pie plate, trim the edges, and flute attractively. Line the pie shell with wax paper and weight the paper down with dried beans, raw rice, or aluminum nuggets. Place the prepared shell in the preheated oven and bake for 10 minutes. Carefully lift off the paper and weights and continue to bake for another 5 minutes, until the crust is pale golden. Remove from the oven and cool completely.

To prepare the filling, squeeze the limes, measure out ½ cup of juice, and strain it. Put the gelatin, sugar, and salt into a small saucepan and stir in the cold water and lime juice. Separate the eggs, putting the whites in a clean, dry bowl. Lightly beat the egg yolks and stir them into the lime-juice mixture. Cook this over low heat, stirring constantly with a whisk, until the liquid reaches the boiling point and begins to thicken. Remove it immediately from the heat; do not allow it to come to a full boil. Transfer this mixture to a bowl, cover tightly with plastic wrap, and chill until it thickens and mounds slightly when dropped from a spoon.

Beat the egg whites until soft peaks form; then gradually add ½ cup sugar and continue to beat until you have a stiff and shiny meringue.

Beat 1 cup heavy cream until thick and stiff. Gently but

thoroughly fold the beaten egg whites and cream into the lime. mixture. Spoon this mixture into the baked pie shell, smoothing over the top. Chill at least 6 hours, or overnight, until set.

Spread the coconut over a cooky sheet and place in a preheated 350° oven. Toast for about 15 minutes, stirring occasionally with a fork, until the coconut is a crisp golden brown. Remove from the oven, cool, and put into a small serving bowl.

Whip the second cup of heavy cream with the sugar and vanilla until it is thick and stiff. Serve the pie cut into wedges with a dollop of whipped cream on top. Sprinkle with toasted coconut. If you like, garnish with very thin slices of fresh lime.

14

Orange and Fennel Salad

Cannelloni

Melon with Raspberry Cream

This menu's entrée substitutes light French crêpes for the pasta usually associated with the dish. Making the crêpes is an extra step, but they may be prepared well ahead and kept for several days in the refrigerator or frozen (stacked and interleaved with wax paper to prevent them from sticking together).

The Sauce Bolognese, Italy's basic and classic meat sauce, probably should be made in extra quantities because it has so many other uses, not the least of which is for saucing spaghetti. It freezes well, and can be kept that way for months.

Poaching the chicken to obtain the needed meat and 2 cups of stock leaves you with a delicious by-product, some 2 quarts of rich chicken stock. It, too, freezes well.

Orange and Fennel Salad

Fresh fennel is a celerylike vegetable with a light aniseed flavor. It is in season in spring and summer and most readily available in Italian markets. If you cannot find it, just increase the proportions of celery and endive correspondingly.

Trim the long slender stems and fernlike ends from the fennel bulb. Slice off the root. Thinly slice the fennel (this will yield about 1 cup). Put it into a salad bowl with the sliced celery and endive. Add the sliced onion.

Carefully peel off the skin and white pith from the oranges and segment them or slice thinly. Add to the salad bowl along with the olives.

Whisk together the oil, vinegar, mustard, salt, and pepper and toss the salad with this dressing just before serving. Garnish with chopped parsley.

1 fresh fennel bulb
4 stalks fresh celery, thinly sliced
2 heads Belgian endive, thinly sliced
1 small red onion, thinly sliced
2 navel oranges
1 cup pitted black olives, cut in half
6 tablespoons olive oil
2 tablespoons red wine vinegar or raspberry vinegar
1 teaspoon prepared Dijon mustard
½ teaspoon salt
Freshly ground black pepper to taste
1 tablespoon chopped fresh parsley

Cannelloni

This recipe makes twenty-four crêpes, enough for twelve average or eight extra-hearty eaters. Because each of the components can be made ahead, and frozen if desired, the recipe is easier than it looks.

Crêpes

Put all the ingredients into the container of an electric blender, or a food processor fitted with the steel blade, and blend for a few minutes until smooth. Chill the batter for 30 minutes.

Heat two 8-inch crêpe pans or skillets and rub them with butter. Pour a small amount of the batter into one of the pans

1 cup flour
A dash of salt
1 egg, plus 2 yolks
1½ cups milk
3 tablespoons melted sweet butter

and swirl to completely coat the bottom. Let this crêpe fry for a minute, loosen the edges with a fork, and flip it over into the second pan. Re-butter the first pan and add more batter. By this time the crêpe in the second pan is ready to turn out onto paper towels. Continue in this manner until the batter is used up. To simplify the buttering of the crêpe pans, use a stick of frozen butter, peeling the paper back as you go. When the crêpes are cool, they can be stacked and refrigerated for several days or frozen. Be sure to put pieces of wax paper between the crêpes before freezing. ◄

Sauce Bolognese

ABOUT 6 CUPS

1 pound ground beef-veal-pork combination
½ pound prosciutto
½ pound fresh mushrooms
¼ pound fresh sweet Italian sausage meat
1 carrot
1 onion
2 cloves garlic
1 ounce dried Italian *porcini* mushrooms (optional)
3 tablespoons olive oil
A 2-pound can of Italian plum tomatoes packed in tomato paste
A 2-pound can of tomato purée
4 tablespoons tomato paste
1 tablespoon dried oregano
1 tablespoon dried basil
1 teaspoon dried thyme
2 bay leaves
1 teaspoon salt
1 teaspoon sugar
Freshly ground black pepper to taste

Have the butcher grind and mix the meats for you. Chop or shred the prosciutto and mince the fresh mushrooms; set them aside. Remove the sausage meat from its casing and crumble the meat. Dice the carrot and onion finely and mash the garlic. Pour about 1 cup of hot water over the dried mushrooms and let them soak for 10 minutes or so to soften. Drain off the liquid, squeeze the mushrooms, then chop them fine.

Heat the olive oil in a deep kettle and add the meat, ham, mushrooms, sausage, carrot, onion, and garlic. Sauté over high heat, stirring and breaking up large chunks of meat with the back of a spoon, until the meat loses its raw color and cooks through. Add the tomatoes, putting them through a food mill or medium sieve to remove seeds. Add all the remaining ingredients, bring the mixture to a boil, reduce the heat to simmer, and cover the pot. Cook for 45 minutes to 1 hour, until the sauce is the consistency of a thick purée. Cool to room temperature. The sauce can be refrigerated for several days or frozen for several months. ◄

Poached Chicken Breasts

6 whole breasts of chicken on the bone
4 large carrots, peeled and cut into chunks
2 large onions, peeled and cut into chunks

Put all the ingredients into a deep soup kettle and bring the liquid to a slow boil. Cover the pot, leaving the cover slightly ajar so steam can escape, and cook over low heat for about 2 hours, or until the chicken and vegetables are fork-tender. Remove from heat. Remove the chicken from the stock and set the pieces in a colander to drain. Cool the stock to room temperature.

When the chicken is cool enough to handle, pull off the skin and discard. Pull the meat away from the bones and discard all bones. Set the meat aside. Strain the stock through a fine sieve and set aside about 2 cups for the recipe. The rest of the stock can be frozen for future use. Or serve it as a first-course soup with some of the cooked carrots and other vegetables, if you like.

2 stalks celery, cut into large pieces
2 parsnips, peeled and cut into chunks
2 leeks, well washed and chopped
Several sprigs of fresh parsley
Several sprigs of fresh dill
2 teaspoons salt
Freshly ground black pepper
3 quarts cold water, or enough to cover everything in the pot

Chicken-Spinach-Ricotta Mixture

Defrost the spinach and squeeze out the excess liquid. Put it into a bowl with the cheeses and salt and pepper. Grind the chicken in a food processor fitted with the steel blade. (You could use a meat grinder instead, or chop the chicken very fine by hand.) Add the chicken to the bowl, mix all the ingredients well, and set aside.

A 7-ounce package of chopped frozen spinach
1 pound ricotta cheese
1 cup grated Parmesan cheese
Salt and pepper to taste
The boned chicken breast meat (see above)

Cannelloni Sauce

Melt the butter in a saucepan until it is hot and foamy. Whisk in the flour, stirring to form a *roux*. Pour in the stock and bring the mixture to a boil. Season with salt and pepper and stir in the cheeses and milk or cream. Allow the mixture to cook and boil for a minute or two. Remove it from the heat and stir in the Sauce Bolognese. When this sauce is finished, stir 2 cups of it into the spinach-chicken-ricotta mixture to form the stuffing. Set the remaining sauce aside.

To assemble the dish for its final baking, fill each crêpe with some of the stuffing and roll it up firmly, enclosing the stuffing. Lay the filled crêpes side by side in a large shallow baking pan, seam side down. When all of the crêpes have been filled and placed in the pan, spoon the reserved Cannelloni Sauce over all and sprinkle the top with additional grated Parmesan cheese.

Bake in a preheated 350° oven for 40 to 45 minutes or until the top is quite brown and bubbly.

6 C U P S

4 tablespoons butter
4 tablespoons flour
1½ cups strained chicken stock (see above)
Salt and pepper to taste
1 cup grated Cheddar cheese
½ cup grated Parmesan cheese
½ cup milk or light cream
4 cups Sauce Bolognese (see page 74)

Melon with Raspberry Cream

1 cup milk
3 egg yolks
¼ cup sugar
¼ cup flour
1 tablespoon sweet butter
1 teaspoon vanilla extract
½ cup heavy cream
4 packages (10 ounces each)
  frozen raspberries
2 tablespoons superfine sugar
2 tablespoons fruit-flavored
  liqueur such as framboise,
  Grand Marnier, or kirsch
1 ripe honeydew melon
1 pint fresh strawberries
4 fresh kiwi fruit (optional)

The delicate pink raspberry sauce is particularly attractive with pale green honeydew melon, but it works well with any fresh fruit. To simplify the sauce and reduce calories, prepare the raspberry purée without adding the custard cream.

Heat the milk to scalding. Set aside. Put the egg yolks into a small saucepan and beat in the sugar and flour with a whisk or a hand-held mixer. Slowly pour in the hot milk. Set the pan over low heat on top of the stove and, whisking constantly, cook until the mixture comes just to the boiling point and thickens into a custard consistency. Remove it from the heat and stir in the butter and vanilla. Transfer the mixture to a small bowl, cover tightly with plastic wrap, and chill for several hours or overnight. When the custard is thoroughly chilled, whip the heavy cream and fold it in.

Defrost the raspberries and drain off all the juice. Purée the pulp and then press it through a sieve to remove the seeds. Sprinkle the superfine sugar over the purée and stir in the liqueur. Mix well and chill.

To serve, combine the raspberry purée with the custard sauce and mix well. Cut the melon in half lengthwise; remove the seeds and peel. Cut each half into thin, crescent-shaped slices and then cut each slice in half. Spoon a small amount of sauce onto a glass dessert plate and arrange the slices of melon over the sauce, pointed side out, like petals of a flower. Place a whole strawberry in the center. Peel and thinly slice the kiwi if you are using it, and interlace the slices of kiwi between the melon slices. Garnish with more strawberries, or pass them in a separate bowl. Pass additional sauce.

If you prefer, the melon, kiwi, and strawberries can be cut up and mixed in a bowl as a salad, and passed with a separate bowl of sauce.

April

LESSON 15

Seafood Quiche
Blanquette of Veal
Crêpes Suzette

LESSON 16

Stuffed Zucchini
Chicken Gismonda
Risotto Milanese
Baked Pears

LESSON 17

Artichokes with Tarragon Mayonnaise
Fillet of Sole Dugléré
Chestnut Cream Dacquoise

LESSON 18

Asparagus Vinaigrette
Stuffed Spring Leg of Lamb
Hot Chocolate Soufflé with Cold Vanilla Sauce

15

Seafood Quiche

Blanquette of Veal

Crêpes Suzette

This menu has great flexibility of preparation. Some parts can be done weeks ahead, others days ahead: The quiche can be fully baked and frozen, the blanquette can be partially cooked the day before, and the crêpes can be made and refrigerated for days or frozen for weeks.

Seafood Quiche

8 tablespoons butter, cut into
  small bits
3 ounces cream cheese, softened
  slightly
1¼ cups flour, sifted with ½
  teaspoon salt
4 tablespoons butter
4 shallots, finely minced
1 cup combined cooked seafood
  (such as shrimp, lobster, and
  crab)
Salt and a dash of white pepper
  to taste
2 tablespoons dry sherry or
  Madeira wine
4 eggs
2 cups heavy cream
1 teaspoon tomato paste
Salt, white pepper, and a dash
  of nutmeg to taste
2 tablespoons chopped fresh
  parsley
1 cup grated Swiss cheese
½ cup grated Parmesan cheese
An additional sprinkling of
  Parmesan cheese (for top)

Cream cheese mixed with butter makes for an extremely savory crust. For first-course or entrée crusts, use salted butter (for dessert crusts, use sweet butter). If the dough is too sticky, add more flour and mix longer; if it doesn't come together in a ball, add a bit more butter and mix. Don't forget to have the dough cold so it will roll out easily.

Put the butter and cream cheese into a bowl for the electric mixer and blend well. Add the flour and continue to mix on low speed until the mixture forms a soft dough. Gather the dough into a ball, wrap it in wax paper, and chill for 30 minutes. Roll it out on a lightly floured pastry cloth or board and fit it into a 10-inch quiche pan with a removable bottom. Trim the edges of the dough and line the pastry with wax paper. Weight the paper down with dried beans, raw rice, or aluminum nuggets. Trim extra wax paper from the sides and bake the prepared pastry in a preheated 400° oven for about 15 minutes. Remove the pan from the oven and carefully lift off the wax paper and weights. The crust is now ready for filling. Reduce the oven temperature to 375°.

Melt the 4 tablespoons of butter in a small skillet and gently sauté the shallots and the mixed seafood for 2 or 3 minutes. Season with salt and white pepper and pour in the sherry or Madeira. Cook for another minute or two until all the liquid is evaporated. Set aside to cool.

Mix the eggs, heavy cream, tomato paste, salt, white pepper, and nutmeg together in a bowl. Sprinkle the sautéed seafood, the parsley, and the Swiss and Parmesan cheeses over the bottom of the partially baked crust. Gently pour the egg-and-cream mixture into the crust and sprinkle the top with a bit of grated Parmesan. This helps to brown the top while baking.

Bake the quiche for 30 minutes or until the top is brown and puffy. When the quiche is done, remove it from the oven and serve immediately. Or cool it, wrap well, and freeze. To prepare the frozen quiche for serving, defrost to room temperature and reheat in a 350° oven for 15 minutes or until hot.

Blanquette of Veal

The French word *blanquette* refers to the fact that this veal dish has a pale, ivory-colored sauce. What makes it different is the dill, and lots of it, along with a julienne of carrot and leek and a light sautéing of the meat before it is braised. The basic recipe also works well with boneless pieces of chicken, but reduce the cooking time in the oven by 30 minutes.

Trim off all fat or gristle from the meat and cut it into even 1-inch cubes. Season with salt and pepper. Heat the butter in a heavy oven-proof kettle or Dutch oven with a tight-fitting lid. Add some of the meat to the hot butter and sauté lightly, making sure the meat does not become too brown. Sauté the meat in small batches, removing each batch as it is done.

Preheat the oven to 350°.

Add the garlic, shallots, mushrooms, and dill to the pot, with more butter if necessary. Sauté for about 5 minutes over low heat, once again taking care not to get anything too brown.

Return the meat to the pot and sprinkle the flour over all, stirring well to incorporate it and coat the meat evenly. Add the wine and enough stock to just cover the meat.

Bury the bundle of vegetables and herbs near the bottom of the pot, cover it, and bring the liquid to a rolling boil on top of the stove. Transfer the pot to the preheated oven and braise for 1 hour or until the meat is fork-tender. The dish can be prepared a day ahead up to this point.

While the meat is braising, drop the pearl onions into boiling water for 1 minute, drain, rinse with cold water, and slip off the skins. Cut off the root end and leave the pointed end intact.

Peel the carrots and cut them into julienne strips. Wash the leeks well in cold water to remove the sand, trim off the green part and the roots, and slice the white part into thin julienne strips. Heat the 2 tablespoons butter in a small skillet and gently sauté the carrot and leek strips for a few minutes until soft and golden.

About 15 minutes before the meat is done, stir in the pearl onions and half the sautéed leek-and-carrot mixture. Reserve the other half for garnish. Continue to braise the meat until tender.

5 pounds boneless shoulder of veal
Salt and pepper to taste
4 tablespoons butter
2 cloves garlic, mashed
6 shallots, finely minced
1 pound small button mushrooms (or larger ones cut in half)
2 tablespoons chopped fresh dill
½ cup flour
1 cup dry white wine
1 cup chicken stock (or enough to just cover the meat in the pot)
2 carrots, 2 ribs of celery, 2 sprigs of parsley, 1 bay leaf (tied together with a piece of string into a bundle for easy removal from the pot after braising)
24 small white pearl onions
3 carrots
3 leeks
2 tablespoons butter
½ cup heavy cream
2 teaspoons fresh lemon juice

When the meat is done, remove the pot from the oven and use a slotted spoon to transfer the meat and vegetables to a large serving casserole or tureen. Discard the bundle of carrot, celery, parsley, and bay leaf. Bring the liquid in the pot to a rolling boil on top of the stove and stir in the cream. Cook a few minutes longer, remove from heat, and stir in the lemon juice. Taste for additional salt and pepper.

Spoon the sauce over the meat and garnish with the remaining julienne of carrot and leek. Snip additional fresh dill over the top if you wish. The blanquette is best served with plain steamed white rice.

Crêpes Suzette

Every cuisine has its pancakes — be they blinis, *palacsinta*, or Mandarin pancakes — but the French have crêpes. They serve them for hors d'oeuvres, entrées, and desserts but hardly ever for breakfast. They have been filling them for centuries with a variety of foods from creamed chicken, lobster, and sweetbreads to real sweets, like jam, pastry cream, and liqueurs. This recipe, with Grand Marnier, orange and lemon juices, and sugar, is one of the most popular of all French desserts.

Since the crêpes arrive hot from the oven, they are easy to flame tableside — if you want to be very grand.

SERVES 8

1 cup flour
1 whole egg plus 2 yolks
A dash of salt
1½ cups milk
3 tablespoons melted sweet
  butter
1 tablespoon sugar
1 teaspoon vanilla extract
8 tablespoons (1 stick) sweet
  butter, frozen
¼ cup sugar
The grated rind of 1 large
  orange and 1 lemon
The juices from the orange and
  lemon
¼ cup Grand Marnier
8 tablespoons sweet butter

Put the flour, egg and yolks, salt, and milk into the container of an electric blender or food processor and blend for a few seconds. Add the melted butter, 1 tablespoon sugar, and vanilla and blend to mix well. Let this mixture rest for 30 minutes in the refrigerator.

To fry the crêpes, heat two 7- or 8-inch skillets until very hot and rub the first one with the stick of frozen butter. (This is an easy way to butter the pans as you work.) Pour a small amount of the batter into the skillet and immediately swirl it around to completely coat the bottom. Let this crêpe cook for a minute or two while you butter the other skillet. Loosen the crêpe around the edges and turn it over into the second skillet. Add butter to the first skillet, pour in more batter, and cook the next crêpe. By this time the crêpe in the other pan is ready to be removed. Slide it out onto a paper towel to cool, butter that skillet, and flip the other crêpe over into it. Butter

82

the first pan and continue this procedure until all of the batter is used up. You should get twenty-four crêpes. As they cool, they can be stacked.

To prepare the Suzette butter, put the ¼ cup sugar, orange and lemon rind and juice, Grand Marnier, and butter into a small pot and heat until the butter is bubbly.

Have ready a shallow gratin dish. Bruch each crêpe liberally with the melted butter mixture, fold it in half, brush again and fold it into a fan shape, and brush the entire outside of the folded crêpe. Place it on the dish and continue brushing and folding the crêpes. Arrange them slightly overlapping in the dish and pour any extra butter mixture over the top. At this point the dish can be refrigerated for several days until you are ready to bake it.

To bake, bring the crêpes to room temperature. Preheat the oven to 400°. Sprinkle powdered sugar over the top of the crêpes and bake them for 15 to 20 minutes or until the tops are crisp and bubbly. Bring the hot dish to the table and, if you like, pour about ¼ cup of warmed Grand Marnier over the crêpes. Ignite, and while the flame dies, serve the crêpes with the juices spooned over.

Note: The entire dish may be assembled and frozen or the crêpes alone can be frozen after frying. Be sure to put pieces of wax paper between each crêpe when stacking them for the freezer.

16

Stuffed Zucchini

Chicken Gismonda

Risotto Milanese

Baked Pears

This is a classic Italian menu that is balanced for color, texture, and preparation time.

The zucchini and the pears can be prepared for baking the day before. The chicken is best served soon after sautéing, but it can be breaded a day ahead. The bed of spinach, a Florentine touch, gets distinctive flavor from the addition of prosciutto and mushrooms.

The *amaretti* in the dessert recipe are the Italian macaroons that caught on in America about the same time amaretto liqueur became so popular. Both are based on almonds and both enhance the pears with this flavor. If you stuff the pears in advance, be sure to cover them tightly with plastic wrap while they are in the refrigerator to keep them from turning brown, but it is really best to stuff them just before baking.

Stuffed Zucchini

The only tricks here are to choose medium-sized zucchini, blanch them for a few minutes in boiling water to make the skin flexible, and scoop out the pulp carefully so as not to break the skins.

Try the dish without the tomato sauce sometime — just stuff the scooped-out shells, cut them into finger-food size, and serve them as a pickup hors d'oeuvre. But don't omit the sauce from your repertoire. It's the true, light Italian tomato sauce that's perfect for thin-cut pasta.

8 medium-sized zucchini
½ pound sweet Italian sausages
6 slices prosciutto
1 clove garlic
½ ounce dried Italian *porcini* mushrooms
4 tablespoons butter (approximately)
½ teaspoon dried rosemary
½ teaspoon dried basil
2 tablespoons chopped fresh parsley
¼ cup heavy cream
½ cup finely grated bread crumbs
½ cup freshly grated Parmesan cheese
Salt and freshly ground black pepper to taste
1 egg yolk, lightly beaten
2 cups fresh tomato sauce (see below)
Additional grated Parmesan cheese

Bring a large pot of salted water to a rolling boil and drop the zucchini in. Allow the water to return to the boil and blanch the zucchini for about 5 minutes, or until they are slightly soft and flexible. Drain immediately and run cold water over them. When they are cool enough to handle, cut off the ends, but do not peel. Slice the zucchini in half lengthwise. Gently scoop out the pulp from each half, leaving a shell about ¼ inch thick. Place the shells upside-down on paper towels to drain, and finely mince the scooped-out pulp. Put the pulp in a strainer and squeeze out the liquid. Set the minced pulp aside.

Remove the sausage meat from its casing and crumble or grind it finely. Shred the prosciutto and mash the garlic. Soak the dried mushrooms in warm water for about 5 minutes, squeeze the liquid out of them, and chop them fine.

Heat about 4 tablespoons of butter in a skillet until hot and foamy and add the sausage, prosciutto, garlic, and mushrooms. Sauté for about 5 minutes. Stir in the chopped zucchini pulp and the herbs. Cook for another 5 minutes. Stir in the heavy cream and allow the mixture to come to a boil and evaporate all liquid. Stir in the bread crumbs, cheese, salt, and pepper. As soon as it is well mixed, remove the mixture from the heat and transfer it to a small bowl. Stir in the egg yolk and mix well. Set aside to cool.

Stuff the zucchini shells with the cooled stuffing, mounding it slightly, and place the stuffed shells in a gratin dish. Spoon the tomato sauce over all, sprinkle the tops with grated Parmesan, and bake in a 400° oven about 20 minutes or until the tops are crisp and brown. Serve as a first course.

◄

5 pounds very ripe tomatoes
½ cup olive oil
1 large onion, finely minced
2 cloves garlic, mashed
1 tablespoon dried oregano
1 tablespoon dried basil
2 tablespoons chopped fresh
parsley
Salt and black pepper to taste
¼ cup drained capers (optional)

Tomato Sauce

Drop the tomatoes into boiling water for 1 minute, drain, and cool. Cut out each stem with the tip of a small knife and pull off the skins. Chop the tomatoes and drain them in a colander to remove the excess liquid.

Heat the olive oil in a deep skillet and sauté the onions and garlic for a few minutes, until golden but not too brown. Stir in the chopped, drained tomatoes and the herbs. Add the salt and pepper and cook over medium heat for 15 to 20 minutes or until the liquid evaporates and the mixture cooks down to a thick purée. Remove from heat and stir in the capers if you are using them.

This sauce freezes well and is delicious served over other sautéed vegetables or pasta.

SERVES 8

Chicken Gismonda

The breading procedure for the chicken is half the secret of this recipe. The spinach accompaniment is the other half. Although the French refer to the breading on the chicken as an *anglaise* covering, the Parmesan cheese in this version makes it Italian. For more flavor, you could add some dried basil and oregano to the crumb mixture. For best results when sautéing the chicken, be sure to chill the breaded pieces for several hours or a day ahead. This helps the crumbs to adhere to the meat while sautéing.

The chicken is sautéed in a combination of hot oil and butter so the heat can be more intense. This also aids in reducing oil absorbency. Turn the chicken pieces carefully while they brown, with tongs if you have them, so the crust won't break.

8 boneless and skinless whole
breasts of chicken
Salt and freshly ground black
pepper to taste
½ cup flour
6 eggs, lightly beaten with 2
tablespoons cold water
1 cup finely grated unseasoned
bread crumbs

Cut each chicken breast in half and season lightly with salt and pepper. Put the flour in one bowl, the egg mixture in another, and the crumbs and cheese mixed together in a third. Dip the pieces of chicken first in the flour, then in the egg, and then in the crumbs. Press the crumbs on with your fingertips. Lay the chicken pieces on a cooky sheet lined with wax paper. *Do not stack them*. Chill the prepared chicken for several hours or overnight.

Heat a few tablespoons each of the butter and oil in a large skillet. Sauté the prepared pieces of chicken in the hot fat until golden brown, turning carefully so as not to break the crust. Turn each piece often, and continue to sauté until the chicken is golden brown all over and cooked through, about 15 minutes in all.

To prepare the spinach, after it has been thoroughly washed and removed of thick stems, place the leaves in a deep kettle with a tight-fitting lid. Do not add any water; the water clinging to the leaves is sufficient. Cover the pot tightly and cook over very low heat for 5 minutes or until the spinach collapses. Remove it from the pot and drain thoroughly. When it is cool enough to handle, squeeze the spinach leaves to remove excess liquid. Then finely chop the spinach. This process can be done early in the day.

Just before the chicken is finished sautéing, melt 4 tablespoons of the butter in a separate skillet and sauté the minced shallots and shredded prosciutto for a few minutes. Add the remaining 4 tablespoons of butter and sauté the sliced mushrooms until soft and golden. Stir in the chopped spinach and season with salt, pepper, and nutmeg. Alternatively, the mushrooms can be sautéed separately and scattered over the top of the chicken for service.

To serve, place a large bed of spinach on a platter with the sautéed chicken pieces on top.

¼ cup freshly grated Parmesan cheese
4 tablespoons butter, or more if needed
4 tablespoons olive oil, or more if needed
2 pounds fresh spinach, well washed, with stems removed
8 tablespoons butter
4 shallots, finely minced
¼ cup prosciutto, shredded or chopped
1 pound fresh mushrooms, thinly sliced
Salt, freshly ground black pepper, and a dash of nutmeg
2 teaspoons fresh lemon juice

Risotto Milanese

SERVES 8

The principle of a risotto is to coat each grain of rice by sautéing the raw rice in butter before braising it in flavored stock. It is a creamy, moist dish, entirely different from American or Oriental rice.

Put the stock, wine, and saffron into a pot and heat to boiling. Let it stand off the heat for a few minutes to soften the saffron.

Melt the 8 tablespoons butter in a deep pot or skillet that has a tight-fitting lid. When it is hot and foamy, add the rice and stir it around in the hot butter until each kernel of rice is well coated. Pour in half the liquid, reduce the heat to very low, cover the pot, and let the rice absorb the liquid. Stir occasionally with a fork. After 15 minutes, add the remaining liquid and the salt and pepper, re-cover the pot, and continue cooking for another 10 to 15 minutes, until all the liquid

4 cups chicken stock (homemade or canned)
1 cup dry white wine
¼ teaspoon saffron threads
8 tablespoons butter
2 cups raw, long-grain, converted rice
Salt and pepper to taste
2 tablespoons butter
½ cup freshly grated Parmesan cheese

has been absorbed and the rice seems moist and creamy.

Immediately stir in the additional 2 tablespoons of butter and the cheese and mix through until the cheese melts. Serve at once.

Baked Pears

Look for ripe pears, preferably Bosc, Bartlett, or Comice. The filling has a brownielike texture after it is baked. The whipped cream topping provides still another texture.

SERVES 8

4 ripe pears
¼ cup sugar
The grated rind of 1 lemon
2 tablespoons unsweetened cocoa
¼ cup blanched almonds, finely chopped
4 *amaretti,* crushed into fine crumbs
1 egg yolk
1 tablespoon amaretto
2 tablespoons sweet butter
1 tablespoon sugar
1 cup heavy cream, whipped with 1 tablespoon sugar and 1 tablespoon amaretto

Peel the pears with a vegetable peeler and cut them in half lengthwise. Carefully remove the core and stem and drop the pear halves into a bowl of cold water containing a bit of lemon juice. This keeps them from darkening.

In a small bowl, combine the sugar, lemon rind, cocoa, almonds, cookie crumbs, and egg yolk. Add the amaretto to bind the mixture. Mix well.

Remove the pears from the water and wipe each dry with a paper towel. Place them on a lightly buttered glass baking dish. Distribute the filling equally among the cavities of the pear halves. Dot each top with butter and sprinkle the tablespoon of sugar over all.

Cover the dish lightly with aluminum foil and place it in a preheated 350° oven for about 15 minutes. Remove the foil and continue baking another 15 to 20 minutes or until a toothpick inserted into a pear moves easily. Remove from the oven and cool to room temperature.

Serve the pear halves with a dollop of the heavy cream whipped with the sugar and amaretto.

17

Artichokes with Tarragon Mayonnaise

Fillet of Sole Dugléré

Chestnut Cream Dacquoise

This menu includes several basic techniques of French cooking: making mayonnaise, oven-poaching fish, and baking meringues to create a cake.

The name Dugléré indicates the presence of mussels and tomatoes in the sauce for the sole. It is just one of a series of sauces for fish whose names depend on the garnish. They all start with the strained poaching liquid, and are thickened with a *roux* and enriched with heavy cream. Green grapes make it Véronique, shrimp make it Marguery, or, as in this case, mussels and tomatoes say Dugléré.

Artichokes with Tarragon Mayonnaise

8 medium-sized fresh artichokes
Half a lemon
The juice of 1 lemon
2 pounds fresh shrimp, cooked, peeled, and chilled
2 egg yolks
1 tablespoon Dijon mustard
A dash each of salt, white pepper, and cayenne pepper
1 tablespoon lemon juice
1 tablespoon tarragon-flavored vinegar
1½ cups oil (half olive oil and half safflower oil)
1 tablespoon finely minced shallots
1 tablespoon chopped fresh herbs (parsley, chives, tarragon)

Purists may say that cold artichokes should only be dressed with a vinaigrette, but this recipe should change their minds. Perhaps it's the tarragon or maybe the shrimp, but the flavor combination is super.

Slice off the top third of the artichokes and cut the stems flush with the bottoms. Immediately rub all cut surfaces with the lemon half to prevent them from darkening. Using a scissors, snip off all the remaining petal points.

Bring several inches of salted water to a boil in a large, wide kettle with a tight-fitting lid. Add the lemon juice. Fit the artichokes into the pot tightly and cover. Reduce the heat to simmer and cook the artichokes for 20 to 30 minutes or until a leaf pulls out easily.

When the artichokes are done, remove them from the kettle and turn them upside-down on a cooky sheet to drain. When they are cool enough to handle, gently separate the outer leaves from the small purple leaves toward the center. Using your fingertips, gently loosen and pull these center purple leaves out in one bunch and discard, thereby exposing the choke, or fuzz, near the bottom center of the artichoke. Scrape out all of this fuzz, using a grapefruit spoon or small knife. Be sure to remove it all. You now have a natural opening in the center of the artichoke, suitable for stuffing.

Reserve at least three whole shrimp for each artichoke you are serving, and chop the remaining shrimp. Set aside.

To make the mayonnaise, put the egg yolks, mustard, salt and peppers, lemon juice, and vinegar into the container of a food processor or an electric blender. Blend for a few seconds. Begin adding the oil, a drop at a time, keeping the machine running. As soon as the mixture begins to thicken, you can increase the oil to a slow, steady stream. Continue in this manner until all the oil has been incorporated and the mixture has become a soft mayonnaise.

Transfer the mayonnaise to a small bowl. Taste for additional seasonings or lemon juice. Stir in the shallots and herbs and mix well. Gently stir in the chopped shrimp.

To serve, fill each artichoke cavity with some of the mayonnaise mixture and drape the reserved whole shrimps over the edges of the artichoke leaves.

Fillet of Sole Dugléré

Poaching fish in wine under wax paper releases tasty juices that form the base of the sauce. You could use any other boned fillet, including flounder, brook trout, or striped bass, in place of the sole.

Begin by preparing the mussels. Discard any that are wide open or have broken shells. Scrub the mussels under running water with a stiff brush until they feel free of sand. Pull off the attached "beards." Soak the mussels for an hour in a bowl or basin of cold water with 1 tablespoon cornmeal. Rinse them. Place the clean mussels in a deep kettle and add about ½ cup white wine (or use water instead). Cover the pot tightly and bring to a boil. Steam the mussels for 5 to 10 minutes, until they are all wide open. Shake the pan occasionally. When they are done, pour them into a colander. When they are cool enough to handle, pull the mussels out of their shells and set them aside. Discard the shells.

Lay out the sole fillets on a board and trim off any skin or bones. Wash them and pat them dry with paper towels. Rinse and dry the shrimp. Be sure the fillets are facing you skinned side up. Lightly salt and pepper the fillets and place a whole shrimp in the center of each fillet, tail out. Fold the fillet in half to enclose the shrimp—with the tail extending out.

Preheat the oven to 350°.

Spread the 2 tablespoons of soft butter over the bottom of a shallow glass baking dish large enough to hold the fish. Sprinkle the chopped shallots over the butter and add the sprigs of parsley. Lay the prepared fish on top and pour in the stock or water and the wine. Butter a piece of wax paper cut to fit inside the dish and place it on top of the fish, buttered side down. Seal the dish completely with aluminum foil and place it over low heat on top of the stove. Bring the juices in the dish to a boil and then transfer the dish to the preheated oven.

Bake the fish for about 15 minutes or until it flakes easily with a fork. Remove the dish from the oven, lift off the foil and wax paper, and gently transfer the fish to a serving platter. Turn off the oven, cover the fish lightly with foil, and return the fish to the turned-off oven to keep warm while you make the sauce. Strain the pan juices and set aside 1 cup.

While the fish is baking, melt 2 tablespoons of butter in

2 pounds fresh mussels
1 tablespoon cornmeal
½ cup dry white wine (optional)
8 slices fillet of sole
8 raw jumbo shrimp, shelled and deveined
Salt and white pepper to taste
2 tablespoons soft butter
6 shallots, chopped
Several sprigs of fresh parsley
½ cup fish stock (page 110) or water
½ cup dry white wine
2 tablespoons butter
4 shallots, finely minced
½ pound fresh white mushrooms, thinly sliced
1 teaspoon fresh lemon juice
1 ripe tomato
2 tablespoons butter
2 tablespoons flour
1 cup heavy cream
Salt, white pepper, and a dash of cayenne pepper
1 teaspoon fresh lemon juice
1 tablespoon chopped fresh parsley

a small skillet and gently sauté the minced shallots and sliced mushrooms for a few minutes, just until the mushrooms begin to release their juices. Do not brown. Transfer them to a small sieve and let the liquid drain off. Toss the teaspoon of lemon juice through the mushrooms to keep them white. Set aside.

Also while the fish is baking, plunge the tomato into boiling water for 1 minute, remove it, and run it under cold water. Gently cut out the core and slip off the skin. Cut the tomato in half crosswise. Holding it over the sink, squeeze out all of the seeds and juice. Chop the remaining pulp and set it aside.

To prepare the Sauce Dugléré, heat the last 2 tablespoons of butter in a saucepan and whisk in the 2 tablespoons of flour, stirring well to form a *roux*. Pour in the reserved cup of fish juices and the heavy cream and bring this mixture to a boil, whisking constantly to prevent lumping. Season with salt, white pepper, and cayenne pepper. Stir in the mussels, mushrooms, chopped tomato, lemon juice, and parsley and heat through.

To serve, nap the fillets with some of the sauce and pass extra sauce separately. Serve with plain white rice.

Chestnut Cream Dacquoise

SERVES 8

Both the nuts and the cooky sheets in this recipe can be prepared ahead of time. In fact, they should be, so the egg whites will not have a chance to deflate after they are whipped. The sheets of meringue can be baked a day ahead and held at room temperature.

1 cup whole nuts (hazelnuts and blanched almonds)
¼ cup sugar
4 egg whites
A pinch of salt
¼ teaspoon cream of tartar
1 cup sugar
2 ounces semisweet chocolate, melted
A 1-pound can of *crème de marrons* (chestnut cream)

Spread the nuts out on a cooky sheet and put them into a 350° oven. Toast them for about 15 minutes, until the skins on the hazelnuts begin to crack and the almonds are a golden brown. Remove from the oven and cool. Gently rub the hazelnuts between the palms of your hands to remove the skins; then finely grate them and the almonds together in a food processor fitted with the steel blade or in a nut grinder. Do not overgrind or you'll get a paste. Sprinkle the ¼ cup sugar over the nuts, mix well, and set aside.

Lightly butter three cooky sheets and cover them with wax

paper. Trim the edges. Using a 9-inch cake pan as a guide, draw three circles in the wax paper with a pencil. (If you can fit two of the circles on one cooky sheet, it will not be necessary to use three separate sheets. Or you could draw three rectangles of about 6 inches by 12 inches. Just design the cake shape to fit the serving tray.) Set aside.

Preheat the oven to 250°. Put the egg whites into a clean bowl for the electric mixer and begin to beat, adding the pinch of salt and the cream of tartar. When they form soft peaks, add the 1 cup of sugar slowly, beating as you add it, and continue beating on high speed until you have a thick and shiny meringue. Fold in the nut mixture by hand.

Divide the meringue evenly over the three circles or rectangles and spread it about ¼ inch thick. Put the meringues in the preheated oven and bake for 30 minutes or until the tops are dry to the touch and pale golden.

Remove them from the oven, immediately invert them onto cake racks, and gently peel off the wax paper. Do this slowly, so that if any one place is sticking you will not tear the meringues apart. Allow the meringues to cool and continue to dry. This can all be done early in the day or the day before.

To assemble the cake, melt the chocolate in the top of a double boiler and beat it with the chestnut cream and the softened butter until the mixture is smooth. Stir in 1 tablespoon cognac.

Whip the heavy cream with the sugar, vanilla, and the remaining cognac until it is quite thick and stiff.

Put one layer of meringue on a serving platter and spread it with half the chestnut mixture. Put one quarter of the whipped cream mixture over this and place a second meringue layer on top. Spread the remaining chestnut mixture over it and another quarter of the whipped cream. Place the third layer of meringue on top and spread with all but ½ cup of the remaining whipped cream. Put this cream into a pastry bag fitted with a rosette nozzle and pipe out decorative rosettes over the top of the cake. Sprinkle with shaved chocolate and refrigerate until ready to serve.

2 tablespoons sweet butter, softened
2 tablespoons cognac
3 cups heavy cream
2 tablespoons sugar
1 teaspoon vanilla extract
Shaved chocolate (for garnish)

18

Asparagus Vinaigrette

Stuffed Spring Leg of Lamb

Hot Chocolate Soufflé with Crème Anglaise

This is a menu to serve an oenophile, because there is no vinegar in the vinaigrette. Lemon is substituted, and sweet gherkins, shallots, and parsley flavor it.

The rosemary in the stuffed leg of lamb is continental, but note that I have avoided the usual abundance of garlic.

To help in timing the soufflé properly, have the bowl prepared and chilling and the base made ahead of time. Be sure to make the *crème anglaise* ahead so it will be properly chilled. Then, just before you serve the lamb, take an extra 5 minutes to beat the whites and put the soufflé together and into the oven. The 40 minutes' baking will give your guests enough time to finish their meal and be ready for dessert. And remember: Escoffier once said, "The guests wait for the soufflé, the soufflé does not wait for the guests."

Asparagus Vinaigrette

They're *asperges* in France, *der Spargel* in Germany, and *asparagi* in Italy. Many of Europe's great houses of gastronomy have their springtime asparagus festivals; every course, with the possible exception of dessert, is made with or from asparagus. In Europe, white is right and the best of the lot is grown under boards or piled high with sand. Sandy growing soil makes the American varieties gritty too, so be sure to wash the asparagus well. If yours is slightly wilted, refresh it by standing the root ends in cold water. Find out where to cut the woody ends off by snapping one. They will break where they're tender.

Blanch the asparagus and make the vinaigrette the day before, if you like. Just don't combine the two until about 3 hours before serving, or the asparagus will start to lose their bright green color.

Snap off the bottoms of the asparagus stalks and trim them to a uniform length. Bring about 1 inch of salted water to a rolling boil in a pot, add the asparagus, cover, and blanch for about 3 minutes. Immediately remove them from the pot and run cold water over them to stop the cooking. Drain well and chill.

Put all the remaining ingredients except the garnishes into a small bowl and whisk well. Pour this marinade over the asparagus and continue to chill.

To serve, place several stalks of asparagus on a glass plate and spoon extra marinade over them. Garnish with crisscross strips of pimiento or bell pepper and sprinkle on the sieved hard-boiled egg.

2 pounds fresh asparagus
6 gherkins, finely minced
2 shallots, finely minced
A small piece of green pepper, seeded and finely minced
1 tablespoon chopped fresh parsley
1 clove garlic, mashed or minced
6 tablespoons olive oil
2 tablespoons fresh lemon juice
½ teaspoon salt
Freshly ground black pepper to taste
Strips of pimiento or red bell pepper (for garnish)
Sieved hard-boiled egg (for garnish)

Stuffed Spring Leg of Lamb

Lamb, stuffed with prosciutto, mushrooms, onions, lemon rind, *and* rosemary? Could be Greek, Italian, French, even Spanish. In fact, it is a variation on them all.

Laying the lamb on a bed of vegetables lets the entire leg brown and crisp while the juices from the vegetables mix with those of the meat, thus forming the base for a simple sauce to serve with the sliced roast.

For a simpler version another time, roast the lamb with the bone in and without the stuffing. Increase your oven time by a few minutes per pound. Lamb should always be cooked medium (pink inside). It has a completely different flavor from the well-done version most Americans are used to.

2 tablespoons olive oil
¼ pound prosciutto, finely minced
½ pound fresh mushrooms, thinly sliced
2 cloves garlic, mashed or minced
1 onion, finely minced
2 tablespoons chopped fresh parsley
4 slices white bread (with crusts removed), cut into small cubes
¼ teaspoon dried rosemary
¼ teaspoon dried thyme
Salt and freshly ground black pepper to taste
2 egg yolks, lightly beaten
A 5-pound spring leg of lamb, boned for stuffing
1 carrot, diced
1 onion, diced
1 stalk celery, diced
¼ cup finely minced fresh parsley
1 teaspoon dried rosemary
1 teaspoon dried thyme
Salt and pepper to taste
1 cup chicken stock (homemade or canned), or more if needed

Heat the olive oil in a skillet and gently sauté the prosciutto, mushrooms, garlic, onion, parsley, and bread cubes until golden brown. Sprinkle with the rosemary, thyme, salt, and pepper. Transfer to a bowl and gently stir in the egg yolks to bind the stuffing. Mix well and set aside to cool.

When the stuffing is cool, gently stuff the leg of lamb and sew the leg closed with kitchen string wherever it seems the stuffing might come out. Do not make any knots in the string — it will be easier to remove when the meat is done. Scatter the diced carrot, onion, and celery in a roasting pan. Sprinkle with the parsley, rosemary, and thyme.

Place the stuffed leg on the bed of vegetables in the roasting pan and season it with salt and pepper. Roast it in a preheated 400° oven for 45 minutes, turning occasionally to brown evenly on all sides. After the first 45 minutes, pour in the chicken stock and roast for another 45 minutes. This will produce lamb with a pink center. Add more stock if the bottom of the pan seems dry while the meat is roasting.

When the meat has reached the desired doneness (140° on a meat thermometer for rare, 155° for medium, 175° for well done), remove it from the oven and place it on a carving board. Strain the pan juices into a small pot and keep the juices warm on top of the stove. The vegetables can be discarded, or you can purée them in a blender or food processor and stir them into the juices to thicken the sauce.

Cut the strings and remove them. Slice the meat, taking care not to let the stuffing fall out. Arrange the slices down the center of a platter; serve the pan juices separately.

Hot Chocolate Soufflé with Crème Anglaise

Served with a chilled custardlike sauce on the side, this soufflé beautifully contrasts hot and cold, chocolate and vanilla.

Spread the tablespoon of soft butter over the bottom and sides of a 6-cup soufflé dish. Sprinkle the sugar over all to coat evenly. Set the dish aside. Tear off a long strip of aluminum foil, fold it in half lengthwise, and butter one side. Wrap it around the outside of the prepared soufflé dish, buttered side in, to create a collar, and attach it firmly in place with string. Chill the prepared dish.

Put the chocolate and coffee together in the top of a double boiler and melt until smooth. Remove the pan from the heat and set it aside.

Put the cornstarch into a small saucepan and pour in a small amount of the milk to dissolve the cornstarch. When well mixed, add the remaining milk and the ⅓ cup sugar. Cook this mixture over medium heat until it thickens and comes to a boil. Remove it from the heat and stir in the melted chocolate mixture. Transfer this to a small bowl and set aside.

Separate the eggs, putting the whites in a clean bowl for the electric mixer. Be sure to add the two additional egg whites, as you might forget them later. The two extra egg yolks can be used in the *crème anglaise*.

Lightly beat the egg yolks into the chocolate mixture, mixing thoroughly. Stir in the 2 tablespoons of sweet butter and cover this mixture tightly with plastic wrap. Refrigerate until ready to use. This portion of the soufflé can be done early in the day.

To complete the soufflé, preheat the oven to 375° and make sure the rack is in the exact center. Add the salt to the egg whites and beat them on high speed until firm peaks form. Fold them gently into the chocolate mixture and spoon the mixture into the prepared soufflé dish.

Bake the soufflé in the preheated oven for exactly 40 minutes. Serve at once with confectioners' sugar sprinkled on the top and the following sauce passed in a separate sauceboat.

1 tablespoon soft sweet butter
1 tablespoon granulated sugar
3½ squares semisweet chocolate
2 tablespoons strong-brewed coffee (preferably espresso)
3 tablespoons cornstarch
1 cup milk
⅓ cup sugar
3 eggs plus 2 extra whites
2 tablespoons soft sweet butter
A dash of salt
Confectioners' sugar

2 CUPS

1½ cups milk
3 egg yolks
¼ cup sugar
2 teaspoons vanilla extract
1 cup heavy cream

Crème Anglaise

Scald the milk in a small saucepan. Put the egg yolks in the top of a double boiler and beat well with a large whisk. Add the sugar and continue to beat until well mixed. Pour in the hot milk and set this mixture over very slowly simmering water. Switch to a wooden spoon and, stirring constantly, cook the custard for 5 minutes or until it thickens and coats the back of the wooden spoon. The custard will be of a pouring consistency when it is done. Do not overcook it, or the egg yolks will lump.

When the custard is done, remove it from the heat and pour it into a small bowl. Stir in the vanilla, cover tightly with plastic wrap, and chill thoroughly.

Just before serving, whip the cream and fold it into the chilled sauce.

May

LESSON 19

Tomato Niçoise Quiche
Stuffed Red Snapper
Chocolate Praline Soufflé

LESSON 20

Gazpacho
Shrimp in Green Sauce
Fresh Lemon Tart

LESSON 21

Shrimp in Ravigote Sauce
Chicken Basquaise
Clafouti

LESSON 22

Antipasto Salad
Chicken Spiedini alla Cacciatore
Ricotta Cheesecake

Tomato Niçoise Quiche

Stuffed Red Snapper

Chocolate Praline Soufflé

This French menu is dripping with Mediterranean colors and flavors — tomato reds, snapper and shrimp pinks, and a rich chocolate brown. It's a perfect weekend collection, just right for a Sunday afternoon. The soufflé and the crust and filling for the quiche can be made well ahead. So can the fish stuffing, but stuff the fish just before baking and make the sauce just before serving.

Tomato Niçoise Quiche

This quiche is an adaptation of two all-time favorites, the classic Mediterranean *pissaladière* (a French pizza?) and the northern French quiche. The eggs and cheese hold the vegetable mixture together, but the flavor is enhanced by oregano, basil, thyme, and the assertiveness of anchovies. The black olives make it Niçoise.

The tomato sauce is basic — rich, fresh, and sweet. Double the recipe, add some sautéed meats or mushrooms to the unused half, and freeze it to use another day as spaghetti sauce.

The quiche filling can be prepared a day in advance and refrigerated. The crust can be prepared and partially baked early in the day or even the day before. Just hold the two separately until ready to bake and serve.

Crust for a 10-Inch Quiche

8 tablespoons soft butter
3 ounces cream cheese, softened
1¼ cups flour, sifted with ½ teaspoon salt

Put the butter and cream cheese in a bowl for the electric mixer and blend well. Add the flour and salt and mix on low speed until the mixture forms a soft ball of dough and leaves the sides of the bowl clean. Gather the dough together and wrap it in wax paper. Chill for at least 30 minutes.

Preheat the oven to 400°.

To roll, lightly flour a pastry cloth or board and place the ball of dough in the center. Flatten it slightly and roll it out to fit a 10-inch quiche pan with a removable bottom. Line the pan with the dough and trim the edges. Line the pastry with wax paper or parchment paper and weight it down with dry beans, raw rice, or aluminum nuggets.

Bake the crust for about 10 minutes. Remove it from the oven and carefully lift off the paper with the weights. Cool slightly. The crust is now ready for filling and continued baking.

Filling

Drop the tomatoes into boiling water for a minute or two; remove and rinse with cold water. Cut the cores out with the tip of a knife and slip off the skins. Chop the pulp.

102

Heat 2 tablespoons of olive oil in a medium-sized skillet and sauté the onion and garlic for about 2 minutes, until they are soft but not brown. Add the chopped tomatoes, oregano, basil, thyme, salt, and pepper. Continue cooking, uncovered, over medium heat, stirring occasionally, until the mixture cooks down to a thick tomato purée. Remove it from the pan and put it in a bowl to cool.

While the tomato mixture is cooling, put the egg, egg yolks, minced anchovies, tomato paste, parsley, paprika, and cayenne pepper into a large bowl and add the reserved anchovy oil and the remaining 2 tablespoons of olive oil. Mix well and add the cooled tomato mixture.

Preheat the oven to 375°.

Pour the filling into the partially baked crust and spread it evenly. Sprinkle the entire surface with the grated cheeses. Distribute the olive halves attractively over the top.

Bake the quiche for about 30 minutes or until the top looks golden brown and puffy.

8 very ripe tomatoes
4 tablespoons olive oil
1 onion, finely minced
2 cloves garlic, finely minced or mashed
1 teaspoon dried oregano
1 teaspoon dried basil
½ teaspoon dried thyme
Salt and freshly ground black pepper to taste
1 whole egg and 3 yolks
A 2-ounce can of flat anchovy fillets, minced (drain and reserve the oil)
2 tablespoons tomato paste
2 tablespoons chopped fresh parsley
1 teaspoon sweet paprika
A dash of cayenne pepper
1 cup grated Swiss cheese
½ cup grated Parmesan cheese
1 cup pitted black olives, sliced in half lengthwise

Stuffed Red Snapper

SERVES 8

Flounder, striped bass, or sea bass would do just as well here, but red snapper is such a beautiful creature, cooked or uncooked, that if you can find it, use it. The recipe needs a large fish to work well and blend the flavors, so save it for a dramatic dinner party. If you wrap the fish in foil, it may be cooked right on top of the coals of an outdoor barbecue. Omit the sauce for this informal service.

Crab meat or spinach may be substituted for the shrimp in the stuffing.

The vegetable bed on which the fish is baked adds the needed moisture and some delicate flavors that enhance the dish. The juices of the wine and fish, plus the vegetables, make the richly flavored base for the Sauce Vin Blanc, which should be presented with, not on, the fish. You may have some dieters among your guests who prefer to skip the sauce.

A 6-pound red snapper
8 tablespoons butter
2 shallots, finely minced
1 small onion, finely minced
1 stalk celery, finely minced
1 pound raw shrimp (cleaned
  and deveined), cut into small
  dice
½ pound fresh white
  mushrooms, thinly sliced
Several sprigs of fresh parsley,
  finely minced
3 slices white bread (crusts
  removed), cut into small dice
3 tablespoons dry white wine
Salt and pepper to taste
1 carrot, sliced
1 onion, sliced
1 stalk celery, sliced
2 bay leaves
4 sprigs of fresh parsley
2 tablespoons melted butter
2 cups dry white wine

2 CUPS

1 cup of the strained pan juices
2 tablespoons butter
2 tablespoons flour
1 cup heavy cream
Salt, white pepper, and a dash
  of cayenne pepper to taste
1 teaspoon fresh lemon juice

Have the fishmonger prepare the fish for stuffing and baking. Ask to have it cleaned and boned, but left whole, "like a book." The head may be left on or removed, but be sure to leave the tail intact for a more attractive presentation.

Melt the butter in a large skillet. When it is hot and foamy, sauté the shallots, onion, celery, shrimp, mushrooms, and parsley for a few minutes until the shrimp turn bright pink and the mushrooms are pale golden. Stir in the diced bread and sprinkle the wine over all. Mix and season lightly with salt and pepper. (If the stuffing seems too dry, add a tablespoon more wine. If it seems too wet and sticky, stir in a few more tablespoons of diced bread.) Transfer the mixture to a bowl to cool.

Lay the fish open flat on a board and gently place the cooled stuffing on the bottom half of the fish. Press to spread evenly and lift the top half of the fish up and over the stuffing. Tie the stuffed fish closed every few inches from head to tail, using a soft kitchen string. Do not fear that the stuffing will come out during baking; as soon as the fish begins to cook, the juices make the fish adhere to the stuffing and to itself.

Preheat the oven to 400°. Line a shallow roasting pan with aluminum foil and place the fish in the center. Scatter the carrot, onion, celery, bay leaves, and parsley around the fish. Brush the top of the fish with the melted butter and pour the white wine into the pan. Bake the fish, uncovered, in the preheated oven for 45 minutes or until the fish flakes easily with a fork. Baste the fish occasionally with the pan juices.

When the fish is done, remove it from the oven and turn off the oven. Carefully transfer the fish to its serving platter and cut and remove the strings. Put the fish on its platter into the turned-off oven while you are making the sauce.

Sauce Vin Blanc

After the fish has been removed to the serving platter, carefully strain the pan juices through a fine sieve into a measuring cup. If you do not have 1 cup of juice, add enough white wine to make 1 cup.

Melt the butter in a small saucepan and when it is hot and foamy, whisk in the flour, stirring to form a *roux*. Pour in the strained juices, whisking constantly until the mixture is smooth. Stir in the cream and bring this mixture to a boil over medium heat, whisking until you have a smooth, thick sauce. Season with the salt and peppers and remove from the heat. Stir in the lemon juice.

Pass the sauce in a separate sauceboat.

Chocolate Praline Soufflé

Did you ever wonder how peanut brittle or almond brittle is made? Well, this recipe tells the secret. A hazelnut praline would be classically French, but almonds make for a delightfully rich flavor.

The sugar and water heats to a much higher temperature than water alone. You will be heating the praline mixture to what is called the hard-crack stage — 280° to 300° on a candy thermometer — so be careful! If you don't happen to have a candy thermometer, you can tell when the sugar is caramelized by its golden, amber-brown color.

Praline candy will absorb moisture and melt if you put it in the refrigerator. So keep leftover crushed crumbs in an airtight container in a cool, dry place. It's great sprinkled on ice cream.

Praline Candy

ABOUT 1 CUP

¾ cup sugar
¼ cup water
¼ teaspoon cream of tartar
½ cup blanched almonds

Combine the sugar, water, and cream of tartar in a small, heavy-weight saucepan. Cook over medium heat, without stirring, until the mixture begins to thicken and becomes syrupy. Add the nuts and continue cooking until the nuts turn a light golden brown and the syrup is amber-brown and caramelized. This should register 280° on a candy thermometer.

Do not overcook the syrup. Once it has reached the caramelized state, remove it from the heat, or it will overcook and taste burnt. Be sure to take precautions, as the syrup is very hot. If you get some on your fingertips, put them under warm water immediately to wash off the caramel.

Have a lightly buttered, shallow cooky sheet ready. Pour the caramel syrup onto the cooky sheet as soon as it is done. Once the caramel has been poured onto the cooky sheet, it will cool and harden. When it is hard, break it up into chunks and crush it in a food processor or blender.

Soufflé

Tear off a strip of aluminum foil or wax paper and fold it in half lengthwise. Lightly butter one side and tie it around a 4-cup soufflé dish, buttered side in, to form a collar. Place the dish in the refrigerator to chill.

105

6 ounces semisweet chocolate
1 tablespoon unflavored gelatin
¼ cup cold water
4 eggs
½ cup sugar
A dash of salt
1 teaspoon vanilla extract
1 tablespoon Praline liqueur, if
  available, or amaretto
1 cup heavy cream, whipped
Crushed praline candy (see
  above)

Melt the chocolate in the top of a double boiler and set it aside to cool. Sprinkle the gelatin over the cold water in a small glass bowl or measuring cup and let it sit for a minute or two. Place the glass bowl in a saucepan and add 2 inches of water to the pan. Bring the water in the pan to a boil on top of the stove and allow the gelatin mixture to absorb enough heat from the boiling water to dissolve completely. Do not let the gelatin mixture come to a boil. Remove the bowl from the saucepan and set it aside to cool.

Separate the eggs and set the whites aside in a clean, dry bowl. Beat the yolks with the sugar and salt until the mixture is very thick and cream-colored. Beat in the vanilla and liqueur and the cooled chocolate.

In a separate bowl, whip the cream until it is thick and stiff. Fold it into the chocolate mixture. Whip the egg whites until stiff peaks form. Fold them into the chocolate mixture. Stir in ¼ cup of the crushed praline mixture.

Pour this mixture into the chilled soufflé dish, allowing the mixture to rise above the rim of the dish into the collar. Chill the soufflé for at least six hours, or overnight if possible.

To serve, carefully run a wet knife between the soufflé and the collar and gently peel the collar away from the dish. Pat additional crushed praline around the sides of the soufflé extending above the rim. Serve with a small bowl of extra crushed praline on the side.

20

Gazpacho

Shrimp in Green Sauce

Fresh Lemon Tart

Spain is the inspiration for this menu. But here the gazpacho calls for some cooking of the vegetables, which lets the soup speak with a new taste. What else could be so hearty and still so healthy? Be sure to use any vegetables available from your own garden.

Salsa verde is the Spanish name for green sauce; pungent, fresh coriander (cilantro) or the more readily available flat Italian parsley make it so. Garlic is also a strong flavor here. The sauce is an excellent accompaniment to cod, sole, and lobster as well as shrimp.

Gazpacho

Most gazpachos taste like a mixed vegetable cocktail, so if that's what you want, buy it by the can. In this recipe, the tomato juice, cooked vegetables, and beef stock create a base that is just the start to a true cold fresh vegetable soup. The diced raw vegetable garnish adds texture.

This recipe is really worth the effort. On a cool day, serve the soup hot with garlic croutons.

¼ cup olive oil
2 cloves garlic, finely minced or mashed
3 green peppers, seeded and coarsely chopped
2 large onions, coarsely chopped
6 very ripe tomatoes, peeled and coarsely chopped
2 cucumbers, peeled, seeded, and coarsely chopped
2 teaspoons sweet paprika
4 cups beef stock (homemade or canned)
2 cups tomato juice
¼ cup wine vinegar
¼ cup dry white wine
Salt and freshly ground black pepper to taste
1 tablespoon each chopped fresh basil, parsley, and chives
1 small onion, finely minced
1 small green pepper, seeded and finely minced
1 small cucumber, peeled, seeded and finely minced

Heat the olive oil in a deep soup kettle and sauté the garlic, peppers, and onions for about 5 minutes, until golden. Stir in the tomatoes and cucumbers, and continue sautéing for another 2 or 3 minutes. Stir in the paprika and mix well.

Add the stock, tomato juice, vinegar, wine, and salt and pepper. Cover the pot and bring to a boil. Reduce the heat to simmer and cook for about 30 minutes or until the vegetables are tender.

Cool the mixture. Then purée it using a food processor or blender. Chill thoroughly.

Prepare a garnish consisting of the herbs, onion, pepper, and cucumber mixed well in a small bowl. Use only fresh herbs. If any of the suggested herbs are unavailable fresh, substitute others (such as scallions in place of chives). Serve the soup in chilled bowls or mugs with a sprinkling of the garnish on top.

Shrimp in Green Sauce

Make your own fish stock, if you possibly can; extra stock freezes well, and any fish dish you make will benefit from it. Once you have all the ingredients assembled, it takes only 5 minutes to put this stock together.

Have all the ingredients for the shrimp dish chopped and measured and ready at the skillet before you start to cook. Since this is a one-pot dish, invite your guests into the kitchen to watch the preparation.

Shell and devein the shrimp or have the fishmonger do this for you. Rinse them well and pat dry with paper towels. Season with the salt and pepper and set aside. Put the ½ cup flour (for dredging) into a bowl.

Mince the onions and put them into a small bowl near the skillet in which you will be preparing the dish. Mash the garlic and add it to the minced watercress and cilantro in a small bowl. Set aside near the onions. (A note about cilantro: It is more pungent than curly parsley. If you cannot find it, substitute flat Italian parsley, which is more readily available.)

Shell the peas and blanch them for about 3 minutes in 1 inch of boiling salted water. Drain immediately and run cold water over them so they stop cooking. Put them into a small bowl near the rest of the ingredients. (If you are using frozen peas, defrost them but do not precook them.)

Measure out all the liquids and the 2 tablespoons flour for the sauce. (Note: If you do not have fish stock, combine 1 cup cold water and 1 cup dry white wine as a replacement for the 1½ cups stock and ½ cup wine.)

Heat the olive oil in a large skillet that has a tight-fitting lid. Lightly dredge the shrimp in the flour, shaking off the excess. When the oil is quite hot, quickly sear the shrimp, turning once when they become bright pink. Remove them from the skillet as they are done and set aside.

Add more oil to the skillet if necessary and stir in the minced onions. Gently sauté them for 2 or 3 minutes, until they are golden but not too brown. Stir the 2 tablespoons of flour over the onions and incorporate it well into the oil. Stir in all of the liquids (stock, wine, and cream) and bring this mixture to a boil over medium heat until it begins to thicken.

48 raw jumbo shrimp
Salt and pepper to taste
½ cup flour
2 onions
4 cloves garlic
⅓ cup each finely minced
  watercress and cilantro
1 pound fresh peas (or a
  package of frozen peas)
⅓ cup olive oil
1 cup heavy cream
1½ cups fish stock (see below)
½ cup dry white wine
2 tablespoons flour
Salt and pepper to taste

109

Using a whisk, add the garlic-herb mixture and additional salt and pepper to taste.

Return the shrimp to the sauce in the skillet, scatter the peas over all, cover the skillet, and cook for about 5 minutes until all the ingredients are heated through.

Serve at once with Risotto Milanese, page 87.

Fish Stock

ABOUT 2 QUARTS

1 pound fish trimmings (heads, bones, skin, and so on); a fishmonger will give you these gladly, free of charge
1 stalk celery, sliced
1 onion, sliced
1 carrot, sliced
2 bay leaves
3 or 4 sprigs of fresh parsley
1 teaspoon whole black peppercorns
1 teaspoon salt
2 cups dry white wine
Enough cold water to cover everything in the pot (about 8 cups)

Put all the ingredients into a deep kettle. Bring to a boil, reduce the heat to simmer, cover the pot, and cook for about 30 minutes. Remove from heat and cool to room temperature. Strain the liquid through very fine damp cheesecloth. Discard the solids. Cool the liquid completely and freeze any extra stock in 1-cup containers for future use.

Fresh Lemon Tart

SERVES 8

Though beauty might call for slicing the lemons with the rind on, eating cries out for cutting away all rind and pith before decorating the top of this lovely dessert. Grating the zest before you slice the lemons and sprinkling it over the lemon slices before you brush on the apricot glaze offsets the sweetness and greatly enhances the flavor.

Sweet Crust for a 10-Inch Tart

1½ cups flour
½ teaspoon salt
2 teaspoons sugar
8 tablespoons sweet butter, cut into small pieces
3 tablespoons ice water

Sift the flour with the salt and sugar and put it into a bowl for the electric mixer. Add the bits of butter, and turn the mixer on to lowest speed. Mix until you have a very grainy consistency.

Add the ice water 1 tablespoon at a time, waiting until the flour has absorbed the water before adding more. Continue mixing the dough on the lowest speed until it forms a soft ball and leaves the sides of the bowl clean. Depending upon the humidity of the day, you may not need all the water, or you may need an additional tablespoon.

Once the dough has formed a ball, gather it together and wrap it in wax paper. Chill the dough at least 30 minutes to "relax" it. This results in a more flaky crust.

To roll it out, lightly flour a pastry cloth or board and place the chilled ball of dough in the center. Flatten it slightly and roll the dough from the center out to the edges, until you have a circle large enough to fit a 10-inch tart pan with a removable bottom. Fit the dough in the pan and trim the edges.

Line the dough with wax paper, parchment paper, or aluminum foil and weight the paper down with raw rice, dried beans, or aluminum nuggets. Trim the edges of paper and bake the crust in a 400° oven for about 10 minutes. Remove it from the oven and carefully lift off the paper and weights. Return the crust to the oven and bake for another 10 minutes or until the crust is golden brown and baked through completely. Remove it from the oven and cool it to room temperature. The crust is now ready for filling and garnishing.

▶ The fully baked crust may be prepared a day in advance and kept at room temperature overnight.

Lemon Filling

Put the cornstarch or arrowroot into a small bowl and pour the ¼ cup cold water over it in a slow stream, mixing well to form a thin paste. Add the egg yolks and whisk lightly. Set this aside.

Put the lemon juice, the ⅔ cup water, and the ⅓ cup sugar into a saucepan and bring to a boil, stirring well. Cook for a minute or two and remove from heat. Slowly trickle about ¼ cup of this hot liquid into the egg yolk mixture, stirring constantly, to warm the yolks. Then return the egg yolk mixture to the remaining hot liquid in the saucepan and stir well. Cook this mixture for a few minutes over low heat, stirring constantly, until it is thickened. Remove from heat and stir in the butter. Cool completely, and cover tightly with plastic
▶ wrap. Chill for several hours.

When the lemon mixture is quite cold, dissolve the gelatin in the ⅓ cup cold water by sprinkling the gelatin over the water in a small glass bowl or measuring cup. Place this bowl or cup into a saucepan and add 1 inch of hot water. Bring the water in the saucepan to a boil on top of the stove and allow

2 tablespoons cornstarch or arrowroot
¼ cup cold water
5 egg yolks
⅓ cup freshly squeezed strained lemon juice
⅔ cup water
⅓ cup sugar
1 tablespoon sweet butter
1 teaspoon unflavored gelatin
⅓ cup cold water
½ cup heavy cream, whipped
2 Italian macaroons (*amaretti***), crushed into fine crumbs**
3 or 4 medium-sized lemons
½ cup apricot jam
1 tablespoon sugar

the gelatin mixture to dissolve completely from the heat of the boiling water. Remove the gelatin mixture from the saucepan and set it aside to cool slightly. Stir this into the chilled lemon mixture. Fold in the whipped cream and the *amaretti* crumbs.

Spoon this mixture into the baked pie shell. Chill thoroughly. ◀

To garnish the top of the tart, grate the zest from the lemons and set it aside. With a sharp knife, remove all white pith from the lemons and discard. Slice the lemons into very thin rounds and remove pits as you see them. Lay the slices of lemon out on paper towels to drain.

Press the apricot jam through a fine sieve into a small saucepan and add the 1 tablespoon sugar. Heat over low heat until the mixture is thin enough for spreading. Cool slightly.

Arrange the slices of lemon in a spiral over the entire top of the tart as attractively as you can, overlapping each slice carefully. Sprinkle the grated lemon zest over all. Carefully brush the apricot glaze over the lemon slices and return the tart to the refrigerator to chill thoroughly before slicing and serving. ◀

If you wish, rosettes of whipped cream may be piped around the edge of the tart, using a pastry bag fitted with a rosette nozzle.

LESSON

21

Shrimp in Ravigote Sauce

Chicken Basquaise

Clafouti

The true Basque claims to be neither Spanish nor French. He is Basque and he is used to hearty fare, like any mountain people. You can see that in the chicken recipe, generous both in quantity and in size of pieces. You can also see the influence of the two countries surrounding the Basques in the use of anchovies, chorizo sausages, and lots of tomatoes. The dessert is a combination of the classic Spanish flan and the rich, baked custard and fruit dessert of the French countryside known as *clafouti*.

Shrimp in Ravigote Sauce

This recipe turns a mayonnaise into something magnificent. Considering the truly tasty herb and spice additions, it really isn't necessary to prepare mayonnaise from scratch, but use fresh herbs whenever they are available. The sauce also makes an excellent dip for cold artichokes and the recipe works equally well for cold poached mussels or even chunk canned tuna or poached chicken. Make the vinaigrette dressing first, so it has a chance to mellow.

6 tablespoons olive oil (or any vegetable oil)
2 tablespoons freshly squeezed lemon juice
1 heaping teaspoon Dijon mustard
½ teaspoon sugar
½ teaspoon salt
Freshly ground black pepper to taste
1 clove garlic, cut in half
2 shallots, finely minced
2 teaspoons capers
1 tablespoon chopped fresh tarragon (or 1 teaspoon dried tarragon)
1 tablespoon chopped fresh chervil (or 1 teaspoon dried chervil)
2 tablespoons chopped fresh parsley
2 cups mayonnaise
A dash of Tabasco
2 pounds cooked shrimp, chilled
1 head Boston lettuce

Put the oil, lemon juice, mustard, sugar, salt, pepper, and garlic into a small plastic or glass container with a tight-fitting lid and shake well. Set aside to allow the flavors to blend while you proceed with the rest of the recipe.

Put the shallots, capers, tarragon, chervil, and parsley into a bowl and whisk in the mayonnaise. Add the Tabasco. Remove the pieces of garlic from the container and stir the oil dressing into the mayonnaise mixture. Whisk together to form a sauce the consistency of thin mayonnaise.

Add the cooked and chilled shrimp to the mayonnaise mixture and allow them to sit in the dressing for several hours to marinate.

To serve, place lettuce leaves on small plates and heap portions of the sauced shrimp in the center of the leaves. Garnish with additional finely minced parsley, if you like.

A few words about the oil dressing in this recipe. The oil, lemon juice, mustard, sugar, salt, pepper, and garlic form a basic French vinaigrette dressing that may be used on any salad, particularly leafy greens. The amounts called for in this recipe can be doubled or even tripled and refrigerated for at least a week. Make up a batch early in the week and you'll have it handy for any salad you serve. A helpful tip for easy removal of the pieces of garlic: put toothpicks in each one. The pieces of garlic may be mashed and incorporated into the dressing, if desired.

Chicken Basquaise

This is the classic chicken dish of the Basque countryside, incorporating chicken, ham, sausages, peppers, and mushrooms. When sautéing all of these, keep the pan uncovered so all will brown evenly. The chorizos are optional but add an authentic flavor to the dish. Sweet Italian sausages can be substituted.

Trim the chicken breasts of excess skin and fat and cut each breast in half so you have sixteen pieces. Put the flour into a bowl or plastic bag and season with salt, pepper, and oregano. Mash the garlic and set aside. Thinly slice the onion, mushrooms, peppers, and sausages. Dice the ham. Drop the tomatoes into boiling water for 1 minute, remove, and cool with cold water. Gently cut out the cores, slip off the skins, and chop the tomatoes. Set them aside. Drain and mince the anchovies and set them aside.

Drop the chicken pieces into the seasoned flour and dredge thoroughly, shaking off the excess. Heat some of the olive oil in a large skillet with a tight-fitting lid. Brown the pieces of chicken evenly, turning frequently until golden brown. As they are done, remove them and continue until all the chicken has been browned.

Add more oil to the skillet if necessary and stir in the garlic, onions, and mushrooms. Sauté for a few minutes, until the mushrooms and onions are golden but not too brown. Stir in the peppers and sauté for another minute or two. Add the ham and sauté for a few minutes.

Return the chicken to the skillet and stir in the chopped tomatoes, tomato paste, anchovies, wine, salt and pepper, and basil. Mix all the ingredients well, cover the skillet, reduce the heat to simmer, and cook for 30 minutes or until the chicken is cooked through.

While the chicken is simmering, add a bit of oil to a small skillet and gently sauté the sliced sausages until they are quite crisp and brown. Transfer them to a paper towel and drain. Scatter the sautéed sausage slices over the top of the skillet while the chicken is simmering, re-cover the skillet, and continue to cook.

When the chicken is tender and cooked through, remove the

8 whole boneless and skinless chicken breasts
½ cup flour
Salt and pepper to taste
½ teaspoon oregano
2 cloves garlic
1 large Spanish onion
½ pound firm fresh white mushrooms
1 large green pepper, seeds removed
1 large red bell pepper, seeds removed
½ pound chorizo sausages (optional)
A ½-pound piece of ham
4 very ripe tomatoes
A 2-ounce can of flat anchovy fillets
¼ cup olive oil
1 tablespoon tomato paste
½ cup dry white wine
Salt and pepper to taste
1 tablespoon chopped fresh basil (or 1 teaspoon dried)
Chopped fresh parsley (for garnish)

pieces to a large platter and, using a slotted spoon, scoop up the vegetables and ham and sausages and scatter them around the chicken. Raise the heat under the skillet and bring the liquid in the pan to a rolling boil. Pour this sauce over the chicken on the platter and garnish with the chopped parsley. This dish is excellent served with Risotto Milanese, page 87.

Clafouti

This "country custard" can also be made by substituting a cup of just about any diced fresh or drained canned fruit — pears, apricots, peaches, or apples, for example. But avoid strawberries. You'll wind up with a puddle of juice in the bottom of the pan.

SERVES 8

2 tablespoons soft butter
A 2-pound can of pitted Bing
 cherries
4 eggs, plus 2 egg yolks
2½ cups milk
A pinch of salt
½ cup sugar
1 cup minus 2 tablespoons flour
1 tablespoon melted butter
1 teaspoon vanilla extract
1 tablespoon soft butter
1 tablespoon granulated sugar
Confectioners' sugar

Butter the bottom and sides of a fairly shallow glass dish about 10 inches in diameter and 2 inches deep.

Drain the cherries and set them aside. You should have about 1 cup of cherries. (The drained cherry juice can be used in fruit punches or as the cold liquid in a gelatin dessert.)

Put the eggs, yolks, milk, and salt into a blender or a bowl for the electric mixer. (Or use a large bowl with a balloon whisk.) Add the ½ cup sugar and mix for a minute or two. Add the flour and stir to mix. Pour in the melted butter and the vanilla and mix until you have a smooth batter the consistency of pancake batter. Let stand a few minutes until the bubbles subside.

Preheat the oven to 350°.

Scatter the drained cherries over the bottom of the buttered dish and gently pour the batter over the cherries. Dot the top of the batter with the tablespoon of soft butter and sprinkle the tablespoon of sugar evenly over the top.

Bake the custard for 45 minutes or until the top is puffy and brown and a clean silver knife inserted in the center comes out clean.

Remove the custard from the oven. The custard tastes best if it is allowed to cool slightly before serving. Sprinkle a little confectioners' sugar over the top just before serving right from its dish.

Antipasto Salad

Chicken Spiedini alla Cacciatore

Ricotta Cheesecake

May is springtime, and this menu reflects the freshest greens and colors available then. *Antipasto* means just that — before the pasta — and here we carry the colors of the salad through to the bright green noodles that form the base of a hearty chicken dish. End your meal sumptuously with the ricotta cheesecake. With its interestingly flavored crust (a hint of lemon and Marsala wine), it is in a category above the ordinary cheesecake.

Antipasto Salad

A salad is only as good as its dressing. By whisking the oil into the vinaigrette slowly, the emulsion will hold together much longer. Dijon mustard is best, but any spicy brand will do. The cream and egg yolk give the dressing consistency and character.

The red bell pepper in the salad will add color — if you can find a nice ripe one. If not, substitute bottled pimiento. Any of the suggested ingredients for the salad may be omitted or substituted. If you don't like salami, use ham instead. Dieting? Omit the potatoes. But since antipasto calls for variety, don't omit too much.

A 1-pound can of chickpeas
6 new potatoes
1 tablespoon olive oil
½ pound fresh green beans
1 small red onion
1 green pepper
1 red bell pepper
¼ pound Genoa salami
¼ pound cheese (Swiss, Gruyère, mozzarella, or a mixture)
2 fresh, ripe tomatoes, cut into thin slices or quarters
An 8-ounce can of pitted black olives
1 tablespoon chopped fresh parsley
1 tablespoon chopped fresh basil (optional)
1 head romaine or Boston lettuce

Drain the chickpeas and put them into a large salad bowl.

Scrub the potatoes and put them into a small pot or steamer. Add an inch of water, cover, and bring to a boil. Lower the heat and simmer for 15 to 20 minutes or until tender. Drain immediately and run cold water over the potatoes. Cool, peel, and dice them. Toss the olive oil through them to lubricate and prevent them from sticking together.

Prepare the green beans by removing the stems and steaming them in 1 inch of salted water for 2 or 3 minutes. As soon as they are done, drain and run cold water over them.

While the potatoes and beans are cooking, dice the onion, peppers, salami, and cheese and add them to the bowl. Slice the tomatoes. Drain the olives and cut each one in half. Add both to the bowl. Add the potatoes and beans and stir in the herbs. When all ingredients are in the bowl, pour the Creamy Vinaigrette Dressing (see below) over all and toss well.

Allow the vegetables to marinate in the dressing in the refrigerator for several hours.

To serve, break the lettuce into separate leaves. Wash and dry the leaves and place them on individual salad plates. Divide the salad evenly on the plates and sprinkle with additional chopped parsley.

Creamy Vinaigrette Dressing

Put the egg yolk, lemon juice, garlic, mustard, salt, pepper, and sugar into a small bowl and whisk to blend. Begin adding the oil, very slowly, whisking constantly. Continue until all the oil has been incorporated. Whisk in the cream and Tabasco.

1 egg yolk
2 tablespoons freshly squeezed lemon juice
1 clove garlic, well minced or mashed
2 teaspoons Dijon mustard
Salt and freshly ground pepper to taste
½ teaspoon sugar
6 tablespoons olive oil
2 tablespoons heavy cream
A dash of Tabasco

Chicken Spiedini alla Cacciatore

SERVES 8

Surrounding a bed of green pasta, this broiled, skewered chicken makes a beautiful dish. The Sauce Espagnole is a brown sauce basic to almost all continental cooking and is worth making. It freezes well, so once you have done it you may forgo canned beef gravy forever.

Cut each piece of chicken in half and cut each half into four small pieces. Cut each slice of prosciutto into four pieces. Season the chicken with salt, pepper, and sage. Thread eight pieces of the chicken alternately with eight pieces of the prosciutto onto eight heat-proof skewers. Set aside.

Using a large skillet or casserole that can go under the broiler, melt the butter on top of the stove and when it is hot, gently sauté the onion, shallots, carrots, celery, and garlic for a few minutes until golden. Stir in the tarragon and thyme. Remove from heat.

Carefully place the eight skewers on top of the sautéed vegetables in the skillet or casserole. Dust the tops of the skewers with some of the melted butter and sprinkle some flour over each one.

Preheat the broiler to medium and put the rack two levels down from it. Broil the chicken skewers for about 10 minutes on one side, turn, and brush with more melted butter and flour. Continue to broil for another 10 minutes or until the chicken seems done. Turn the skewers occasionally if necessary to brown the chicken evenly on all sides.

8 whole boneless and skinless breasts of chicken
16 slices prosciutto
Salt, pepper, and rubbed sage to taste
4 tablespoons butter
1 large onion, finely chopped
4 shallots, peeled and finely chopped
2 carrots, peeled and finely chopped
2 stalks celery, finely chopped
2 cloves garlic, mashed or minced
1 tablespoon chopped fresh tarragon (or 1 teaspoon dried tarragon)
¼ teaspoon dried thyme
4 tablespoons melted butter
¼ cup flour
1 pound mushrooms

4 quarts water with 1 teaspoon
salt and 1 tablespoon oil
1 pound thin *tagliarini verde* or
any thin green pasta
4 tablespoons melted butter
½ cup freshly grated Parmesan
cheese
½ cup dry white wine
4 ripe tomatoes, peeled and
chopped
2 cups fresh Sauce Espagnole
(see below)

4 CUPS

3 tablespoons butter
1 carrot, diced
1 onion, diced
1 stalk celery, diced
4 strips bacon, diced
4 tablespoons flour
4 cups beef stock (homemade or
canned)
1 small bunch fresh parsley
2 bay leaves
¼ teaspoon whole black
peppercorns
2 tablespoons tomato paste

SERVES 8

While the chicken is broiling, wipe the mushrooms clean with a damp paper towel and slice off the stems flush with the caps. Thinly slice the caps. Sauté them in a few tablespoons of butter in a small skillet for a few minutes until golden brown. Set aside.

Also while the chicken is broiling, bring the water, salt, and oil to a rolling boil in a large pot and drop in the pasta. Cook for 6 to 8 minutes if using fresh pasta, 10 to 12 minutes if dried. When the pasta is done, drain it in a colander and stir the 4 tablespoons of melted butter through it. Toss with the grated cheese.

When the chicken is done, remove the skewers from the top of the casserole, set them on a platter, turn off the oven, and place the chicken in the oven to keep warm. Put the skillet or casserole with the vegetables in it on top of the stove and stir in the wine, tomatoes, Sauce Espagnole, and mushrooms. Bring to a boil over high heat and cook for about 2 minutes to blend the flavors.

To serve the dish, heap the pasta in the center of a deep platter. Place the skewers of chicken around the pasta and spoon the sauce over the pasta and the chicken skewers. Pass additional Parmesan cheese.

Sauce Espagnole

Melt the butter in a large saucepan and add the diced carrot, onion, celery, and bacon. Cook for about 5 minutes, until everything is golden brown. Remove from heat and sprinkle the flour over all. Stir to incorporate the flour. Add the remaining ingredients, bring to a boil, cover, and reduce the heat to simmer. Cook for about 30 minutes, stirring occasionally. Cool and then strain through a fine sieve. The sauce may be frozen.

Ricotta Cheesecake

One or two passes at this delicious Italian cheesecake should qualify you as a pastry specialist. The crisscross pattern on the top is the sign of an authentic Italian cheesecake.

Crust for One 9-Inch Cake

Put the flour into a bowl for the electric mixer. Add the bits of butter and mix on low speed until grainy. Add the egg yolks, sugar, Marsala, lemon rind, and salt. Continue mixing until the mixture forms a soft ball of dough and leaves the sides of the bowl clean.

Gather the ball together and wrap it in wax paper. Chill for at least 1 hour to firm up the butter.

Cut off one quarter of the dough to be used later for the crisscross topping and return it to the refrigerator. Lightly flour a pastry cloth or board and put the ball of dough in the center. Roll out the dough, making it about ⅛ inch thick and 12 inches in diameter.

Fit the dough into a 9-inch cake pan with a removable bottom or a 9-inch springform. Press the dough down firmly into the corners and up the sides of the pan. Trim the edges. Set the prepared pan aside while you make the filling.

2 cups sifted flour
12 tablespoons (1½ sticks) sweet butter, cut into small bits
4 egg yolks
¼ cup sugar
3 tablespoons sweet Marsala
Grated rind of 1 lemon
½ teaspoon salt

Filling

Put all the ingredients up to the raisins into a bowl for the electric mixer and mix well until smooth and creamy. Stir in the raisins, orange peel, and citron.

Use a small pastry brush to brush the inside bottom and sides of the prepared crust with the egg white beaten with the water. Allow the egg white to dry slightly on the pastry, then pour in the ricotta mixture. Sprinkle the pine nuts over the top of the filling and set aside. Preheat the oven to 325°.

Remove the piece of dough remaining in the refrigerator and flour the pastry cloth or board again. Roll this piece of dough out into a rectangle about 12 inches by 6 inches.

Cut this rectangle into eight long strips and trim off the rough edges. Place four of the strips across the filling in the pan and press edges to sides. Trim excess dough. Turn the pan one quarter turn away from you, counterclockwise, and lay the remaining four strips of dough across the top, creating a crisscross effect. Press edges to sides and trim excess dough.

Brush these strips with some of the egg white mixture. The cake is now ready for the oven.

Bake the cake for 2 hours or until the filling seems firm and puffy and brown on top. Cool for about 10 minutes.

When cool enough to handle, put the cake on a coffee can and allow the sides of the pan to drop away, or if using a springform, release the sides. Cool the cake completely; then slide it off the bottom of the pan onto a serving tray.

3 pounds fresh ricotta cheese
½ cup sugar
1 tablespoon flour
½ teaspoon salt
1 teaspoon vanilla extract
Grated rind of 1 lemon or orange
4 egg yolks
¼ cup white raisins
2 tablespoons finely diced candied orange peel
2 tablespoons finely diced candied citron
1 egg white lightly beaten with 1 tablespoon cold water
2 tablespoons pine nuts

June

LESSON 2 3

Beet and Endive Salad
Lobster d'Été
Lemon Mousse with Raspberry Sauce

LESSON 2 4

Salade Niçoise
Bouillabaisse à la Provençale
Strawberry Walnut Cream Roulade

LESSON 2 5

Vegetables Bagna Cauda
Lobster Fra Diavolo
Strawberries with Zabaglione Sauce

LESSON 2 6

Salade Nouvelle
Lobster Soufflé à la Plaza-Athénée
Fresh Fruits with Crushed Caramel

Beet and Endive Salad

Lobster d'Été

Lemon Mousse with Raspberry Sauce

Although pasta forms the base for the pink and creamy mor-sels of lobster, this entrée is fare for an elegant meal. Be sure to use a very thin pasta, and for a beautiful color contrast to the lobster, scatter some sautéed asparagus tips over the top.

Make the lemon mousse and the raspberry sauce a day in advance.

Beet and Endive Salad

In this salad, the snow-white endive sets off the rich beet red. Parsley and red onion are good taste and color additions too. In looking for Belgian endives, try to avoid those that are yellowing at the tips, a sign of age.

A 1-pound can of shoestring
  beets
6 Belgian endives
1 red onion
2 tablespoons chopped fresh
  parsley
6 tablespoons olive oil
2 tablespoons fresh lemon juice
1 heaping teaspoon Dijon
  mustard
1 teaspoon salt
½ teaspoon sugar
Freshly ground black pepper to
  taste

Drain the beets well and spread them out on a paper towel to continue to drain. (If you prefer, six fresh, medium-sized beets may be steamed for about 1 hour, drained, peeled, and cut into thin julienne strips.)

Trim the root ends of the endives, wash the leaves, and dry them well. Stack the leaves and cut them lengthwise into thin julienne strips.

Finely dice the onion. Put the beets, endive, onion, and parsley into a large salad bowl and chill.

Put the oil, lemon juice, mustard, salt, sugar, and pepper into a small plastic or glass container with a tight-fitting lid, and shake well until thoroughly mixed. Pour the dressing over the salad ingredients and toss to mix well. Chill thoroughly and serve with a sprinkling of chopped parsley on top.

Lobster d'Été

If you have no fresh fish stock, bottled clam juice diluted with an equal amount of water may be substituted. Also, be sure to use a fairly decent cognac because when the liquid boils down and the alcohol evaporates, it's the grape flavor that's left. Cognac does magical things to cooked foods — as in this recipe, for example, or a pâté where it helps to turn what is basically a baked meat loaf into a French masterpiece.

When buying the pasta, look for something called *cappa d'angelo* (angel's hair). Or use the thinnest you can find.

Bring about 2 inches of salted water to a rolling boil in a large pot with a tight-fitting lid. Drop the live lobsters into the pot, cover, and steam for about 15 minutes. (If you are using frozen lobster tails, steam them for only 10 minutes.) When the lobsters are done, remove them from the pot and let them drain. When they are cool enough to handle, crack the shells and carefully remove all the meat. Cut the meat into small chunks and set aside.

Heat the 3 or 4 tablespoons of butter in a large skillet and sauté the mushrooms and shallots for 3 to 5 minutes, until they are soft and golden but not brown. Stir in the lobster pieces and sauté for another minute or two. Season with salt and white pepper and stir in the tarragon. Pour the cognac over all and reduce the liquid slightly over high heat. Turn off the heat and set the skillet aside.

Melt the 4 tablespoons of butter in another saucepan and when it is hot and foamy whisk in the flour, stirring to form a *roux*. Whisk in the fish stock and the heavy cream; add the tomato paste, seasonings, and mustard. Bring this mixture to a rolling boil, whisking constantly, and simmer for a few minutes. When the sauce is done, pour it over the lobster and heat through.

Have a large pot of salted water at a rolling boil and add 1 tablespoon oil. Drop in the pasta and cook it for 6 to 7 minutes if it is fresh, 10 to 12 if dried. Drain it and immediately toss with the melted butter.

To serve the dish, place a ring of pasta on a large round platter and spoon the hot lobster mixture into the center of the ring. Pass grated Parmesan cheese.

2 live lobsters (or 4 frozen, defrosted lobster tails)
3 or 4 tablespoons butter
1 pound mushrooms, thinly sliced
6 shallots, finely minced
Salt and a dash of white pepper to taste
1 teaspoon dried tarragon (or 1 tablespoon chopped fresh tarragon)
2 tablespoons cognac or Armagnac
4 tablespoons butter
4 tablespoons flour
2 cups fish stock (page 110)
1 cup heavy cream
2 tablespoons tomato paste
Salt, white pepper, and a dash of cayenne pepper to taste
A dash of ground nutmeg
½ teaspoon dry Colman's mustard
1 tablespoon cooking oil
1 pound very thin pasta
2 tablespoons melted butter
Freshly grated Parmesan cheese

Lemon Mousse with Raspberry Sauce

This recipe tastes like a cool summer breeze. A pinch of cream of tartar beaten into the egg whites will help hold the peaks. If you have fresh raspberries, it seems a shame to purée them for sauce; serve them whole as an accompaniment to the mousse. Blueberries, just coming into season, may also be substituted, either whole or puréed.

SERVES 8

127

4 fresh lemons
2 tablespoons unflavored gelatin
8 eggs
⅔ cup sugar
2 cups heavy cream
4 packages (10 ounces each)
   frozen raspberries, defrosted
1 tablespoon cornstarch or
   arrowroot
4 tablespoons sugar
2 tablespoons kirsch, framboise,
   or Grand Marnier

Cut a piece of aluminum foil or wax paper long enough to fit around the sides of a 6-cup soufflé dish. Fold it in half lengthwise and lightly butter one side. Tie the foil around the bowl, buttered side in. Refrigerate the bowl. If you prefer, use individual sherbet or champagne glasses and omit the collar.

Grate the rind of two of the lemons and set it aside. Juice all the lemons into a heat-proof glass measuring cup or bowl and sprinkle the gelatin over the lemon juice. When the gelatin is soft, put the cup or bowl into a saucepan. Add an inch of hot water to the pan. Place over low heat until the gelatin mixture is dissolved and smooth. Remove the cup or bowl from the pan and set it aside to cool.

While the gelatin is cooling, separate the eggs and begin beating the yolks. Add the ⅔ cup sugar slowly and continue to beat the mixture until it is thick and creamy.

Beat the heavy cream in a chilled bowl and set it aside. Beat the egg whites in a clean, dry bowl and set them aside.

Stir the gelatin mixture into the beaten yolk mixture and then gently fold in the lemon rind, whipped cream, and egg whites until all is well mixed.

Pour this mixture into the prepared soufflé dish and chill it overnight. ◀

To prepare the raspberry sauce, drain the raspberries (reserving the juice) and purée until smooth. Press the puréed raspberry pulp through a fine sieve to remove the seeds. Dilute the cornstarch in a tablespoon of the reserved juice. Put the sieved raspberry purée, diluted cornstarch mixture, sugar, and liqueur into a small saucepan and add 2 tablespoons of the juice. Mix well and bring to a boil. Stir and remove from the heat. Cool and chill overnight. Serve it with ◀ the mousse.

Salade Niçoise

Bouillabaisse à la Provençale

Strawberry Walnut Cream Roulade

This is a menu from France's Côte d'Azur, featuring the epitome of Marseilles cooking, bouillabaisse. It started with unsold fish from the fisherman's daily catch, which wound up in the family soup kettle each evening — heads, tails, bones, and all. French chefs, always eager to build refinements into the basics, adopted it, adapted it, and added elegance; now it is the number-one menu choice from Saint-Tropez to Monte Carlo.

Salade Niçoise

4 eggs
12 red-skinned new potatoes
1 pound fresh green beans
1 package (9 ounces) frozen
  artichoke hearts
A 7-ounce can of tuna fish
1 pint fresh cherry tomatoes
A 6-ounce can of pitted black
  olives or ½ pound small
  Niçoise olives (available in
  specialty food shops)
1 small red onion
1 green pepper
1 red bell pepper
A 1-pound can of shoestring
  beets
A 2-ounce can of rolled anchovy
  fillets
1 head romaine lettuce
1 head Boston lettuce
2 tablespoons chopped fresh
  parsley
1 recipe Creamy Vinaigrette
  Dressing (see below)

A medley of vegetable flavors and a beautiful and bountiful appearance are the keys to this sumptuous salad. Preparation of any or all ingredients can be done a day ahead, including the vinaigrette dressing. Do not assemble the salad until ready to serve.

Hard-boil the eggs. When they are cool, shell them and cut them into quarters.

Scrub the potatoes and put them into a pot with about 2 inches of water. Cover the pot and steam the potatoes for about 20 minutes or until tender. Cool, but do not peel. Slice them thinly and toss the slices with a tablespoon or two of olive oil to lubricate them. This prevents them from sticking together. Set aside.

Snap the ends off the beans and steam them in an inch of boiling, salted water, covered, for about 3 minutes. Immediately drain and run the beans under cold water to refresh. Drain again and set aside.

Steam the frozen artichoke hearts in an inch of boiling, salted water, covered, for about 3 minutes. Drain and refresh with cold water. Drain again and set aside.

Drain the tuna well and flake it. Cut the cherry tomatoes in half. Drain the olives. Slice the onion and peppers into thin rings. Drain the canned beets, rinse them with cold water, and let them continue to drain to remove the excess liquid. Drain the anchovies well and pat them with paper towels to absorb the excess oil.

To present the salad, wash the lettuce leaves well, dry them, and arrange them in the bottom of a large glass or Lucite salad bowl. Begin arranging all the prepared ingredients in layers on top of the lettuce. Do this attractively in terms of color, size, and texture of the ingredients. Sprinkle the chopped fresh parsley over all.

Chill the prepared bowl until just before serving. Bring the bowl to the table and toss the salad with the dressing.

Creamy Vinaigrette Dressing

Put all ingredients except the oil into a bowl and whisk together. Whisk in the oil slowly to create a creamy consistency — similar to thin mayonnaise. Just before using, whisk again.

1 egg yolk
1 tablespoon heavy cream
3 tablespoons fresh lemon juice
1 clove garlic, mashed
1 heaping teaspoon Dijon
  mustard
1 teaspoon salt
½ teaspoon sugar
Freshly ground black pepper to
  taste
½ cup olive oil

Bouillabaisse à la Provençale

SERVES 8

All Marseilles housewives and most Parisian chefs have their own bouillabaisse recipes, each a little different, and most of them would probably say this is not the classic recipe. But chances are they would approve of its flavor, with such tasty additions as shrimp and lobster. The Pernod or anisette is traditional, but optional, because the light licorice flavor is not to everyone's liking.

Look for littlenecks in preference to cherrystone clams, because they don't toughen up quite as much.

The fish stock is a basic recipe that freezes well and can be used in several other recipes in this book. As long as you are buying a lot of fish, ask the fishmonger to give you the heads and trimmings and try making the stock.

4 fresh, live lobsters, cut up in
their shells into small pieces
(remove and discard the eyes,
antennae, and tomalley)
1 dozen each littleneck clams
and fresh mussels
2 pounds raw shrimp, peeled to
the fantail and deveined
3 or 4 pounds firm, white fleshy
fish (such as striped bass,
snapper, sea bass, or halibut),
cut into large chunks
3 tablespoons olive oil
2 leeks, well washed and
chopped
3 large onions, chopped
3 cloves garlic, mashed
A 2-pound can of Italian plum
tomatoes packed in purée
2 tablespoons tomato paste
½ teaspoon dried thyme
3 large Idaho potatoes, peeled
and sliced
3 or 4 sprigs of fresh parsley
and 2 bay leaves, tied together
for easy removal
1 teaspoon saffron threads
1 quart fresh fish stock (see
below)
Salt and black pepper to taste
A *beurre manié* made of 4
tablespoons soft butter and 4
tablespoons flour mixed
together to form a paste
A dash of Tabasco
1 tablespoon Pernod or anisette
(optional)
1 recipe *aïoli* (page 133)
1 recipe fresh garlic toasts (page
133)
Freshly grated Parmesan cheese

If you have a reliable fishmonger, he will prepare all the seafood for you according to your instructions. Be sure fleshy fish is filleted and free of bone, but leave the skin on, as it helps to hold the fish together. If you cannot get him to cut up the lobster for you, just plunge the live lobsters into an inch of boiling water and steam for 3 minutes, covered. This will kill them instantly and then make them much easier to cut up.

Scrub the mussels and clams under cold running water. Set the clams aside. Pull the "beards" off the mussels and put them in a basin of cold water. Add a tablespoon of cornmeal and let the mussels soak for an hour and rid themselves of excess sand. Rinse again before using. Prepare all the other ingredients as directed.

Heat the oil in a large deep kettle and add the leeks, onions, and garlic. Cook for 3 to 5 minutes until they are soft but not brown. Add the tomatoes (broken up into large chunks) with their juice, the tomato paste, thyme, potatoes, parsley–bay leaf bundle, saffron, fish stock, salt, and pepper. Cover and bring the mixture to a boil. Reduce the heat to simmer and cook for about 15 minutes. Uncover, remove the parsley and bay leaves, and discard. The bouillabaisse can be made a day ahead up to this point.

Bring the liquid to a rolling boil and whisk in the *beurre manié* a small bit at a time, using a balloon whisk, until it is all incorporated and the mixture has thickened. Add the lobster pieces, cover the pot, and cook for about 10 minutes. Then add the shrimp, clams, mussels, fish chunks, Tabasco, and Pernod. Cook for an additional 10 minutes or until the clams and mussels are all open wide.

To serve, put the seafood onto a large platter and spoon the broth with the vegetables into a soup tureen. Put the hot garlic toasts in a basket and the *aïoli* into a sauceboat. Guests should help themselves to seafood and soup. The bouillabaisse is served with the croutons placed on top of the soup bowl, *aïoli* spooned on top of the croutons, and grated Parmesan cheese sprinkled over all.

Fish Stock

Heat the butter in a deep kettle and add the carrot, onion, celery, shallots, and garlic. Sauté these vegetables over low heat until they are soft and pale golden. Add the remaining ingredients, cover the pot, bring to a boil, reduce to simmer, and cook for about 30 minutes. Cool and strain through fine cheesecloth. Any unused stock can be frozen.

ABOUT 2 QUARTS

2 tablespoons butter
1 carrot, sliced
1 onion, sliced
1 stalk celery, sliced
Several shallots, sliced
2 cloves garlic, cut in half
Heads, bones, and trimmings of about 4 pounds of fish
2 bay leaves
1 teaspoon whole black peppercorns
1 teaspoon salt
2 cups dry white wine
Enough cold water to cover everything in the pot

Garlic Toasts

Put the butter and garlic into a small saucepan and heat until the butter is completely melted. Let stand for at least 15 minutes so the butter can absorb the garlic flavor. Remove the garlic and discard. Lay the slices of bread out flat on a cooky sheet and brush them liberally with the garlic-flavored butter. Toast the slices in a 350° oven for about 15 minutes, until crisp and golden brown. The toasts can be made ahead. Store them in a plastic bag.

16 TOASTS

8 tablespoons butter
3 or 4 cloves garlic, peeled and cut in half
1 loaf French bread, cut into 16 thick slices

Aïoli

Put the egg yolks and the mashed garlic into a blender or a food processor fitted with the steel blade. Blend for a few seconds. Begin adding the oil a drop at a time, until the mixture begins to thicken. Then increase the oil to a slow, steady stream, until it is all incorporated and the mixture has the consistency of mayonnaise. *Aïoli* is the Provençal term for garlic mayonnaise, and it keeps in the refrigerator for several days.

ABOUT 1 CUP

3 egg yolks
3 cloves garlic, mashed
1 cup olive oil (or use a combination of oils)

133

Strawberry Walnut Cream Roulade

7 eggs
¾ cup sugar
1 teaspoon baking powder
2 teaspoons powdered instant
 coffee (not freeze-dried)
1 cup finely ground walnuts
½ cup apricot jam
2 tablespoons Grand Marnier
1 teaspoon sugar
1 cup heavy cream
1 tablespoon sugar
1 pint fresh ripe strawberries,
 hulled and sliced
Confectioners' sugar

Walnuts and strawberries seem like an improbable combination. The addition of Grand Marnier to flavor the apricot jam mixture and the whipped cream is also a bit out of the ordinary, but that is what makes this cake roll *very* extraordinary.

Butter an 11-by-16-inch jelly-roll pan lightly and line the buttered pan with wax paper. Butter the wax paper and trim it at the edges. Set aside. Preheat the oven to 350°.

Separate the eggs and set the whites aside. Begin beating the yolks and gradually add the sugar, continuing to beat at high speed until the mixture thickens and turns a pale vanilla color. Stir in the baking powder and the instant coffee. Remove from the mixer and gently fold in the ground nuts. Set this mixture aside.

Beat the egg whites in a clean, dry bowl until stiff peaks form. Gently fold them into the egg yolk mixture and spread this over the prepared pan.

Bake the cake for 25 minutes or until the top is golden brown and springs back lightly when you touch it. Remove the cake when it is done and place a damp linen towel over it. Invert the cake onto the towel and gently peel off the wax paper. Roll up the cake in the damp towel and let it sit until it comes to room temperature.

While the cake is cooling, sieve the apricot jam into a small pot and add 1 tablespoon of Grand Marnier and the 1 teaspoon of sugar. Melt over medium heat until smooth. Remove from heat and allow to cool.

When ready to fill the cake, whip the cream with the 1 tablespoon of sugar and the remaining Grand Marnier until thick and stiff. Have the sliced berries ready. Unroll the cake and spread the apricot glaze over it. Fold the sliced berries into the whipped cream and spread this mixture over the cake. Reroll the cake and transfer it to a serving platter. Chill thoroughly. The cake can be filled and refrigerated for several hours before serving.

Sprinkle the cake liberally with confectioners' sugar just before serving.

25

Vegetables Bagna Cauda

Lobster Fra Diavolo

Strawberries with Zabaglione Sauce

This is the menu an Italian hostess would probably concoct if lobster was her choice for the main course. The appetizer is light, healthy, colorful, and a very different way of serving *crudités*.

If you have a small warmer or fondue pot from another decade's culinary gadgetry, this is a good time to use it — to keep the *bagna cauda* from becoming tepid.

Vegetables Bagna Cauda

8 tablespoons butter
½ cup olive oil
3 cloves garlic, minced or
  mashed
A 2-ounce can of flat anchovy
  fillets, drained and mashed
2 tablespoons wine vinegar
An assortment of raw or
  blanched vegetables:
  cauliflower, broccoli, green
  beans, celery, carrots, fennel,
  peppers, and so on
Lemon wedges and sprigs of
  parsley (for garnish)

Hot bath is what *bagna cauda* means, because you dip the vegetables of your choice into a warm sauce.

Whether you blanch the vegetables is up to you, with the exception of green beans, which might be a bit too crunchy without 3 minutes of blanching.

Heat the butter and oil in a small saucepan and add the garlic. Sauté the garlic in the hot oil and butter for a minute or two, taking care not to burn it. Stir in the mashed anchovies and cook for another minute. Add the vinegar and heat through. Pour the hot sauce into a small bowl or crock that fits over a flame.

Surround the bowl with an assortment of vegetables and garnish with the lemon wedges and parsley sprigs. Put it in the center of a table and allow your guests to dip the vegetables into the hot sauce.

Lobster Fra Diavolo

Look for fresh basil for this recipe. It should be available in June.

The plum tomato sauce, red lobster shells, and red peppers make this recipe richly colored and devilishly spicy, hence the name Fra Diavolo, "Brother Devil."

Digging out those succulent morsels of lobster from their shells amid the rich tomato-based sauce can be a bit messy. But cooking the lobster in the shells adds considerably to the flavor of the sauce, which can be as spicy as you like, depending on how much hot pepper and Tabasco you use.

Have the fishmonger cut up the lobsters. When you get them home, rinse each piece and pat it dry. Remove the antennae and scrape out and discard the tomalley. Sprinkle the pieces of lobster with salt and pepper.

Heat the olive oil in a deep kettle and sauté the lobster pieces until they turn bright red all over. Remove them from the pan and set aside.

Add the garlic, onion, and shallots to the pan and sauté for a minute or two until they are pale golden. Add the diced peppers and sauté for another minute or two, mixing well. Sprinkle the cognac over all and allow it to come to a boil and reduce slightly. This burns off the alcohol. Return the lobsters to the pot and add the wine, pepper flakes, tomatoes, tomato paste, herbs, Tabasco, and additional salt and pepper. Bring this mixture to a boil, breaking up the larger pieces of tomato. Cover the pot, reduce the heat to simmer, and cook for about 10 minutes. Remove the bay leaf.

Serve with spaghetti or white rice.

4 live lobsters, cut up in the shells (or 4 frozen lobster tails cut into pieces in the shells)
Salt and freshly ground black pepper to taste
4 tablespoons olive oil
3 cloves garlic, minced or mashed
1 onion, finely minced
6 shallots, finely minced
1 green pepper and 1 red bell pepper, seeded and diced
3 tablespoons cognac
½ cup dry white wine
½ teaspoon dried red pepper flakes (optional)
A 2-pound can of Italian plum tomatoes packed in tomato purée
2 tablespoons tomato paste
½ cup chopped fresh parsley
1 teaspoon each dried oregano and basil (or 1 tablespoon each chopped fresh oregano and basil)
½ teaspoon dried thyme
1 bay leaf
A dash of Tabasco or to taste
Additional salt and freshly ground black pepper to taste

Strawberries with Zabaglione Sauce

1 pint fresh strawberries
2 egg yolks
6 tablespoons sugar
¼ cup sweet Marsala
1 cup heavy cream, whipped
4 ounces semisweet chocolate
2 tablespoons sweet butter

Sweet Marsala wine is basic to *zabaglione*. The constant beating over low heat doubles the volume and thickens the sauce. Folding whipped cream into the chilled sauce gives a light texture and smooths out the heady wine flavor. The final touch, chocolate, is an exquisite addition, but be sure that the chocolate is not too hot — just syrupy enough to dribble over the top.

Wash, hull, and dry the berries. Cut the large ones in half and set them aside to chill.

Put the egg yolks in the top of a double boiler and beat them with a wire whisk. (A hand-held mixer also works well.) Beat in the sugar and Marsala and continue to beat until the mixture begins to thicken. Place the pot over barely simmering water and continue to beat until it thickens and doubles in volume. The sauce is ready when it is thick, slightly warmer than room temperature, and thoroughly coats the back of a wooden spoon. This takes a while, so do not hurry the procedure by increasing the heat, or you will end up with scrambled eggs.

When the sauce is finished, transfer it to a bowl, cover tightly with plastic wrap, and chill thoroughly. The sauce can be made up to this point several days ahead.

To serve, whip the cup of heavy cream until thick and stiff and fold it into the chilled sauce. Melt the chocolate and butter together in the top of a double boiler until smooth. Distribute the berries among individual serving dishes, spoon some of the sauce over each, and dribble the melted chocolate over all. Serve at once.

26

Salade Nouvelle

Lobster Soufflé à la Plaza-Athénée

Fresh Fruits with Crushed Caramel

Some years ago, on a visit to Paris, I indulged myself in luxury for a couple of days by staying at the famous Hôtel Plaza-Athénée. It was June and the summer garden dining room had just opened. Though it was impossible to persuade my two young daughters to stray very far from a simple steak, I ordered the lobster soufflé, and what a choice it turned out to be! Everything was right — the day, the time, the place, and, most of all, the soufflé.

After lunch, I introduced myself to the maître d'. He wasn't about to let me into the kitchen on such short notice, but he did give me the highlights of the chef's recipe and procedure.

So, here, several years and half a dozen trial tests later, is the recipe that duplicates that ambrosial taste. To go with such a repast, I have chosen a Salade Nouvelle and fresh fruit with a sprinkling of crushed caramel.

Salade Nouvelle

Putting cold roast meat together with vegetables and adding a truffle garnish is a mainstay procedure of the *nouvelle cuisine*. It certainly elevates a basic salad into a presentation of elegance. With this recipe you do not drown the salad in dressing. Rather, the delicate lemon-egg-oil dressing is used to add piquancy to the beans, mushrooms, and radishes, while the shredded duck meat is savored as is. Make this recipe another time as a main course and substitute celeriac for the radishes. You lose some color, but gain texture.

A 3-pound duckling, cut into quarters
Salt and pepper to taste
½ cup chicken stock
2 pounds thin and small fresh green beans, ends removed
2 tablespoons fresh lemon juice
1 egg yolk
1 clove garlic, mashed
2 teaspoons Dijon mustard
A dash of Tabasco
Salt and freshly ground black pepper to taste
½ teaspoon sugar
2 tablespoons heavy cream or *crème fraîche*
6 tablespoons olive oil
1 pound very firm white mushrooms
8 small red radishes, ends trimmed
1 small truffle, thinly sliced or shaved with a vegetable peeler (optional)
Chopped parsley (for garnish)

Preheat the oven to 400°. Trim off all visible fat from the pieces of duckling and season with salt and pepper. Place the pieces of duck on a rack in a shallow roasting pan and pour in the chicken stock. Roast the duck, skin side down, for 30 minutes. Turn over and roast an additional 30 minutes or until the duck is quite crisp and golden brown. Remove from the oven and set aside to cool.

Skim the fat from the roasting pan and pour the remaining juices into a small bowl and reserve. When the duck is cool enough to handle, gently pull off the skin and discard. Cut the meat away from the bone and shred it into thin julienne strips. Moisten the strips with the reserved juices; set aside.

Put the prepared green beans into an inch of boiling, salted water, cover, and blanch for about 2 minutes. Drain when done and immediately run cold water over the beans to stop the cooking process. Drain again and set aside.

Make the dressing by putting the lemon juice, egg yolk, garlic, mustard, Tabasco, salt, pepper, and sugar into a small bowl. Whisk in the cream and then the oil in a slow, steady stream until the dressing thickens slightly. Pour a few tablespoons of the dressing over the beans and chill them.

Cut off the stems of the mushrooms flush with the caps and slice the caps. Lay the slices on a board and cut into thin matchsticks. Do the same with the radishes. Toss the remaining dressing through the mushrooms and radishes and chill.

To serve, place a small round of the mushroom-radish mixture in the center of a salad plate and arrange some beans in a circle around the mound. Sprinkle the top with strips of duckling meat and shaved truffle. Garnish with chopped parsley and serve at once.

Lobster Soufflé à la Plaza-Athénée

This recipe is a two-for-the-price-of-one special. The lobster part is basically *homard à l'amoricaine*, while the soufflé also can stand on its own.

There is dispute over the term *amoricaine*; is it the restaurant which might have unveiled it, the ancient name for the department in France that is famous for lobster, or does the dish, also known as *homard à l'americaine*, have some association with America? Whatever, it is classic, good, and worth cooking.

It is also well worth getting the lobsters in the shells for this recipe, since the shells have great flavor.

If you want to prepare the soufflé without the lobster sometime, you might want to increase the amount of Gruyère cheese; and be sure to use a 6-cup soufflé dish. Use real Gruyère, cut from the wheel, not the preportioned, processed triangles done up in foil. Good as they are for snacks, they don't grate well and they don't have the nutty bite of true Gruyère.

2 lobsters, cut into pieces in the shell
3 or 4 tablespoons olive oil
Salt and freshly ground black pepper to taste
2 carrots, minced
2 onions, minced
2 stalks celery, minced
4 shallots, minced
¼ cup cognac
2 cloves garlic, mashed
2 whole cloves
12 black peppercorns
½ teaspoon dried thyme
1 teaspoon dried tarragon
½ cup tomato paste
4 very ripe tomatoes, chopped
1 cup dry white wine
1 cup fresh fish stock (page 110)
4 sprigs of fresh parsley
2 tablespoons soft butter
3 tablespoons flour

If you can't get live lobsters cut up in the shell or don't want to work with them, use steamed lobsters. Pull the lobster meat out of the shell of the steamed lobsters before you begin the recipe and set it aside. Then chop the cooked shells into smaller pieces and use them to flavor the sauce. You may also substitute frozen lobster tails, defrosted and cut up in the shells.

Heat the oil in a large, deep kettle and add the pieces of lobster. Cook over high heat, stirring, until the shells turn a bright pink. Sprinkle with salt and pepper. Add the carrots, onions, celery, and shallots. Cook until all of the moisture in the pot is evaporated and the vegetables are soft and golden. Pour in the cognac and let it come to a boil and reduce slightly. Add the garlic, cloves, peppercorns, thyme, tarragon, tomato paste, tomatoes, wine, stock, and parsley. Cover the pot, bring to a boil, reduce the heat to simmer, and cook for about 15 minutes.

At this point, remove the pieces of lobster and set them aside to cool. When they are cool enough to handle, remove the lobster meat from the shells and dice it. Set it aside and discard the shells.

Put the softened butter into a small bowl and work in the flour with your fingertips or a fork to form a *beurre manié*. Bring the sauce mixture in the kettle to a rolling boil and gently whisk in the *beurre manié* a small bit at a time, until it is all incorporated and the sauce has thickened. It should be the consistency of medium white sauce. If it is still not thick enough, make more *beurre manié* and add it. Be sure the sauce is boiling when you add it. After the sauce has thickened, remove it from the heat and cool slightly.

When the sauce is cool, put the entire mixture through a fine sieve, pressing against the solids with the back of a wooden spoon to extract all juices. Set aside about 1 cup of the strained sauce to pass with the finished soufflé and stir the diced lobster meat into the remaining sauce.

Cheese Soufflé

2 tablespoons soft butter
¼ cup freshly grated Parmesan cheese
3 tablespoons butter
3 tablespoons flour
1 cup milk
Salt, white pepper, and a dash of cayenne pepper
A dash of nutmeg
2 teaspoons cornstarch diluted in 3 tablespoons water
6 eggs
A pinch of salt
1 cup grated Gruyère or Swiss cheese
¼ cup freshly grated Parmesan cheese

Butter the bottom and sides of a 2-quart soufflé dish with the softened butter and sprinkle the grated Parmesan cheese over all to coat the dish completely. Chill the dish until ready to use. Preheat the oven to 375°.

Melt the 3 tablespoons of butter in a small saucepan and whisk in the 3 tablespoons flour, stirring to form a *roux*. Slowly pour in the milk and bring this mixture to a boil. Stir in the salt, peppers, nutmeg, and the diluted cornstarch. Cook for another minute or two and remove from the heat.

Separate the eggs and put the whites in a clean, dry bowl and set them aside. Lightly beat the yolks and spoon some of the hot sauce into the egg yolks to warm them. Then return this mixture to the remaining sauce and mix well. Transfer it to a small bowl. If you want to make this base sauce early in the day and refrigerate it, cover the bowl tightly with plastic wrap.

To finish the lobster soufflé, spoon the lobster mixture (above) into the bottom of the chilled soufflé bowl. Put the reserved cup of lobster sauce into a small saucepan to heat while the soufflé is baking.

Beat the egg whites with a pinch of salt until stiff peaks form. Fold the grated Gruyère and Parmesan cheeses into the base of the cheese soufflé and then fold in the whipped egg whites. Gently spoon this mixture over the lobster mixture in the dish and bake the soufflé for exactly 40 minutes in the center of the oven. Serve at once with the reserved, heated lobster sauce on the side.

Fresh Fruit with Crushed Caramel

A food processor is a very handy tool for crushing the cooked caramel, though a clean hammer and a strong arm also work wonders. Cover the caramel with several layers of wax paper or put it into a paper bag before you begin to pound so it doesn't fly in all directions.

Prepare the fruits up to the oranges according to directions and put them into a large glass serving bowl.

Carefully cut the zest of the oranges away from the white pith in long pieces. Set the pieces of zest aside and continue to peel all the pith away from the oranges. When the oranges are completely peeled, slice or segment them. Do this over the fruit bowl to catch the juices. Put the pieces of orange in with the other fruits and chill the bowl.

Lay the pieces of zest strips on a board and thinly slice them into julienne strips. Put these strips into a heavy saucepan and add the water, sugar, and cream of tartar. Bring this mixture to a boil and continue to cook for 30 minutes or until the liquid is quite syrupy and the strips of rind are soft and sweet. Remove from heat, cool slightly, and stir in the ½ cup Grand Marnier. Spoon the entire mixture over the fruits in the bowl. Chill. The fruit can be prepared to this point a day ahead.

To prepare the caramel, put the 1 cup of sugar and the ½ cup of water into a small heavy saucepan and bring to a rolling boil. Continue to cook over medium heat until the mixture turns amber brown and is very thick and caramelized. This should take 15 to 20 minutes, and the mixture should register about 270° on a candy thermometer if you wish to check it. Have a lightly buttered cooky sheet with shallow sides ready and pour the liquid caramel out onto the buttered sheet. It will begin to harden as soon as it cools. Set it aside until it is completely cool and hard; then it can be crushed into small pieces. The crushed caramel will keep for several days stored in a tightly sealed jar or plastic container at room temperature.

Whip the cream with the sugar and Grand Marnier.

To serve, pass the bowl of fruit, a bowl of the crushed caramel, and a bowl of the whipped cream.

1 ripe honeydew melon, peeled and cut into small cubes
1 ripe cantaloupe, peeled and cut into cubes
1 ripe pineapple, peeled and cut into cubes
1 pint fresh blueberries, washed and dried
1 pint fresh strawberries, washed, hulled, and dried
4 large seedless oranges
2 cups water
2 cups sugar
¼ teaspoon cream of tartar
½ cup Grand Marnier or any orange-flavored liqueur
1 cup sugar
½ cup water
1 cup heavy cream
2 teaspoons sugar
1 tablespoon Grand Marnier

July

LESSON 27

Salade Francillon
Vitello Tonnato
Chocolate Mold with Glazed Strawberries

LESSON 28

Ratatouille Niçoise
Fillet of Striped Bass in Fillo Pastry
Peach Mousse with Raspberries

LESSON 29

Guacamole
Paella
Spanish Flan, Flamenco Style

LESSON 30

Terrine of Fish with Sauce Andalouse
Bombay Chicken Curry
Fresh Raspberry Tart

27

Salade Francillon

Vitello Tonnato

Chocolate Mold with Glazed Strawberries

The name Salade Francillon implies mussels and new potatoes. Cooked rice or cold pasta could be substituted for the potatoes. The Vitello Tonnato gains more flavor if the anchovies and capers are scattered over the dish with some abandon. One warning about the dessert: If it is a humid day, the glaze on the strawberries may not set. As an alternative, soak the berries in Grand Marnier and then dip them in melted chocolate.

Salade Francillon

Mussels are the most delicate and perishable of all the mollusks, so buy or collect them the day you plan to serve them. If asparagus is unavailable, use green beans. Regular sugar peas can be substituted for the snow peas. Instead of serving the salad in the tomato shell, you might want to serve it sometime simply surrounded by tomato wedges.

8 red-skinned new potatoes
5 pounds fresh mussels
½ cup dry white wine
½ pound fresh asparagus
½ pound fresh snow peas
1 small red onion
1 tablespoon chopped fresh
  parsley
1 teaspoon fresh-snipped chives
  (optional)
8 medium-sized ripe tomatoes
2 tablespoons fresh lemon juice
6 tablespoons olive oil
1 heaping teaspoon Dijon
  mustard
Salt and freshly ground black
  pepper to taste
A pinch of sugar

Scrub the potatoes well with a vegetable brush and put them into a steamer or saucepan with an inch or two of boiling salted water. Steam them for about 20 minutes, or until they are tender when pierced. Drain immediately and let them cool. When the potatoes are cool enough to handle, peel and dice or slice them and toss with a tablespoon or two of olive oil to keep them moist.

Discard any mussels that have broken shells or are open. Scrub the mussels under running cold water and pull off the "beards." Fill a basin or bowl with cold water and add a sprinkling of cornmeal. Drop the mussels in the water and let them soak for about an hour. Rinse and transfer them to a deep kettle and add the white wine. Cover and bring to a boil. Reduce the heat and steam the mussels for about 10 minutes or until they are all wide open. Shake the pan once or twice during the steaming. Pour the mussels into a colander to drain. When they are cool enough to handle, gently pull them out of their shells and discard the shells, but reserve a few in their shells for garnish.

Break off the thick white stem ends of the asparagus and slice the remaining stems and tips on the diagonal, into ½-inch pieces. String the snow peas and cut each one in half. Heat about a tablespoon of peanut or safflower oil in a small skillet. Gently sauté the asparagus pieces for about 3 minutes; then add the snow peas and sauté for another 2 minutes. Transfer to a strainer and cool.

Mince the red onion and set it aside with the parsley and chives. Slice off the tops of the tomatoes and gently scoop out the pulp and discard. Leave the shell of the tomato intact for stuffing. Slice a small piece off the bottom of each tomato so it will stand upright. Turn the tomato shells upside-down on paper towels to drain. The tomatoes can be scooped and set to drain a day ahead.

Put the lemon juice, olive oil, mustard, salt, pepper, and

sugar into a small container with a tight-fitting lid and shake well. Combine the potatoes, mussels, vegetables, onions, herbs, and dressing in a large bowl and toss gently. Stuff the drained tomato shells with the mixed salad and place them on individual salad plates. Garnish each plate with one or two of the reserved mussels in the shell and sprinkle additional chopped parsley over the top of each tomato. Serve slightly colder than room temperature.

Vitello Tonnato

SERVES 8

Often the crowning glory of a great northern Italian restaurant's cold buffet table, this dish combines several improbable companions, including humble canned tuna and aristocratic veal. You can economize a bit if you choose leg over loin, even more if you use boneless shoulder.

This dish may be made one or two days ahead, for both time and taste's sake. Give it at least 24 hours to meld flavors and thoroughly chill the reduced cooking liquids before adding them to the mayonnaise.

Tie the piece of veal so it forms a long cylinder. Season it with salt and pepper. Heat the olive oil in a deep Dutch oven or roasting pan and brown the meat on all sides, turning gently, until it is golden brown all over. Remove the meat from the pot and set it aside. Add the onions and celery to the hot oil in the pot and sauté for a few minutes. When they are golden, sprinkle the flour over all and stir to incorporate it. Add the stock, wine, tuna, anchovies, dried herbs, and parsley sprigs and mix well. Return the meat to the pot, cover, and bring the mixture to a boil. Reduce the heat to simmer and braise the meat for 1 hour or until it is fork-tender. Remove the bundle of parsley from the pot and discard. Remove the meat and allow it to drain and cool. Cut off the strings and discard. Then wrap the meat tightly in plastic wrap and refrigerate it
▶ for at least 24 hours.

Put the pan juices back on top of the stove and cook over very high heat until the liquid has reduced to 2 or 3 cups. It will thicken as it reduces. This will take some time, possibly as long as 20 minutes. Cool this reduction and then purée it until smooth in a blender or food processor. Chill for at least
▶ 24 hours.

A 5-pound piece of boneless veal, cut in a long, narrow piece
Salt and black pepper to taste
½ cup olive oil
1 medium onion, diced
2 stalks celery, diced
6 tablespoons flour
2 cups chicken stock (homemade or canned)
1 cup dry white wine
A 7-ounce can of tuna fish, drained
A 2-ounce can of flat anchovy fillets, drained
¼ teaspoon dried thyme
¼ teaspoon dried sage
A few sprigs of fresh parsley, tied together for easy removal
2 cups mayonnaise (see page 150)
Fresh lemon juice to taste
Capers
Chopped fresh parsley
Rolled anchovies

149

To finish the sauce for serving, put the mayonnaise into a bowl and whisk in the puréed mixture. Stir in a bit of lemon juice to taste and additional salt and pepper. The sauce should be of spooning consistency, not quite as thick as mayonnaise.

Remove the meat from the refrigerator, unwrap it, and slice it very thinly — slightly on the diagonal. Arrange the slices of meat attractively on a platter and nap the tops of the slices with some of the sauce. Scatter capers, chopped parsley, and rolled anchovies over the top and pass the remaining sauce in a separate sauceboat.

Mayonnaise

ABOUT 1 CUP

2 egg yolks
1 tablespoon fresh lemon juice
2 teaspoons Dijon mustard
Salt, white pepper, and a dash
  of cayenne pepper to taste
1½ cups oil (combined olive and
  safflower or corn oils)

Put the egg yolks, lemon juice, mustard, salt, and peppers into the container of a food processor fitted with the steel blade, or an electric blender, and mix for a few seconds. Begin adding the oil, a drop at a time, until the mixture starts to thicken. Then increase the addition of the oil to a slow, steady stream until it is all incorporated. Taste the mixture for additional salt, pepper, or lemon juice.

SERVES 8

Chocolate Mold with Glazed Strawberries

Remember the warning about humid days and glazed fruits. Here are a few more caveats:

When you make the glaze for the berries, be careful with temperatures. The caramelizing sugar keeps drawing heat from the pot and can turn dark brown quickly, so get it off the heat as soon as it begins to turn amber and pour it into a small metal bowl. If the caramel begins to harden while you are dipping, put the bowl of caramel glaze into a larger bowl of hot water to soften it. See the recipe for Chocolate Praline Soufflé (page 105) for more tips on caramelizing sugar.

When unmolding, dip a knife in hot water and work it around the edge carefully, so as not to spoil the molded design.

The Grand Marnier in this recipe may be optional for some, a necessity for many, but it is an obsession of mine. Especially with chocolate. You could substitute Cointreau, Triple Sec, or amaretto.

Lightly oil a 6-cup mold of any attractive shape and chill the mold.

Put the chocolate and butter in the top of a double boiler and add 3 tablespoons of the superfine sugar. Melt this mixture until smooth. Set aside to cool.

Separate the eggs; put the whites in a clean, dry bowl and set aside. Begin beating the yolks with an electric mixer until they thicken and then add the chocolate mixture in a slow stream until it is all incorporated. Continue to beat this mixture on high speed for about 5 minutes, until it is very thick and stiff.

Beat the egg whites until soft peaks begin to form, add the remaining tablespoon of superfine sugar, and continue to beat until stiff but not too dry. Stir the whites into the chocolate mixture with the 2 tablespoons Grand Marnier. Continue beating for another 5 minutes.

▶ Spoon this mixture into the oiled mold and chill for at least 6 hours, but preferably overnight.

To unmold, dip the mold in a basin of hot water and count to ten. Loosen around the sides of the mold with a clean knife dipped in hot water and then invert it onto a serving platter. Tap the bottom of the mold hard with the handle of a knife. It should slide out. If not, dip in hot water for another 10 seconds and try again.

To garnish, whip the heavy cream with the 1 tablespoon sugar and 1 tablespoon Grand Marnier and fill a pastry bag fitted with a rosette nozzle with the mixture. Pipe out attractive rosettes over the top and sides of the mold. Garnish with shaved chocolate or candied violets and refrigerate while you prepare the strawberries.

To make the caramel glaze, put the 2 cups of sugar and ⅔ cup water into a small heavy saucepan and cook over medium heat until the mixture dissolves and then begins to caramelize, turning a light amber. This should be at 270° on a candy thermometer. Immediately pour this liquid caramel into a small stainless steel or glass bowl and set this bowl into a larger bowl of hot water. Have ready the pint of strawberries, washed and dried, but not hulled.

Holding each berry by its stem, gently dip *halfway* into the glaze and then set it down immediately on a buttered or oiled cooky sheet to harden. Be sure not to dip farther down than halfway, or you will burn your fingertips. The glaze will begin to harden immediately on the berries. Serve them as soon as possible after they have been dipped. Do not refrigerate, or the glaze will melt. You may place the dipped berries attractively around the platter of the mold or pass them on a separate tray.

8 ounces semisweet chocolate
1 cup (2 sticks) sweet butter
4 tablespoons superfine sugar
6 eggs
2 tablespoons Grand Marnier
1 cup heavy cream
1 tablespoon sugar
1 tablespoon Grand Marnier
Shaved chocolate or candied violets (for garnish)
2 cups sugar
⅔ cup water
1 pint fresh ripe strawberries

28

Ratatouille Niçoise

Fillet of Striped Bass in Fillo Pastry

Peach Mousse with Raspberries

Here is a southern European mélange: Provence is represented by the ratatouille and Greece by the fillo pastry. Raspberries and/or blueberries, both in season, work well as a finish for the mousse. All of the dishes may be made a day ahead, even the wrapping of the fish.

Ratatouille Niçoise

The light cooking keeps the vegetables crisp. Black olives are more authentically Niçoise than green. The anchovies are optional, but remember, they decrease in intensity when they are cooked.

After trimming off the ends, cut the eggplant and zucchini into small cubes. Dice the peppers and onions. Drop the tomatoes into boiling water, leave for 1 minute, and rinse with cold water. Gently cut out the stems with the tip of a knife and slip off the skins. Chop the pulp.

    Heat several tablespoons of olive oil in a deep skillet and add the cubed eggplant and zucchini. Sauté for a few minutes until soft and golden. Remove from the skillet and set aside. Add more oil if needed and sauté the peppers and onions until soft but not brown. Return the eggplant and zucchini to the skillet and stir in the garlic, chopped tomatoes, tomato paste, herbs, salt, pepper, anchovies, and olives.

    Let this mixture cook, uncovered, over medium heat, until the liquid begins to evaporate and cook down and the mixture forms a thick consistency — about 15 minutes. Remove from the heat and cool to room temperature. Taste for additional salt and pepper and stir in the capers. Chill until serving.

1 medium-sized eggplant, unpeeled
2 zucchini, unpeeled
2 green peppers
2 red bell peppers
3 medium-sized onions
6 very ripe tomatoes
Several tablespoons olive oil
4 cloves garlic, mashed
2 tablespoons tomato paste
2 tablespoons chopped fresh parsley
2 tablespoons chopped fresh basil (or 1 tablespoon dried basil)
1 teaspoon dried thyme
1 tablespoon dried oregano
2 bay leaves
Salt and freshly ground black pepper to taste
A 2-ounce can of flat anchovy fillets, drained and chopped
1 cup pitted black olives, chopped
¼ cup capers

Fillet of Striped Bass in Fillo Pastry

This recipe was created in New York City by chef Seppi Renggli of the Forum of the Twelve Caesars Restaurant. His recipe also included poached oysters, but at the School of Contemporary Cooking many students felt that oysters were gilding the lily. On the other hand, adding watercress to the spinach is my idea. For an even tangier taste, use half watercress and half sorrel.

A 3-pound striped bass, filleted, boned, and skinned
Salt and black pepper to taste
A 1-pound package of frozen fillo dough
1 pound salted butter
½ cup fresh, finely grated bread crumbs
4 tablespoons salted butter
4 shallots, finely minced
2 packages chopped frozen spinach, defrosted and squeezed dry
1 tablespoon chopped fresh parsley
1 cup fresh watercress, stems removed and leaves chopped fine
2 teaspoons anisette or Pernod
A few dashes of Tabasco
Salt, pepper, and a dash of nutmeg
Paprika

Fillo, those ever-so-thin pastry sheets, are delicate to handle but not difficult to work with if you remember to follow the package instructions — keep the unused leaves covered with a damp cloth — and use at least six leaves of dough for each fillet package. They will bake up crisp and buttery.

Have the fishmonger prepare the fish for you. Be sure it is well boned and skinned. If striped bass is unavailable, any firm, fleshy fish such as grouper, flounder, snapper, or whitefish can be substituted. Cut each fillet into four small pieces and sprinkle each piece with salt and pepper. Set aside.

Remove the fillo dough from the freezer and bring it to room temperature. Put the pound of butter in a small saucepan for melting. Set the bread crumbs aside.

Melt the 4 tablespoons of butter in a small skillet and gently sauté the shallots, spinach, parsley, and watercress until all is well incorporated, about 3 minutes. Stir in the anisette or Pernod and the Tabasco, salt, pepper, and nutmeg. Mix well and set aside to cool.

To wrap the fish, open the fillo dough and arrange it in a stack on a flat surface. Cover it with a damp kitchen towel to prevent it from drying and cracking. Melt the butter in the saucepan until it is very hot and smooth.

Place a layer of the fillo on a board and brush it liberally with melted butter. Place another layer on top of this and brush again with melted butter. Do this for six layers. Fold the rectangle of dough in half and brush again with butter. Sprinkle the surface of the dough with a few bread crumbs and place a piece of fish in the center. Spoon some of the spinach mixture on top and press it against the fish.

Wrap the dough completely around the fish, and tuck the end flaps under. Brush the top of the package with more melted butter and sprinkle it lightly with paprika. Place on a buttered cooky sheet and proceed until all eight pieces of fish have been wrapped — using forty-eight pieces of fillo in all. Be sure the packages are placed on the cooky sheet with the flaps under, so the packages won't open up while baking. Refrigerate, but bring back to room temperature before baking.

Bake the fish packages in a 375° oven until puffy and golden brown, 20 to 30 minutes.

Peach Mousse with Raspberries

I seem to be emphasizing raspberries in this chapter, but when they come they come, and they never stay around long. Other summer berries are reasonable substitutes: blackberries, blueberries, huckleberries, and strawberries.

Drop the peaches into boiling water and let them sit in the water for about 1 minute. Then drain and immediately run cold water over them. When they are cool enough to handle, gently peel off the skins and cut the peaches in half. Remove the pits and chop the pulp. Put the chopped pulp into a food processor fitted with the steel blade, or an electric blender, and purée until smooth. Sprinkle the purée with 1 cup of the sugar, mix well, and set aside.

Put the remaining cup of sugar into the top of a double boiler and add the egg yolks. Beat this mixture with a hand-held mixer or a balloon whisk until it is thick and creamy. Pour in the warm milk and mix well. Cook this custard over barely simmering water, stirring constantly, until it begins to thicken and coats the back of a wooden spoon. Do not let the mixture come to a boil, or it will curdle.

When the mixture has thickened sufficiently, remove it from the heat and stir in the vanilla extract and the liqueur. Pour the custard into a bowl and set it aside.

Put the cold water into a heat-proof glass measuring cup. Sprinkle the gelatin over the water. Place the cup in a saucepan and pour 1 inch of water into the pan. Bring the water in the pan to a boil and heat until the gelatin mixture is completely dissolved. Remove the gelatin mixture and set it aside to cool. Mix it into the custard.

Beat the egg whites with a pinch of salt until they are stiff but not too dry. Whisk them into the custard, using a balloon whisk. Chill this mixture until it begins to set and mounds slightly when dropped from a spoon. When it reaches this point, whip the heavy cream until it is thick and stiff and fold it into the chilled custard along with the peach purée. Mix well and carefully fold in the berries — taking care not to break them.

Spoon this mixture into a crystal bowl or individual dessert glasses or bowls. Chill for at least 6 hours, or overnight, and serve with additional berries.

3 pounds fresh ripe peaches
2 cups sugar
8 eggs, separated
2 cups warm milk
2 teaspoons vanilla extract
2 tablespoons framboise, Grand Marnier, kirsch, or any fruit-flavored liqueur
6 tablespoons cold water
2 tablespoons unflavored gelatin
2 cups heavy cream
1 pint fresh raspberries
Additional raspberries to pass on the side

29

Guacamole

Paella

Spanish Flan, Flamenco Style

Although Paella involves many ingredients, separately sautéed, the entire dish can be prepared and assembled and then held for several hours or refrigerated overnight before the final baking and presentation. Both the guacamole and the flan can be prepared a day ahead, making this menu simple but very colorful and impressive.

Guacamole

The addition of chopped fresh tomato gives this recipe its own character. The flavor is heightened and the texture is delightful. Placing the avocado pits on top until serving will keep the color and flavor bright and fresh.

Peel the avocados, pit them, and save the pits. Drop the tomato into boiling water for 1 minute, remove, and rinse with cold water. Cut out the stem with the tip of a knife and slip off the skin. Cut the tomato in half horizontally and squeeze out the juice and seeds. Chop the pulp. Set aside. Put the avocados into a food processor fitted with a steel blade, or a blender, and purée for a few seconds. Add the onion, garlic, lemon juice, Tabasco, mayonnaise, Worcestershire, jalapeño, and salt; continue to blend until smooth.

Transfer the mixture to a small bowl and stir in the chopped tomato pulp. Taste for additional seasonings. If you like it hotter, add more Tabasco. You might want to add more salt or lemon juice.

Spoon the guacamole into a serving bowl or crock, place the pits on top of the mixture, and cover tightly with plastic wrap. Refrigerate until serving.

To serve, prepare any of your favorite *crudités*, such as carrots, celery, zucchini sticks, or cauliflower, or serve with a bowl of tostados on the side. Be sure to remove the avocado pits before serving!

2 very ripe avocados
1 very ripe tomato
1 small onion, finely minced
1 clove garlic, mashed
3 teaspoons fresh lemon juice (or more to taste)
A dash of Tabasco
1 heaping tablespoon mayonnaise
1 teaspoon Worcestershire sauce
1 jalapeño pepper, scraped of all seeds and chopped
½ teaspoon salt
Assorted raw vegetables, or tostados (for dipping)

Paella

The Spanish make three kinds of paella: all-chicken, all-seafood, or a combination of the two. In this country most of us think it's not real paella if it doesn't contain both. Lobsters and artichoke hearts make this dish very special.

A couple of hints: Wait until the oil is very hot before beginning to sauté — otherwise it will be absorbed by the food. And coat the rice with oil so you will be sure to get slippery, not sticky, rice.

1 frying chicken (or 4 whole
  boneless breasts)
1 pound sweet Spanish or
  Italian sausages (or combined
  sweet and hot)
2 lobsters, cut in the shell into
  small, maneuverable pieces
1 pound raw shrimp
2 pounds fresh mussels
2 pounds littleneck or
  cherrystone clams
1 large onion
2 cloves garlic
2 cups chicken stock
  (homemade or canned)
¼ teaspoon saffron threads
3 very ripe large tomatoes, cut
  into thin wedges
1 pound shelled fresh peas,
  steamed about 3 minutes (or
  1 package frozen peas)
1 package frozen artichoke
  hearts (or drained canned
  artichoke hearts)
2 whole pimientos, thinly sliced
  into strips
¼ cup olive oil
2 cups raw rice
1 teaspoon salt
Freshly ground black pepper to
  taste

Cut up the chicken into small pieces. If you are using breasts, cut each whole breast in half and then into smaller pieces. Slice the sausages and set them aside. Have the fishmonger cut up the lobster for you. Rinse the lobster pieces, pat dry with a paper towel, and set aside. Peel the shrimp, leaving the last segment of shell and the tail on. Devein them, rinse, and pat dry with paper towels. Put the mussels in a basin, scrub well, and pull off all the "beards." Cover them with cold water, add a dash of cornmeal, and let the mussels soak for a while to rid them of excess sand. Scrub the clams well and set them aside.

Chop the onion and mash the garlic. Put the chicken stock into a small saucepan and add the saffron. Heat to boiling, remove from heat, and allow the broth to stand so the saffron will soften.

Prepare the tomatoes, peas, artichoke hearts, and pimientos and set them aside for final assembly of the paella. (It is not necessary to cook frozen peas or artichoke hearts; just defrost them to room temperature.)

Heat some of the olive oil in a large, deep skillet and sauté the pieces of chicken until they are golden brown all over. (If you dredge the chicken pieces lightly in flour before sautéing, they will not splatter as much while they cook.) As the chicken is done, remove it from the skillet and set aside.

Add more oil to the skillet, if needed, and sauté the pieces of lobster, turning until they are bright red all over. Remove them from the skillet and set them aside with the chicken. Add the shrimp to the skillet and sauté until they turn bright pink. Set them aside with the lobster and chicken.

Add the onions and garlic to the skillet, with more oil if

needed, and sauté them for a few minutes, until they are soft and golden. Add the rice and stir it well to coat it completely with oil. Pour in half the chicken stock mixture, reduce the heat to very low, cover the skillet, and let the rice cook for 7 or 8 minutes and begin to absorb the stock.

While the rice is cooking, sauté the slices of sausage in a separate skillet. When they are crisp and brown, remove them and drain on paper towels.

When the 7 or 8 minutes are up, remove the rice from the heat. The dish is now ready for final assembly.

Using a large, round casserole or paella pan, spoon some of the rice over the bottom of the pan and arrange half of the chicken, lobster, shrimp, sausages, tomatoes, peas, artichoke hearts, and pimiento over it. Season with salt and pepper and add more rice. Arrange more chicken and so on over the rice and scatter the remaining rice over all. Arrange the mussels and clams attractively over the top, hinge side down, and cover the pan with aluminum foil. Place it in a preheated 375° oven and bake the paella, covered, for at least 45 minutes, until the chicken and rice are tender and the clams and mussels are wide open. Serve the paella right from its pan so as not to disturb the arrangement.

Spanish Flan, Flamenco Style

1½ cups sugar
¼ cup water
1 large navel orange
2 cinnamon sticks
3 cups half-and-half or light cream
6 whole eggs plus 4 yolks
A dash of salt
1 teaspoon vanilla extract
1 pint fresh strawberries (or any berries or combination), washed and hulled

Sometimes called *leche* flan because of the milk, this recipe, which uses half-and-half or light cream, is richer than the usual Spanish flan. The word *flamenco* is pure whimsy — the red berries used as garnish remind me of the flying red skirts of flamenco dancers. This is practically the national dessert of Spain and most of her former colonies from the Philippines to South America.

Have ready a 6-cup ring mold and a pan large enough to hold the mold that can be used as a *bain-marie*, or water bath.

Put 1 cup of the sugar into a heavy saucepan and add the water. Set this over medium heat and allow the sugar to melt thoroughly and the mixture to come to a boil. Continue to cook until it begins to caramelize and turn amber, thick, and bubbly. Immediately pour this liquid caramel into the mold and swirl it around to completely cover the bottom. Set the mold aside to let the caramel harden while you make the custard.

Peel the rind off the orange and put it into a saucepan with the cinnamon sticks and the half-and-half. Bring this mixture just to the scalding point, remove it from the heat, and let it stand to blend the flavors. Be sure to strain out the rind and cinnamon before using.

Put the eggs, yolks, and salt into a bowl and mix with a balloon whisk. Add the vanilla and slowly pour in the strained hot milk. Mix well. Pour this mixture over the hardened caramel in the mold and gently set the mold into the *bain-marie*. Place on a rack in a preheated 325° oven and pour boiling water into the *bain-marie* until it comes halfway up the side of the mold. Bake the flan for 1 hour or until a clean silver knife inserted in the center of the custard comes out clean. Remove it from the oven, carefully lift it out of the *bain-marie*, and let it cool to room temperature. Chill the mold overnight.

To serve the flan, run a knife around the edge of the custard to loosen and carefully invert it onto a serving platter that has shallow sides to contain the caramel that will run as a liquid over the flan. Fill the center of the mold with the berries and serve chilled.

Terrine of Fish with Sauce Andalouse

Bombay Chicken Curry

Fresh Raspberry Tart

Don't let the "Bombay" in the curry entrée fool you. It's just a name. It could be Curry Athena, Milano, Marseilles, or Barcelona, or herpahs, *à l'indienne*. Every European cuisine has adopted curry and smoothed out the edges, usually with the addition of cream and apples. Europeans feel that a curry should not attack you with spice; rather it should caress you with a spiced flavor. This one does just that.

The fish terrine, rich with cream and eggs, calls for sole, but pike, trout, or flounder may be substituted.

The surfeit of raspberries in the dessert speaks for itself. A tart like this, combining framboise, jam, and fresh berries is an ultimate in raspberry delight.

Terrine of Fish with Sauce Andalouse

1 tablespoon soft sweet butter
½ cup fish stock (page 110), or a
 combination of water and
 bottled clam juice
2 tablespoons sweet butter
A dash of salt
½ cup flour
1 pound fillet of sole, boned and
 skinned
4 tablespoons sweet butter, very
 cold, cut into small bits
A ½-pound piece of boneless
 and skinless fresh salmon
2 teaspoons chopped fresh
 parsley
1 teaspoon snipped fresh chives
1 whole egg plus 2 whites
Salt, white pepper, and a dash
 of cayenne pepper to taste
1 cup very cold heavy cream

You really need a blender or food processor to be able to make this recipe. The dish could be served hot, but then would need a hot sauce, say a hollandaise or a *sauce vin blanc*, or a rich Nantua (shrimp) sauce. The cold Sauce Andalouse gets its name from the addition of pimientos and tomato paste and the color is a beautiful match for the mosaic terrine.

Using the tablespoon of butter, lightly butter the bottom and sides of a 6-cup loaf pan or mold. Cut a piece of wax paper to fit the bottom of the pan and place it on the bottom. Lightly butter the wax paper. Cut another piece of wax paper to fit the top of the mold, butter it on one side, and set the mold and the buttered wax paper aside — preferably in the refrigerator. Have ready a larger pan to serve as a *bain-marie*, or water bath.

Put the stock, or water and clam juice, into a small saucepan with the 2 tablespoons of butter and the dash of salt. Bring this to a rolling boil and boil until the butter is completely melted. Remove from heat and add the flour—all at once — stirring hard with a wooden spoon until the mixture comes together and forms a soft ball of shiny dough. This is called a *panade*. Transfer the *panade* to a small buttered bowl, cover it tightly with plastic wrap, and chill thoroughly.

Wash and dry the fillet of sole. Cut it into small pieces and put it into a food processor fitted with the steel blade, or an electric blender. Purée until the fish is smooth. Add the cold butter, a small bit at a time, and continue to mix until the butter is incorporated. Transfer this mixture to a small buttered bowl, cover it tightly with plastic wrap, and chill.

Wash and dry the piece of salmon. Cut it into small dice. Set it aside with the chopped parsley and snipped chives.

When the *panade* and fish purée are thoroughly chilled, put both together into the food processor and blend. Add the whole egg, the whites, and the salt and peppers; continue to mix. While the machine is running, add the heavy cream, a tablespoon or two at a time, and continue to mix until all the cream has been incorporated and the mixture is well blended. It should be thick and shiny and hold firm peaks.

Transfer the mixture to a bowl and stir in the diced salmon and the herbs. Spoon this mixture into the prepared mold and place the buttered wax paper, buttered side down, on top of the fish in the mold. Cover the entire top of the mold tightly with aluminum foil and place in the *bain-marie*. Place on the center rack in a preheated 350° oven and pour boiling water into the *bain-marie* to come *halfway* up the side of the mold. Bake for 1 hour or until the top of the fish is firm to the touch. Remove from the oven, carefully lift the mold out of the *bain-marie*, unwrap it, and let it come to room temperature.

Cover the top of the mold tightly with foil again. Refrigerate overnight.

To serve, remove the foil and run a knife around the edge of the mold. Invert it carefully onto a serving platter and peel off the bottom wax paper. Sprinkle with chopped parsley. Slice and serve with the following sauce.

Sauce Andalouse

ABOUT 2 CUPS

Put the egg yolks, mustard, lemon juice, salt, and peppers into a blender or food processor and blend for a few seconds. Add the oil a drop at a time until the mixture begins to thicken. Then increase the addition of the oil to a slow, steady stream, until it is all incorporated.

Remove this mayonnaise to a small bowl and stir in the chopped pimiento, herbs, tomato paste, Worcestershire, cognac, and paprika and mix well. Fold in the whipped cream and chill the sauce before serving.

If necessary, 1 cup of bottled mayonnaise may be used in place of the homemade version.

3 egg yolks
1 tablespoon Dijon mustard
1 tablespoon fresh lemon juice
Salt, white pepper, and a dash of cayenne pepper to taste
1 cup oil (combined olive and safflower or corn oils)
1 small canned pimiento, drained and seeds removed, chopped
1 teaspoon finely chopped fresh parsley
1 teaspoon finely snipped fresh chives
1 teaspoon tomato paste
1 teaspoon Worcestershire sauce
2 teaspoons cognac
A dash of paprika
½ cup whipped cream

Bombay Chicken Curry

Though this recipe calls for chicken, the curry itself is a basic adaptation that could be made with lamb cubes or shrimp just as well. If you use shrimp, cook them last, without the flour dredging, but be sure to do the cornstarch step at the end to thicken the curry sauce.

The yogurt-and-cucumber condiment is particularly refreshing and crunchy. The smoked eggplant chutney is an intriguing touch, as the charred skin permeates the eggplant with flavor. It could become a house specialty of yours for cocktail appetizers and other side dishes.

8 whole boneless and skinless breasts of chicken
Salt and pepper to taste
1 cup flour
Several tablespoons olive oil
Several tablespoons butter
3 onions, chopped fine
4 very ripe tomatoes
4 cloves garlic, well mashed
1 bay leaf
1 teaspoon ground cinnamon
¼ teaspoon ground cloves
2 tablespoons curry powder, or more if desired
1 teaspoon white pepper
1 teaspoon ground cumin
1 tablespoon sweet paprika
1 teaspoon ground coriander
1 cup chicken stock (homemade or canned)
2 large apples, peeled and diced
1 cup heavy cream
1 or 2 tablespoons cornstarch diluted in 1 tablespoon cold water

Cut each piece of chicken in half and season lightly with salt and pepper. Dredge the pieces with flour and shake off the excess. Heat the oil and butter in a deep kettle and sauté the chicken until golden brown on both sides. Remove it from the pot as it is done and set aside.

Add more butter and oil if necessary and stir in the onions. Sauté for a few minutes until soft and golden. Drop the tomatoes into boiling water, let stand for 1 minute, then rinse with cold water. Cut out the stems with the tip of a knife and peel off the skins. Cut the tomatoes in half horizontally. Squeeze out the seeds and chop the pulp. Add the garlic, tomatoes, bay leaf, and all the spices and sauté for a few minutes, stirring well. Return the pieces of chicken to the kettle and pour in the chicken stock. Cover the pot and simmer for 30 minutes or until the chicken is tender.

Stir in the diced apples, the cream, and the cornstarch mixture and mix well. Cook for an additional 5 minutes until heated through.

Serve the curry with plain boiled white rice and any of the following: chopped peanuts, grated coconut, chopped candied ginger, chopped fresh parsley, grated orange peel, white raisins, chopped hard-boiled egg, Major Grey's chutney, and either or both of the following condiments.

Yogurt with Cucumbers

2 CUPS

Prepare the cucumber, taking care to remove all seeds. Put all the ingredients into a small bowl, mix well, and chill.

1 medium-sized cucumber, peeled, cut in half lengthwise, seeded, and finely diced
2 cups plain yogurt
1 clove garlic, mashed
Salt and freshly ground black pepper to taste
The juice of half a lemon

Smoked Eggplant Chutney

ABOUT 2 CUPS

Put the unpeeled eggplant in the center of a gas burner or under a broiler. Turn the heat to low and allow the eggplant to cook, turning occasionally, until the skin is charred and beginning to split. Remove the eggplant from the heat and wrap it in aluminum foil. Return to heat and continue to cook about 10 minutes longer, until it is very tender.

Remove the eggplant from the heat, unwrap it, and gently peel away the charred skin. Chop the pulp fine and stir in remaining ingredients. Mix well and chill.

1 large eggplant
2 teaspoons fresh lemon juice
1 tablespoon finely minced onion
Salt and black pepper to taste
A tablespoon or two of olive oil

Fresh Raspberry Tart

This tart might be made with puff pastry, but it is such a long-drawn-out affair that I have avoided a recipe for puff pastry in this collection. At the School of Contemporary Cooking my students and I agree it is far more important to teach recipes and procedures that a student will be likely to repeat at home than some of the classic and intricate ones that are seldom attempted when one is cooking alone.

For a more elegant finish to this tart, reserve the most perfect raspberries and stud the top with them after you spoon the rest into the shell.

8 tablespoons sweet butter
1 egg
2 to 3 teaspoons milk
1⅓ cups flour, sifted with 1
  teaspoon sugar and ½ teaspoon
  salt
1 cup currant jelly or seedless
  red raspberry jam
1 teaspoon sugar
1 tablespoon framboise
  (optional)
Several pints fresh raspberries
1 cup heavy cream, whipped
  with 1 teaspoon sugar and 1
  tablespoon framboise

Put the butter, egg, and milk into a bowl for the electric mixer and mix on low speed for a minute or two until well blended. Add the sifted flour mixture and continue to mix on low speed until the mixture forms a soft ball of dough and leaves the sides of the bowl clean. Remove the dough from the bowl, form a ball, and wrap it in wax paper. Chill for 30 minutes.

Lightly flour a pastry cloth or board and roll out the ball of dough to fit a 10-inch flan or tart pan with fluted sides. Transfer the dough to the pan and gently fit it into the bottom. Press the dough to the edges of the pan to prevent shrinkage; cut off excess dough.

Line the dough with wax paper and weight it down with raw rice, dried beans, or aluminum nuggets. Bake the shell in a preheated 400° oven for 10 minutes, remove the wax paper and weights, and continue to bake for another 5 to 8 minutes or until the crust is golden and crisp. Remove it from the oven and cool thoroughly at room temperature.

Melt the jelly, sugar, and framboise together in a small saucepan until smooth. Brush a small amount of it over the bottom of the baked pie shell. Mix the remaining jelly mixture with the raspberries and heap this into the pie shell. Chill, and serve with the whipped cream.

August

LESSON 3 1

Shrimp Arrabbiata
Tortellini and Swiss Chard Salad
Frozen Profiteroles

LESSON 3 2

Cucumber Mousse with Red Caviar Sauce
Fillet of Beef in Aspic
Baked Fruit Pudding

LESSON 3 3

Savory Stuffed Tomatoes
Poached Fish Salad with Tarragon Mayonnaise
Fresh Plum Crisp with Hot Brandy Sauce

LESSON 3 4

Chilled Cucumber and Zucchini Bisque
Pâté-Stuffed Breast of Veal
Cold Rice Salad
Blueberry Sour Cream Tart

Shrimp Arrabbiata

Tortellini and Swiss Chard Salad

Frozen Profiteroles

This menu has great flexibility. The shrimp and tortellini dishes are interchangeable in usage. You can double the shrimp amount and make it the main course, while serving the pasta as a starter. Both can become part of an expanded buffet table. Together, the three recipes work as a simple lunch, light dinner, or easy-to-serve buffet supper.

Shrimp Arrabbiata

Here's proof that not every hot, spicy, and tomatoey Italian shellfish dish is "Fra Diavolo." *Arrabbiata* means "enraged" in Italian, and with all that pepper and Tabasco it probably does stir up the blood a bit. But on a warm summer's day, hot on the inside can help cool the outside.

6 fresh clams and 6 fresh
  mussels for garnish (optional)
1 onion
6 shallots
4 cloves garlic
1 green pepper
1 red bell pepper
2 pounds fresh raw shrimp
⅓ cup olive oil
3 tablespoons cognac
1 cup dry white wine
2 tablespoons chopped fresh
  parsley
1 tablespoon chopped fresh basil
  (or 1 teaspoon dried basil)
A 2-pound can of Italian plum
  tomatoes packed in tomato
  purée
2 tablespoons tomato paste
¼ teaspoon dried hot red pepper
  flakes
1 teaspoon dried oregano
Salt and freshly ground black
  pepper to taste
A few dashes of Tabasco

If you are using the clams and mussels, discard any that are open or have broken shells. Scrub them clean under cold running water. Put the cleaned clams into a bowl and refrigerate until ready to use. Pull the "beards" off the mussels and drop them into a basin of cold water. Add a handful of cornmeal and let the mussels soak for an hour to release their sand. Rinse them again and set aside with the clams.

Mince the onion and shallots. Mash the garlic. Seed and dice the peppers. Peel and devein the shrimp. Rinse them well with cold water and pat them dry with paper towels. Set aside.

Heat the olive oil in a deep skillet that has a tight-fitting lid. When it is very hot, stir in the onions, shallots, garlic, and peppers and sauté for about 3 minutes, until the onions are soft and golden. Add the shrimp and continue to sauté until they turn bright pink. Pour in the cognac and let it come to a boil and reduce down to a tablespoon or two.

Stir in the remaining ingredients, breaking up the tomatoes with the back of a wooden spoon. Mix well and place the clams and mussels on the top, hinge side down.

Cover the skillet and cook until the clams and mussels have opened. Discard any that are not open after about 10 minutes. Serve the shrimp in deep bowls with hot Italian bread.

Tortellini and Swiss Chard Salad

You can gather ingredients for this recipe a day in advance. Prepare and assemble the salad hours ahead so it can chill properly. Just don't pour on the dressing until ready to serve.

The mortadella, listed as optional, is almost a must if you use any small pasta other than the tortellini. You will need the meaty flavor that it brings.

You will have to look for fresh or frozen tortellini. They are not generally available in dried form. If they are unavailable, 1 pound of any small dried pasta will do. Cook the tortellini in a large amount of boiling salted water for 6 to 8 minutes. For small dried pasta, cook for 10 to 12 minutes. Drain when done and rinse with cold water. When the pasta is well drained, stir a few tablespoons of oil through it to keep it from sticking. Set aside.

Mash the garlic. Wash the Swiss chard thoroughly, break off the thick stems and discard, and dry the leaves with paper towels. Heat the oil in a small skillet and add the garlic and chard, sautéing for a few minutes until the chard is limp. Remove it from the skillet and set it aside to cool. If you cannot find chard, fresh spinach can be substituted.

Dice the pepper, celery, and onion. Prepare the olives and tomatoes according to directions. Chop the anchovies and dice the mortadella. Put these ingredients into a bowl with the chopped herbs, the cooled pasta, and the cooled chard. If the chard leaves are too large, chop them coarsely. Refrigerate the salad for several hours.

Make the dressing by whisking together the vinegar, salt, pepper, sugar, and oil. Before serving, toss the dressing through the salad. Serve chilled.

2 pounds green or white tortellini (or a combination)
2 cloves garlic
1 bunch Swiss chard
2 tablespoons olive oil
1 red bell pepper
2 stalks celery
1 small red onion
1 cup pitted black olives, cut into quarters
2 very ripe tomatoes, peeled, seeded, juiced, and chopped
3 or 4 anchovy fillets, drained (optional)
½ pound finely diced fresh mortadella (optional)
1 tablespoon chopped fresh parsley
1 tablespoon chopped fresh basil
2 tablespoons tarragon vinegar
Salt and pepper to taste
½ teaspoon sugar
6 tablespoons olive oil

Frozen Profiteroles

1 cup water
A dash of salt
6 tablespoons sweet butter
1 cup flour
3 large eggs
1 egg
1 tablespoon cold water
Vanilla ice cream
2 ounces unsweetened chocolate
6 tablespoons water
½ cup sugar
3 tablespoons sweet butter
1 teaspoon vanilla extract
1 tablespoon dark rum
 (optional)

This is the dough the French call *pâte à choux*. It is a boiled mixture that's a snap to make — no kneading or rolling necessary. Just drop onto baking sheets by spoonfuls, like cookies. As sary. Just drop onto baking sheets by spoonfuls, like cookies. As you drop the dough from the spoon, give it a twirl, or use a ensure evenly shaped mounds. This helps to cut a perfect cap when filling the profiteroles.

The hot chocolate sauce helps the frozen puffs to soften slightly for easier eating. If you like, decorate the profiteroles with a few toasted almond slices.

Put the water, salt, and butter into a small saucepan and bring to a rolling boil. When the butter is completely melted, remove the pan from the heat and add the flour all at once. Stir to form a soft ball of dough. Transfer this ball of dough to a food processor fitted with the steel blade and beat in the three eggs, one at a time. Or beat them in by hand with a wooden spoon.

Lightly butter a cooky sheet. Preheat the oven to 450°. Fill a pastry bag fitted with a plain ¼-inch nozzle with the pastry dough and pipe out spirals of dough onto the cooky sheet. Make the puffs as large as you like, but keep in mind that they will double in size as they bake. Space the puffs about 1 inch apart to allow for expansion.

Mix the egg with the cold water to form an egg wash, or *dorure*. Lightly brush this over the top of each puff with a pastry brush or goose feather, making sure that the egg wash does not drop down the sides of the puffs onto the cooky sheet. The egg wash will give a shiny, finished look to the puffs.

Bake the puffs in the hot oven for about 10 minutes, and then reduce the temperature to 350°. Continue to bake the puffs an additional 30 minutes or until they are golden brown, shiny, and crisp to the touch. Shut off the oven and leave the puffs in the turned-off oven for another 15 minutes to continue to crisp. Remove them from the oven.

When they are cool enough to handle, slice off a piece from the top of each puff, using a serrated knife. Pull out any soft dough from the inside center to create a space for filling.

Fill each puff with softened vanilla ice cream or any flavor of your choice. Replace the caps and put the filled puffs in the freezer until serving.

▶ To prepare the chocolate sauce, put the chocolate and water together in the top of a double boiler and melt until smooth. Stir in the sugar and mix until you have a glaze consistency. Stir in the butter, vanilla, and rum and mix well. Keep hot until serving.

To serve, put one large puff or three miniature ones on individual plates and spoon hot sauce over them.

Cucumber Mousse with Red Caviar Sauce

Fillet of Beef in Aspic

Baked Fruit Pudding

Fillet of beef is the most expensive cut of meat, but in this recipe it is the kindest cut of all because you slice it very thin, thereby stretching the portions. When trimming the fillet, be sure to cut away all visible fat and silvery membrane. Leaving it on makes the slicing difficult and the chewing a chore.

Cucumber Mousse with Red Caviar Sauce   SERVES 8

To set properly, this mousse should chill overnight. Be sure to squeeze and drain the juice from the shredded cucumbers, or there will be too much liquid for the mixture to solidify. Considering all the blended flavors, homemade mayonnaise just doesn't seem worth it here, so use a good commercial variety.

Fold is the key word for the caviar sauce. Be careful of the grains. They have such a wonderful texture, as well as a mini-explosion of flavor, if they are broken in the mouth instead of in the sauce.

2 large cucumbers (or enough to make 1 cup shredded pulp)
1 tablespoon unflavored gelatin
¼ cup cold water
2 small scallions
½ cup mayonnaise
1 teaspoon Worcestershire sauce
The juice of half a lemon
Salt and freshly ground black pepper to taste
1 teaspoon chopped fresh parsley
1 cup heavy cream
1 cup sour cream
1 tablespoon freshly grated onion
Salt and freshly ground black pepper to taste
4 ounces red caviar

Lightly oil a 4-cup mold. Wipe out all excess oil and chill the prepared mold.

Peel the cucumbers, cut them in half lengthwise, and with a small spoon, carefully scoop out all the seeds. Shred the flesh on a medium-sized shredder or use a food processor fitted with the shredding blade. Put the shredded cucumber in a colander and press it with the back of a wooden spoon to extract all the liquid. Let it drain.

In a heat-proof glass bowl or measuring cup sprinkle the gelatin over the cold water and allow it to dissolve slightly. Place the gelatin mixture in a small pan with an inch of water and bring that water to a boil on top of the stove. Boil until the gelatin mixture is completely dissolved. Remove the gelatin mixture from the pot and set it aside to cool.

Mince the scallions. Combine the mayonnaise, Worcestershire sauce, lemon juice, cooled gelatin, salt, and pepper. Stir in the scallions, chopped parsley, and drained cucumber. Whip the heavy cream until it is thick and stiff and fold it gently into the cucumber mixture.

Spoon this mixture into the prepared mold and chill overnight, or at least 6 hours, until set.

To prepare the sauce, put the sour cream, onion, salt, and pepper in a small bowl and mix. Gently fold in the caviar, taking care not to break the eggs. Chill.

To serve, unmold the mousse onto a serving platter. Decorate the platter with thin slices of cucumber, lemon wedges, and parsley sprigs. Pass the sauce on the side.

Fillet of Beef in Aspic

This dish offers a field day for the culinary artist, since it looks beautiful decorated with vegetables. They'll sparkle under the clear aspic and above the rich brown sauce. Since most truffles are grown in Perigord, the addition of them to a Sauce Espagnole turns it into a Sauce Périgourdine. The cognac and Madeira enhance the sauce even more. Try it sometime without adding the gelatin and serve it hot with a roast fillet of beef or grilled sliced steak.

The dish can be prepared up to two days ahead. You should definitely start the day before so the aspic covering has a chance to set overnight. Be sure the meat is thoroughly chilled before you begin to coat it with the aspic.

1 whole fillet of beef (about 5 pounds), well trimmed
Salt, pepper, and a dash of celery salt
4 tablespoons butter
1 onion, sliced
1 carrot, sliced
2 cloves garlic, sliced
¼ cup Madeira
¼ cup cognac
4 cups Sauce Espagnole (page 120)
2 tablespoons unflavored gelatin
1 small truffle (optional)
3 cups chicken stock (homemade or canned)
1 cup tomato juice
4 tablespoons unflavored gelatin
Salt and freshly ground black pepper to taste
1 teaspoon sugar
Several sprigs of fresh tarragon (or 1 teaspoon dried tarragon)
2 egg whites, lightly beaten
2 egg shells, crushed
2 tablespoons Madeira
Blanched and cut fresh vegetables (for garnish)

Trim the fillet of beef well, taking care to remove all signs of fat, gristle, and membrane. Season it with salt, pepper, and celery salt. Melt the butter in a shallow roasting pan and roll the meat around in the melted butter. Scatter the sliced onion, carrot, and garlic over the bottom of the pan and roast the meat in a preheated 400° oven for 15 minutes for very rare, 20 minutes for medium, and 30 minutes for well-done. When the meat is done, remove it from the oven and transfer it to a small platter. Wrap the meat in plastic wrap and chill.

Put the roasting pan with the vegetables on top of the stove across two burners. Pour in the Madeira and cognac and bring to a rolling boil. Boil over high heat for a few minutes until the liquids reduce to about 2 tablespoons. Stir in the Sauce Espagnole and 2 tablespoons of gelatin and blend well. Bring to a boil and allow to cook for a minute or two.

Purée this entire mixture through a fine sieve into a small bowl and set aside. Drain the truffle well and mince it. Stir into the strained sauce mixture. Cool slightly.

When the sauce has cooled somewhat, pour it into the bottom of a shallow oval serving dish. Chill the dish until the sauce has set firm.

To prepare the aspic glaze, put the chicken stock, tomato juice, 4 tablespoons gelatin, salt, pepper, sugar, tarragon, egg whites, and crushed egg shells into a saucepan and bring this mixture to a boil. Stir well and remove from the heat. The egg white and crushed shell will clear the mixture to a golden liquid. Strain carefully through fine cheesecloth, stir in the Madeira, and cool to room temperature. Set aside.

Slice the chilled beef into thin slices and arrange the slices in a spiral over the chilled sauce in the serving dish. Brush the top of the beef slices with a thin coating of the cooled aspic. Chill thoroughly. When chilled, spoon another layer of aspic over the beef and chill again. Do this several more times until the beef is completely coated with shiny aspic.

Cut out decorative flowers, leaves, and stems from carrots, turnips, pimiento, tarragon or other herb leaves, and blanched leek stems. Arrange them attractively over and around the beef and coat them with aspic. Rechill the dish.

▶ Pour any remaining aspic into a flat dish and chill.

To serve, unmold the flat dish of aspic and chop it. Scatter the chopped aspic around the edge of the beef dish.

Baked Fruit Pudding

SERVES 8

Pudding? This dessert will banish the negative connotations of that word forever. The dish is easily done in two steps — 20 minutes for baking the fruit and another 20 minutes for the meringue topping. If you are in a hurry, you can spread the meringue over the baked fruit and slide it under the broiler for a few minutes to brown. But watch it carefully; you don't want the pudding to look like a marshmallow charred on the cookout fire.

Peel, core, and dice the apples and/or pears. Melt the butter in a skillet and add the diced fruit, the cup of sugar, and the water and cook for about 10 minutes, until the fruit begins to get tender. Sprinkle it with the cinnamon and nutmeg and mash it slightly with a fork. Transfer this to a 1-quart shallow, oven-proof dish and stir in the berries, raisins, nuts, and diluted cornstarch. Beat the egg yolks lightly with a fork and stir them through the fruit. Bake the pudding in a preheated 375° oven for 20 minutes or until the eggs are set.

While the fruit is baking, put the egg whites into a clean bowl for the electric mixer and beat them with the ¾ cup sugar until stiff peaks form. Spread or pipe this meringue over the fruit when it is done and return the dish to the oven (reduce the temperature to 250°). Bake for another 20 minutes or until the meringue feels dry. Serve the pudding right from the dish at room temperature or slightly warmer.

2 pounds fresh apples or pears (or some of each)
8 tablespoons sweet butter
1 cup sugar
3 tablespoons water
1 teaspoon cinnamon
A dash of nutmeg
2 cups fresh blueberries or blackberries (or some of each)
½ cup raisins
¼ cup finely chopped walnuts or almonds
2 tablespoons cornstarch diluted in 2 tablespoons kirsch
3 egg yolks
3 egg whites
¾ cup sugar

177

33

Savory Stuffed Tomatoes

Poached Fish Salad with Tarragon
Mayonnaise

Fresh Plum Crisp with Hot Brandy Sauce

This all-cold menu gets flavor and character from the inter-
play of five different seafoods. Tuna and anchovies are the en-
hancers that make the stuffed tomatoes the treats they are.
Mussels and shrimp add their flavors to the poached fish
salad.

Both the appetizer and the entrée can be completed a day
ahead. Then you can concentrate your last day's energies on
preparing the dessert. Thus you will retain the crispness of
both the bottom crust and the crumb topping. The brandy
sauce, however, can be made a day ahead and reheated.

Savory Stuffed Tomatoes

Be careful when scooping the tomatoes not to pierce the shells, or they won't hold up well while baking. In this recipe the tomatoes are baked a day ahead and chilled before serving, but they are equally delicious served hot from the oven. Try it for another occasion.

Cut off a slice from the top of each tomato and carefully scoop out and discard the juice and pulp. Slice off a very thin piece from the bottom of each tomato so it will stand upright. Salt the insides of the tomatoes and turn them upside down on paper towels to drain.

Mince the onion and garlic. Heat the olive oil in a skillet and sauté the onion and garlic for a minute or two. Stir in the anchovies, tuna fish, tomato paste, herbs, capers, and olives and sauté for a few minutes more. Stir in the bread crumbs, cheese, salt, and pepper and mix well to form the stuffing. If the mixture is too dry, add a bit more olive oil to moisten.

Spoon the mixture into the tomato shells and sprinkle the tops with additional Parmesan cheese. Drizzle a bit more olive oil over the top of each tomato and place them in a shallow baking dish.

Bake the tomatoes in a preheated 375° oven for about 20 minutes. Be careful not to overbake, or the shells of the tomatoes will collapse. Remove the tomatoes from the oven and bring to room temperature. Chill before serving.

8 firm, ripe tomatoes
1 onion
2 cloves garlic
2 tablespoons olive oil
A 2-ounce can of flat anchovy
  fillets, drained of oil and
  chopped
Two 7-ounce cans of tuna fish,
  drained of oil and flaked
1 tablespoon tomato paste
¼ teaspoon each dried
  marjoram, thyme, and sage
1 tablespoon chopped fresh basil
  (or 1 teaspoon dried basil)
2 tablespoons chopped fresh
  parsley
2 tablespoons capers
1 cup pitted black olives,
  chopped
1 cup fresh, finely grated bread
  crumbs
¼ cup freshly grated Parmesan
  cheese
Salt and freshly ground black
  pepper to taste

Poached Fish Salad with Tarragon Mayonnaise

The tarragon in the sauce for this dish is a subtle but unmistakable flavor. Fresh tarragon should be available in August, in the markets if not in your own garden.

Bone and flake the fish carefully, but try to keep the chunks as large as possible. As you remove the meat near the head of the fish, be especially careful to remove the featherlike bones on the upper fillets. The best way to find them is to feel for them with your fingers.

The first three paragraphs in the instructions are basic to poaching whole fish. On some other occasion you might like to try poaching one to serve whole. Garnished with lemon wedges and parsley sprigs and served with the tarragon mayonnaise on the side, it is a lovely presentation.

1 onion, sliced
2 carrots, peeled and sliced
1 stalk celery, sliced
Several sprigs of fresh parsley
1 bay leaf
1 clove garlic, peeled and cut in half
¼ teaspoon whole black peppercorns
1 teaspoon salt
2 cups dry white wine
A 3- to 4-pound striped bass (or any firm, fleshy white fish suitable for poaching whole)
8 small red-skinned new potatoes
2 pounds fresh mussels
½ cup dry white wine
1 pound fresh shrimp
1 cup Tarragon Mayonnaise (see page 181)
2 scallions, finely minced
2 tablespoons chopped fresh parsley
2 tablespoons chopped fresh tarragon

Put the onion, carrots, celery, parsley, bay leaf, garlic, peppercorns, salt, wine, and enough cold water to cover the fish into a fish poacher with a rack large enough to hold the fish. Bring the liquid to a rolling boil on top of the stove. Reduce the heat to simmer and cook for a few minutes to blend the flavors.

If the fish is too large to fit into the poacher, remove the head. Or, if you prefer, have the fishmonger remove it before you bring the fish home. Wrap the fish tightly in cheesecloth.

Gently lower the wrapped fish onto the rack in the slowly simmering liquid and cover the poacher tightly. Bring the liquid back to a slow simmer and time the fish, about 6 minutes to the pound. Lift the rack from the poacher and lay the fish on a tray to cool to room temperature. The poaching liquid can be strained and frozen for future use in poaching other fish or as a base for a sauce or fish soup.

While the fish is poaching and then cooling, scrub the potatoes, put them into about 2 inches of lightly salted boiling water, cover the pot, and steam them for 20 minutes or until tender. Immediately drain and run cold water over them to stop the cooking process. When the potatoes are cool enough to handle, peel the skins off and dice them. Toss a few tablespoons of olive oil through the diced potatoes to prevent them from sticking together. Put them into a large salad bowl and set aside.

Also while the fish is poaching, scrub the mussels under running water and pull off the "beards." Put them into a basin of cold water and add a handful of cornmeal. Let them soak for about 1 hour, rinse, and put them into a deep kettle. Add the ½ cup white wine, cover the kettle tightly, and steam the mussels over high heat until they are all wide open, about 10 minutes. Discard any that do not open, and drain the remaining mussels. When they are cool enough to handle, pull them out of their shells, discard the shells, and add the mussels to the potatoes.

Rinse the shrimp and drop them into a pot of lightly salted boiling water. Bring the water back to a boil and cook the shrimp for exactly 3 minutes. Drain and rinse them with cold water. When they are cool enough to handle, peel and devein them and add to the salad bowl.

When the poached fish is cool enough to handle, unwrap it from the cheesecloth and gently pull the skin away from the meat. Discard the skin, and using your fingers and feeling carefully, pull large chunks of the fish away from the bone, taking care to feel for very thin bones in the flesh. Put the boned and chunked fish into the salad bowl as you proceed.

Prepare the tarragon mayonnaise and stir into it the scallions, parsley, tarragon, Tabasco, salt, and pepper. Taste for additional salt and pepper. Gently toss the mayonnaise through the other ingredients in the salad bowl. Chill the fish salad before serving.

▶ To serve, place washed and dried Boston lettuce leaves on a glass salad dish and heap the chilled fish salad on it. Garnish with hard-boiled egg wedges, tomatoes, olives, and additional chopped parsley.

A dash of Tabasco
Salt and freshly ground black
  pepper to taste
1 head Boston lettuce
Hard-boiled egg wedges
Cherry tomatoes or tomato
  wedges
Black or green olives
Additional chopped parsley

Tarragon Mayonnaise

Put the egg yolks, salt, peppers, mustard, lemon juice, and vinegar into the container of an electric blender or a food processor fitted with the steel blade. Mix for a few seconds. Add the oil a drop at a time until the mixture begins to thicken. Then increase the addition of the oil to a slow, steady stream until it is all incorporated. Taste the mayonnaise for additional salt, pepper, or lemon juice.

ABOUT 1 CUP

3 egg yolks
Salt, white pepper, and a dash of
  cayenne pepper
1 tablespoon Dijon mustard
1 tablespoon fresh lemon juice
1 tablespoon tarragon vinegar
1 cup oil (half olive oil and half
  vegetable or safflower oil)

Fresh Plum Crisp with Hot Brandy Sauce

Bottom Crust

1 cup flour
A dash of salt
4 tablespoons sweet butter,
  softened to room temperature
½ cup sugar
1 teaspoon vanilla extract
1 egg
1 teaspoon baking powder

Plum Filling

2 pounds ripe plums
4 tablespoons sweet butter
½ cup sugar
2 tablespoons plum brandy (or
  any fruit-flavored brandy)
A dash each of ground
  cinnamon, nutmeg, and cloves

Topping

¾ cup flour
6 tablespoons sweet butter,
  softened to room temperature
½ cup sugar
A dash each of ground
  cinnamon and nutmeg
¼ cup chopped walnuts

Plum Brandy Sauce

10 ounces apricot preserves
1 tablespoon cornstarch or
  arrowroot
1 cup apple cider (or apple
  juice)
2 tablespoons plum brandy (or
  any fruit-flavored brandy)
The juice of 1 lemon
A dash of ground ginger
  (optional)

The crust, the plums, and the crunchy, crumbly nut topping all bake at once. This recipe works equally well with apples, apricots, pears, or nectarines. Whichever fruit you use, be sure it is very ripe. It doesn't have to be peeled.

Mix together the ingredients for the bottom crust in a small bowl until they reach the consistency of cooky dough. (This can also be done in an electric mixer.) Press the dough into a 9-by-13-inch baking dish so it is even on the bottom and comes about ¼ inch up the sides of the dish. Set aside.

Cut the plums in half and carefully remove the pits. Melt the butter in a skillet and stir in the sugar. Cook until the sugar is melted. Add the plums, cut side down, and cook for a few minutes until they begin to soften. Sprinkle the brandy over all and stir in the cinnamon, nutmeg, and cloves. Remove from heat and allow to cool to room temperature.

Mix the ingredients for the topping in a small bowl, using your fingertips to get a crumbly consistency.

When the plums are cool, spread them over the crust in the baking dish and spoon any extra juices over all. Sprinkle the crumbed topping over the pan and bake in a preheated 350° oven for 45 minutes to 1 hour or until the top is very brown and crisp. Remove from the oven and cool to room temperature.

To make the sauce, press the apricot preserves through a sieve into a small saucepan. Dissolve the cornstarch in a tablespoon of the cider and mix until a paste is formed. Add this to the pan, along with the remaining cider. Stir in the brandy, lemon juice, and ginger. Cook over low heat on top of the stove until the sauce comes to a boil, thickens, and clears.

Cut the crisp into squares, serve vanilla ice cream on the side, and pass the hot sauce.

34

Chilled Cucumber and Zucchini Bisque

Pâté-Stuffed Breast of Veal

Cold Rice Salad

Blueberry Sour Cream Tart

In the main course of this menu the word *pâté* is the key. The veal-pork-and-ham stuffing is a true *pâté* nestled within the veal. When it is chilled and sliced, a mosaic of pistachio nuts, peas, ground meats, and hard-cooked eggs is displayed. The cold rice salad complements the stuffed veal wonderfully, as it would most cold meat dishes.

All the dishes can be prepared well in advance — the soup as much as two days, the pâté and the veal a day or two. And the crust for the tart may be rolled and assembled for baking a day ahead. Fill and bake the tart the same day you plan to serve it. This will prevent the bottom crust from getting soggy.

Chilled Cucumber and Zucchini Bisque

A blender or food processor is important for this recipe in order to achieve a smooth, velvety consistency. Be sure to seed the cucumbers. If the zucchini are extra large, seed them too.

6 tablespoons butter
1 large onion, chopped
4 scallions, trimmed and chopped
3 large Idaho potatoes, peeled and chopped
1 clove garlic, peeled and cut in half
3 cucumbers, peeled, seeded, and chopped
3 zucchini, peeled, seeded (if necessary), and chopped
A small bunch of fresh watercress, thick stems removed
½ cup chopped fresh dill
Salt and freshly ground pepper to taste
8 cups chicken stock (homemade or canned)
1 cup heavy cream
Freshly snipped dill (for garnish)
1 small cucumber, peeled, seeded, and finely minced (for garnish)

Melt the butter in a deep soup kettle and add the onion, scallions, potatoes, garlic, cucumbers, zucchini, watercress, and dill. Sauté for about 5 minutes over low heat until the vegetables release their juices and begin to soften. Add the salt and pepper and pour in the chicken stock. Cover the pot, bring to a boil, reduce heat to simmer, and cook for 30 minutes or until the potatoes are tender. Remove from the stove and cool slightly.

Purée the entire mixture in batches, using a blender or food processor and adding a bit of heavy cream with each batch. Chill the soup thoroughly.

To serve, ladle into chilled mugs or bowls and pass the dill and the finely chopped cucumbers. A dollop of sour cream could also be added.

184

Pâté-Stuffed Breast of Veal

Though preparation of this dish is hardly more than a 2-hour affair, it can be broken down into stages and the work spread over several days. Just remember that you should completely assemble and bake the veal at least a day ahead of time so it can be thoroughly chilled for slicing.

Another wonderful thing about this dish is that leftovers stay fresh in the refrigerator for several days and freeze well for several weeks.

Soak the bread in the milk. Melt the butter in a skillet and sauté the chopped onions for a few minutes until they are soft and golden. Transfer to a bowl and add the ground meats, cheese, spinach, herbs, salt, and eggs. Mix well with your hands. Squeeze excess milk from the bread and add the bread to the mixture. Continue to mix, using a kneading motion with the heel of your hand until all is well combined. Fold in the nuts and set aside.

Shell the peas and blanch them in an inch of boiling, salted water for about 3 minutes. Drain, rinse with cold water, and stir them into the stuffing mixture. (Frozen peas may be substituted — just defrost and drain well. It is not necessary to cook them.)

When you buy the veal, have the butcher cut a pocket in the meat for you. Be sure to trim off most of the fat from the top. Gently stuff half of the mixture into the pocket, pressing it flat against the bottom of the meat. Arrange the hard-boiled eggs in a line on top of the stuffing and then press the remaining stuffing into the pocket on top of the eggs. Sew the pocket closed with kitchen string or use skewers to hold it closed.

Season the stuffed veal well with salt and pepper and place it in a deep roasting pan. Scatter the chunked onions and carrots around it and pour in the chicken stock and the wine. Cover the roasting pan and braise the meat in a preheated 350° oven for 2 hours, or until the meat is fork-tender.

When the meat is done, remove it from the oven and take it out of the roasting pan. Cool it to room temperature, wrap tightly in plastic wrap, and chill thoroughly.

To serve, slice thinly down to the bone. Serve with cold rice salad.

3 slices firm white bread, with crusts removed
⅔ cup milk
2 tablespoons butter
1 onion, chopped
¼ pound coarsely ground pork
¼ pound coarsely ground veal
¼ pound coarsely ground ham
½ cup freshly grated Parmesan cheese
1 cup chopped spinach (frozen or freshly cooked)
½ teaspoon each dried rosemary, thyme, sage, and marjoram
1 tablespoon salt
2 eggs, lightly beaten
½ cup shelled pistachio nuts
1 pound fresh peas
A 5-pound breast of veal on the bone, with a pocket for stuffing
3 hard-boiled eggs
2 onions, cut into large chunks
2 carrots, cut into large chunks
1 cup chicken stock
1 cup dry white wine

Cold Rice Salad

Make the vinaigrette for this salad first. That way the garlic has a chance to add its flavor to the dressing. Several days of garlic maceration would not be out of order if you appreciate the flavor.

Leftover rice is fine for this dish, but if none is available, start early enough to cook and thoroughly chill it.

A double batch of this salad makes sense because it holds as long as a potato salad in the refrigerator. The dish is a wonderful accompaniment to picnic-style meals and most cold meats and chicken.

6 tablespoons olive oil
2 tablespoons fresh lemon juice
1 heaping teaspoon Dijon
  mustard
1 teaspoon salt
½ teaspoon sugar
Freshly ground black pepper to
  taste
1 clove garlic, peeled and cut in
  half
1 red onion, finely diced
1 green pepper, seeded and
  finely diced
1 red bell pepper, seeded and
  finely diced
2 very ripe tomatoes, cut into
  thin wedges
1 cup pitted black olives, cut
  into quarters
1 tablespoon chopped fresh
  parsley
1 tablespoon chopped fresh
  basil
1 teaspoon freshly snipped
  chives
1 pound fresh green beans, cut
  into 1-inch pieces
4 cups cooked rice
Salt and freshly ground black
  pepper to taste

Combine the oil, lemon juice, mustard, salt, sugar, pepper, and garlic in a plastic or glass container with a tight-fitting lid and shake well. Let it stand for at least several hours to allow the garlic to macerate. Be sure to remove the garlic before using.

Prepare the onion, peppers, tomatoes, and olives and herbs according to directions. Put the pieces of green beans into an inch of lightly salted boiling water, cover, and steam for about 2 minutes. Drain and rinse with cold water. Drain again.

Put all the prepared ingredients into a large salad bowl and stir in the cooked rice and some salt and pepper. Mix well. Several hours before serving, toss the dressing through the salad and chill again until serving.

Blueberry Sour Cream Tart

SERVES 8 TO 10

Adding lemon rind to the pastry crust gives it extra flavor. There are several pastry crust recipes in this book. In some I use all butter, and in others, such as this one, I cut back on the butter and add some solid vegetable shortening. This results in a less rich crust and is designed to complement the filling it holds. Using solid hydrogenated shortening is important. Oil will produce a heavier, less manageable or malleable crust. You will lose flakiness and pick up an oily aftertaste.

Sift the flour with the salt and sugar and put it into a bowl for the electric mixer. Add the butter, cut into small bits, the shortening, and the lemon rind. Mix on lowest speed until the mixture resembles fine cornmeal. Then add the ice water, 1 tablespoon at a time, until the dough forms a soft ball and leaves the sides of the bowl clean. Gather the dough together, wrap it in wax paper, and chill it for about 30 minutes.

Lightly flour a pastry cloth or board and roll the ball of dough out to fit a 10-inch fluted flan pan. Transfer the dough to the pan and fit it carefully down the sides. Press the dough to the sides of the pan to prevent shrinkage and cut off excess dough.

Line the dough with wax paper and weight it down with raw rice, dried beans, or aluminum nuggets. Put the prepared pan into a preheated 400° oven and bake for about 10 minutes. Remove it from the oven and carefully lift off the wax paper and weights. Cool the crust slightly before filling.

Put the sugar, cinnamon, nutmeg, and salt together in a bowl. Pick the blueberries over and remove leaves and stems. Toss them into the sugar mixture and mix well.

Put the eggs, sour cream, honey, and sugar in another bowl and beat with a whisk until well mixed. Stir the blueberry mixture through the egg mixture, taking care not to break the berries. Pour the mixture into the partially baked pie shell and put it into a preheated 350° oven. Bake for 45 minutes or until a clean knife inserted in the center comes out clean.

Serve the pie at room temperature — with whipped cream or ice cream, if you wish.

1½ cups flour
½ teaspoon salt
1 teaspoon sugar
6 tablespoons sweet butter
2 tablespoons solid vegetable shortening
The grated rind of 1 lemon
2 or 3 tablespoons ice water
3 tablespoons sugar
¼ teaspoon each ground cinnamon and nutmeg
A dash of salt
1 pint fresh blueberries
6 eggs
2 cups sour cream
½ cup honey
½ cup sugar

187

September

35

Artichokes Romana

Salmon en Papillote

Braised New Potatoes with Dill

Boccone Dolce

The highlight of this menu is the lightly browned packet of salmon, holding in its delicious flavors and aroma until the paper is unfolded. Since it is a simple dish and not too filling, you'll have plenty of room to indulge in the divinely rich but airy dessert.

Artichokes Romana

Steaming, cleaning, and stuffing the artichokes can be done as much as two days ahead. This stuffing, which freezes well, is also delicious in baked stuffed mushrooms.

8 medium-sized fresh artichokes
1 lemon, cut in half
¼ cup olive oil
1 onion, finely minced
½ pound mushrooms, finely minced
2 cloves garlic, mashed
A 2-ounce can of flat anchovy fillets, drained of oil and chopped
2 tablespoons chopped fresh parsley
½ teaspoon dried basil
½ teaspoon dried oregano
¼ teaspoon dried thyme
1 cup small pitted black olives, chopped
2 tablespoons capers
2 cups finely grated bread crumbs (unseasoned)
½ cup grated Parmesan cheese
2 to 3 tablespoons dry white wine
Salt and freshly ground black pepper to taste
Several additional tablespoons grated Parmesan cheese
¼ cup olive oil
¼ cup dry white wine
¼ cup chicken stock or water

Pull off the small leaves at the base of the artichokes and discard them. Slice off the stems flush with the artichokes so they will stand upright. Immediately rub the cut sides with a lemon half to prevent darkening. Slice off about one third of the leaves from the top of each artichoke, and use scissors to snip off any remaining sharp tips on the leaves. Rub the tops of the cut artichokes with a lemon half.

Bring about 2 inches of water to a boil in a deep kettle and add a dash of salt. Place the artichokes in the kettle, fitting them in as snugly as possible to prevent them from falling over while they are cooking. Cover the pot and steam the artichokes for 30 minutes or until a leaf pulls out easily. When the artichokes are tender, gently remove them from the kettle and place them upside-down on a rack to drain and cool.

When the artichokes are cool enough to handle, gently pull the center leaves away from the choke, and using the tips of your fingers, pull out the choke, leaving a cavity in the center. Use a small spoon to scrape away all the fuzz. The artichokes are now ready for stuffing.

To prepare the stuffing, heat the olive oil in a skillet and sauté the onion, mushrooms, garlic, anchovies, and herbs for about 3 minutes, until they are soft and golden. Add the olives, capers, bread crumbs, and cheese and mix well. Spoon the 2 to 3 tablespoons wine over the mixture to moisten it slightly and mix until it reaches a stuffing consistency. Add the salt and pepper.

Remove the stuffing from the heat and cool it slightly. To stuff each artichoke, put a small amount of the stuffing in the cavity and then pack it between the leaves. Wrap each artichoke with plastic wrap and refrigerate until ready to use.

To bake, sprinkle additional Parmesan cheese over the top of each prepared artichoke and place them side by side in a flat baking dish. Drizzle the olive oil over the tops and combine the wine and stock or water. Pour this liquid into the bottom of the baking dish and bake the artichokes in a preheated 350° oven for 30 minutes or until the tops are crisp and brown. Serve hot or at room temperature.

Salmon en Papillote

The technique of wrapping and baking in parchment paper or aluminum foil allows you to cook fish in its own sealed-in juices. The addition of a mushroom-and-tomato-based sauce enhances the flavor. The sauce is equally good served over broiled salmon steaks.

The fish can be prepared, wrapped, and readied for the oven earlier in the day. Just refrigerate the packages and bring to room temperature before baking.

Melt the butter in a saucepan and sauté the shallots, garlic, and mushrooms for a few minutes until they are soft and golden. Add the cognac and allow it to come to a boil. Cook for a minute or two to reduce the liquid. Then sprinkle the flour over all and stir to incorporate. Add the wine, cream, tomatoes, tomato paste, herbs, salt, and pepper. Bring this mixture to a boil, reduce the heat to simmer, and cook for a minute or two. Remove from heat and cool slightly.

Sprinkle the pieces of salmon with salt and pepper. Melt several tablespoons of butter in a small pan and have it ready with a pastry brush at hand. Fold each piece of parchment paper in half crosswise, open it, and brush the entire surface with melted butter.

Place a piece of the salmon on each paper, at the fold, and spoon a few tablespoons of the cooled sauce on top of the salmon. Bring the top and bottom edges of the paper together and roll them down toward the fish. Brush the top of the paper with the beaten egg mixture and fold the side flaps up and over, pressing them down on the egg wash to seal the paper closed.

Place the prepared packets, seam side down, on a lightly buttered cooky sheet. Brush the tops of the packets with the remaining melted butter.

Bake the packets in a preheated 375° oven for 20 minutes or until the paper is very puffy and brown. Serve at once in the paper.

3 tablespoons butter
6 shallots, finely minced
1 clove garlic, mashed
½ pound mushrooms, thinly sliced
2 tablespoons cognac
2 tablespoons flour
⅓ cup dry white wine
1 cup heavy cream
2 very ripe tomatoes, peeled, seeded, juiced, and chopped
1 teaspoon tomato paste
1 tablespoon chopped fresh parsley
1 tablespoon chopped fresh tarragon (optional)
Salt and freshly ground black pepper to taste
8 pieces boneless and skinless fresh salmon (8 ounces each)
Salt and pepper to taste
Several tablespoons butter
1 whole egg beaten with 1 tablespoon cold water
8 sheets parchment paper or aluminum foil (11 by 14 inches each)

Braised New Potatoes with Dill

What could be simpler than new potatoes, peeled or un-peeled, braised in a bit of chicken stock? The carrots and chopped fresh dill give considerable color and flavor to this dish.

24 small red-skinned new
  potatoes
1 teaspoon salt
3 tablespoons butter
2 cups thinly sliced fresh carrots
⅓ cup chicken stock
1 tablespoon chopped fresh dill
1 tablespoon soft butter

Scrub the potatoes well with a vegetable brush. You may peel them or not. Put them in a large kettle and add the salt, butter, carrots, and stock. Cover and cook the potatoes, over low heat, for 20 minutes or until they are tender when pierced.

Add the chopped dill and the soft butter and toss the potatoes gently.

Boccone Dolce

In Italian, *boccone* means mouthful and *dolce* is sweet. And this dessert is truly a mouthful of sweet tastes and many textures: meringue, whipped cream, chocolate, and sliced strawberries.

The layers of meringue can be prepared as much as three days in advance, in any shape you like. Just be sure you have a comparably shaped serving platter.

4 egg whites
¼ teaspoon cream of tartar
A dash of salt
1 cup sugar
6 ounces semisweet chocolate
3 tablespoons water
1 pint fresh strawberries
3 cups heavy cream
⅓ cup sugar
1 teaspoon vanilla extract

Butter three cooky sheets and line them with wax paper. Do not butter the wax paper. Draw three circles (9 inches in diameter) or three rectangles (9 by 4 inches) or any shape you desire on the wax paper. Use a cake pan or a ruler as your guide. After the cooky sheets have been prepared, set them aside.

Preheat the oven to 250°.

Beat the egg whites with an electric mixer until soft peaks begin to form; then add the cream of tartar and salt. Add the cup of sugar gradually, continuing to beat until you have a stiff, shiny meringue.

Divide the meringue evenly over the three shapes and spread smoothly. Bake in the preheated oven for 40 minutes

194

or until the tops feel dry and are a very pale golden color.

Remove the meringues from the oven. Holding the wax paper by the ends, lift them off the cooky sheets and invert them onto cake racks. Gently peel away the wax paper from the baked meringues and let them cool to room temperature. Keep the meringues at room temperature, lightly covered or wrapped with foil, until you are ready to assemble the cake.

To assemble the cake, melt the chocolate and the water in the top of a double boiler until smooth. Wash, hull, and slice the strawberries. Set the chocolate to cool slightly while you whip the cream.

Whip the cream until it begins to thicken; then slowly add the ⅓ cup sugar and vanilla. Continue to whip until thick and stiff. Reserve about ½ cup of the whipped cream.

Spread the cooled chocolate thinly over each layer of meringue. Put the first layer on a serving platter and spread a small amount of the whipped cream over the chocolate. Cover with half of the sliced berries. Place the second layer of meringue on top of this and spread more whipped cream over the chocolate. Cover with the remaining sliced berries, reserving a few slices for garnishing the top of the cake.

Put the third layer of meringue on top and frost the entire sides and top of the cake with the remaining whipped cream. Put the reserved ½ cup of whipped cream into a pastry bag fitted with a rosette nozzle and pipe out decorative rosettes over the top and sides of the cake. Garnish with the reserved sliced berries and refrigerate the cake until ready to serve. The cake can be assembled early in the day and refrigerated until serving.

36

Mussels with Hazelnut Butter

Braised Duckling

Apple Tart

This menu's entrée is another approach to duckling: braising in a rich brown sauce with a variety of vegetables. Simple buttered noodles are a good accompaniment.

Mussels with Hazelnut Butter

Mussels acquire a rich nutty flavor when baked with a hazel-nut-and-butter topping. Mix this compound butter a day or two in advance to meld the flavors.

Discard any mussels that are open or have broken shells. Scrub them under cold running water and pull off the "beards." Drop them into a basin of fresh cold water and add a handful of cornmeal to the water. Allow mussels to soak for about 1 hour; then rinse them again.

Put the clean, scrubbed mussels into a deep kettle and add the wine or water. Cover the kettle and steam the mussels, over high heat, for 10 minutes or until all the shells are wide open. Remove the mussels with a slotted spoon, discarding any that did not open.

When the mussels are cool enough to handle, gently remove each top shell, leaving the mussel intact on the bottom shell. Place the mussels on a cooky sheet.

Combine the remaining ingredients in a small bowl. Place a small ball of the butter mixture on top of each mussel and flatten it slightly.

Slide the mussels under a preheated broiler for a few minutes, until the tops are brown and bubbly. Serve at once with hot bread.

48 fresh mussels
¼ cup dry white wine or water
2 tablespoons fresh lemon juice
4 shallots, finely minced
½ pound (2 sticks) butter
Freshly ground black pepper to taste
¼ cup shelled hazelnuts, finely chopped
2 cloves garlic, mashed
6 tablespoons fresh finely grated bread crumbs
2 tablespoons chopped fresh parsley
2 tablespoons chopped fresh chives (optional)

Braised Duckling

Roasting the pieces of duck before braising helps to render the excess fat so the completed dish will be relatively fat-free. This process can be done early in the day.

The French-style braising with red wine and vegetables bears a family resemblance to *boeuf bourguignon* and *coq au vin*. As with those dishes, the braising can be done ahead and the duck reheated with the vegetable garnish.

For informal serving, cook and serve the duckling in an attractive casserole.

Two 4- to 5-pound ducklings,
  cut into quarters
Salt and freshly ground black
  pepper to taste
2 tablespoons butter
2 carrots, diced
2 onions, diced
2 cloves garlic, diced
¼ cup cognac
1 cup red Burgundy
4 cups Sauce Espagnole (page
  120)
1 bay leaf
1 tablespoon chopped fresh
  parsley
½ teaspoon dried thyme
24 small white pearl onions
24 whole button mushrooms
6 white turnips
24 pimiento-stuffed green olives
  (optional)
2 tablespoons butter
2 tablespoons sugar
Freshly cooked and buttered
  noodles
2 heaping tablespoons Dijon
  mustard
1 tablespoon green peppercorns
Salt, black pepper, and a dash of
  cayenne pepper
Chopped fresh parsley (for
  garnish)

Trim off all visible fat from the pieces of duckling. Salt and pepper them and place them, skin side down, on a rack over a shallow roasting pan. Pour about ½ cup of hot water into the bottom of the roasting pan and place the duck in a preheated 450° oven. Roast for 30 minutes, turn the duck skin side up, and roast for another 30 minutes or until the duck pieces are crisp and brown. Add more water if the pan seems dry at any point during the roasting; this keeps the fat from splattering and smoking. When the duck is done, remove it from the oven and set it aside.

Melt the 2 tablespoons of butter in an oven-proof deep kettle or Dutch oven. Sauté the carrots, onions, and garlic in the hot butter for a few minutes until soft and golden. Add the cognac and let it come to a rolling boil. Reduce the liquid by half.

Put the pieces of duck into the pot and add the wine and Sauce Espagnole. Add the bay leaf, parsley, and thyme. Cover the pot and place in a preheated 350° oven. Braise for 1 hour or until the duck is fork-tender. The dish can be prepared ahead up to this point.

While the duck is braising, drop the pearl onions into a pot of boiling water. Boil for 1 minute, remove, and drain. When the onions are cool enough to handle, gently slice off the root ends and peel off the skins. Trim the hard bottoms off the mushroom stems, wipe the mushrooms clean with a damp paper towel, and set aside. Peel the turnips and cut them into small pieces (about 24 altogether). Drain the olives.

Heat the 2 tablespoons of butter in a small skillet and add the mushrooms. Sauté for a minute or two until golden. Remove them to a small bowl. Add more butter to the skillet if necessary and sauté the onions and turnips for a few minutes until golden. Sprinkle the sugar over them and toss to caramelize and coat. When the sugar has turned golden brown, scrape the contents of the skillet into the bowl of mushrooms.

About 15 minutes before the duck is done, add the sautéed vegetables and the olives to the braising pot. Continue to cook until the duckling and onions are fork-tender. Remove the pieces of duck to a serving platter, and surround them with the vegetables and buttered noodles.

Place the braising pot on top of the stove and bring the liquids to a rolling boil. Stir in the mustard, green peppercorns, salt, pepper, and cayenne. Cook for a minute, skim any excess fat from the surface, and serve this sauce in a gravy boat to accompany the duckling. Scatter the chopped parsley over the top of the serving platter just before serving.

Apple Tart

The apple-raisin filling in this two-layer tart can be cooked a day ahead and refrigerated.

Golden Delicious apples behave best in baking this shallow, French-style tart. If proof is needed, the French are now growing them in their own country.

Put the butter, egg, and milk into a bowl for the electric mixer and blend for a few seconds. Add the sifted flour mixture and mix on lowest speed until the mixture forms a soft ball of dough and leaves the sides of the bowl clean. Gather the dough together into a ball, wrap it in wax paper, and refrigerate for at least 30 minutes. Lightly flour a pastry cloth or board and roll out the ball of dough to a circle large enough to fit the bottom and sides of a 10-inch flan pan with a removable bottom.

Transfer the dough to the pan and carefully fit it around the sides and edges, pressing the dough to the top edge to prevent shrinkage. Trim excess dough and line the pastry with wax paper. Weight the paper down with raw rice, dried beans, or aluminum nuggets.

Partially bake the pie shell in a preheated 400° oven for 10 minutes. Remove from oven and carefully lift off the weights and the wax paper. The crust is now ready for filling.

Peel, core, and dice four of the apples and put them into a saucepan. Add the ⅓ cup of sugar, 2 tablespoons of lemon juice, the cold water, and the raisins. Cover the pot and cook over very low heat for 15 minutes or until the mixture is the consistency of applesauce. Remove from the heat and cool.

Peel, core, and thinly slice the remaining apples. Put them into a bowl and sprinkle with the remaining lemon juice.

Spoon the cooled applesauce mixture into the bottom of the pie shell and spread it evenly. Arrange apple slices in a spiral over the entire top of the tart, making it as attractive as you can. Beat the egg white with a fork until bubbly and brush this over the apple slices to prevent them from burning while baking.

Bake the tart in a preheated 375° oven for 30 minutes or until the top is golden brown. Set it aside to cool slightly.

Press the apricot jam through a fine sieve into a small saucepan. Stir in the sugar and apple brandy. Bring this mixture to a boil and stir until smooth. Brush the glaze over the entire top of the apple tart and set it aside to cool. Serve with whipped cream or vanilla ice cream if you wish.

Crust

8 tablespoons soft sweet butter
1 egg
2 to 3 teaspoons milk
1½ cups flour, sifted with ½ teaspoon salt and 2 teaspoons sugar

Filling and Topping

8 large Golden Delicious apples
⅓ cup sugar
4 tablespoons fresh lemon juice
2 tablespoons cold water
¼ cup raisins
1 egg white
1 cup apricot jam
1 tablespoon sugar
1 tablespoon apple brandy (optional)

199

Marinated Mushrooms

Veal with Pesto and Pasta

Chilled Grand Marnier Soufflé

By September, basil is in full bloom, and *pesto* sauce is the best way to savor this pungent herb. Along the Genoa coast, the home of *pesto*, Italian families put up a supply of *pesto* every fall to last them through the winter. You could do the same.

A 24-hour marinade for the mushrooms and a chilled soufflé dessert make it possible to spread the work load for this menu over two or three days.

Marinated Mushrooms

The recipe suggests a 24-hour rest in the refrigerator, but as long as 48 hours would be fine. If you want to double the recipe, these piquant mushrooms make delicious cocktail appetizers that will keep for up to a week.

Wipe the mushrooms clean with a damp paper towel and trim the bottoms of the stems. Place the mushrooms in a deep saucepan and cover them with boiling water. Add ½ teaspoon salt. Cover the pot and cook over low heat for about 5 minutes. Do not boil. Drain off the hot water and rinse the mushrooms in cold water to stop the cooking process. Drain well and put them in a bowl.

Mix the dry mustard with the cold water. Let the mustard soak for 5 minutes; then add the remaining ingredients and mix well. Pour this mixture over the mushrooms, cover the bowl tightly, and let the mushrooms marinate for 24 hours or longer. Serve the mushrooms on lettuce leaves as a cold first course or on toothpicks as an accompaniment to cocktails.

1 pound fresh, firm button
  mushrooms
Boiling water
½ teaspoon salt
1 teaspoon dry Colman's
  mustard
2 teaspoons cold water
2 tablespoons red wine vinegar
6 tablespoons olive oil
½ teaspoon salt
Freshly ground black pepper to
  taste
½ teaspoon sugar
1 tablespoon chopped fresh
  parsley
½ teaspoon dried coriander
¼ teaspoon dried cumin

Veal with Pesto and Pasta

In this recipe, *pesto*'s rich green color and basil flavor is enriched by the ricotta cheese and the cream. The dish is given substance by the addition of veal cubes to the sauce. Cubed boneless chicken breast may be substituted for the veal.

Pesto must be made in season with fresh basil leaves, but it freezes well. Omit the cheese before freezing and freeze in small batches for convenience. To use after freezing, defrost to room temperature and stir the grated cheese through before serving on any hot cooked pasta.

2 pounds boneless veal, cut
  from the leg or shoulder
Salt and pepper to taste
½ cup flour
2 tablespoons butter
2 tablespoons olive oil
4 shallots, finely minced
1 clove garlic, mashed
¼ pound prosciutto, chopped or
  shredded
½ cup chicken stock
  (homemade or canned)
1 pound fresh peas
2 cups tightly packed fresh basil
  leaves
3 tablespoons pine nuts
1 tablespoon walnuts
2 cloves garlic, mashed
A dash of salt
½ cup olive oil
¼ cup grated Parmesan cheese
½ cup ricotta cheese
1 cup heavy cream
1 pound thin spaghetti
2 tablespoons melted butter
Freshly grated Parmesan cheese

Cut the meat into small cubes and season with salt and pepper. Dredge the meat lightly in the flour and shake off the excess. (This works best if you sprinkle the flour over the meat in a colander and let the excess flour fall through.) Heat the butter and oil in a skillet and sauté the cubes of meat until they are golden brown on all sides. Add the shallots, garlic, and prosciutto and sauté for another minute or two.

Pour in the stock, cover the skillet, and simmer for 10 minutes or until the meat is tender.

Shell the peas and cook them in 1 inch of boiling, salted water for about 3 minutes. Rinse them under cold water to refresh them, and drain. (If you prefer, use one package of defrosted frozen peas. It is not necessary to cook them.)

While the meat is cooking, put the basil leaves, pine nuts, walnuts, garlic, and salt into the container of an electric blender or a food processor fitted with the steel blade and purée until smooth. Add the oil and blend well. Add the cheeses and mix for another few seconds. Do not overmix.

When the meat is tender, add the basil sauce, stir, and add the heavy cream and the peas. Stir to combine. Cover the skillet again and allow the entire mixture to cook a few minutes longer to heat through.

Bring a large pot of salted water to a rolling boil and add a tablespoon of oil. Drop the pasta into the boiling water and cook it for 6 to 8 minutes if fresh, 10 to 12 minutes if dried. Drain the pasta and toss it with the melted butter.

To serve, toss the sauce through the pasta and pass additional grated Parmesan cheese.

Chilled Grand Marnier Soufflé

This dessert might just as well be called a mousse, except for its appearance. It looks like a soufflé because a collar is used to extend the mixture above the rim of the dish, as if it had risen.

Put the cold water and the Grand Marnier into a heat-proof glass measuring cup or small bowl. Sprinkle the gelatin over the liquid. Place the cup or bowl in a small saucepan and add about an inch of water to the pan. Bring the water in the pan to a boil on top of the stove and let the heat of the boiling water dissolve the contents of the cup. When the gelatin mixture seems quite dissolved, remove it from the pan and set it aside to cool.

Put the eggs and yolks into a bowl for the electric mixer. Set the whites aside in a clean, dry bowl. Begin beating the eggs and yolks together, and gradually add the sugar, continuing to beat at high speed until the mixture is thick and very pale. Beat in the gelatin mixture and the vanilla. Set this mixture aside.

Whip the heavy cream in a chilled bowl until it is thick and stiff. Fold it gently into the egg mixture. Whip the egg whites with the salt until they hold firm, stiff peaks. Fold them gently into the egg mixture.

Tear off a long strip of aluminum foil or wax paper and fold it in half lengthwise. Butter one side and tie it around a 4-cup soufflé dish, buttered side in. Spoon the soufflé mixture into the prepared dish, allowing it to come up beyond the rim into the collar. Chill for at least 6 hours, or overnight.

Wash, hull, and slice the berries. Peel and cut the oranges into segments or slices. Sprinkle the Grand Marnier over all and allow to marinate for several hours.

To serve, carefully run a clean knife between the collar and the soufflé in the dish and pull the collar gently away. Serve the soufflé with the bowl of marinated fruit on the side.

¼ cup cold water
¼ cup Grand Marnier
2 tablespoons unflavored gelatin
4 large eggs plus 3 yolks
3 egg whites
¾ cup sugar
1 teaspoon vanilla extract
2 cups heavy cream
A dash of salt
1 pint fresh strawberries
3 or 4 large navel oranges
2 tablespoons Grand Marnier

Fresh Tomato Bisque

Seafood Florentine

Chocolate Velvet

This menu suits the season. Fall colors are resplendent, with variations of reds plus vibrant and golden yellows. The tomato bisque is perfectly timed because fresh tomatoes are at their juiciest and most plentiful in September. The main course, lying on a bed of spinach, provides varied seafood and a rich sauce covering. It can be assembled and held up to several hours before it goes into the oven.

Fresh Tomato Bisque

This recipe gets an added boost of flavor from the curry and the garnish of toasted garlic croutons. It is worth repeating that fresh, extra-ripe tomatoes are what make this soup taste so good.

Heat the 4 tablespoons butter in a deep soup kettle and add the onions and the mashed garlic. Sauté them for a few minutes, over low heat, until they are golden. Stir in the curry powder and cook for a few minutes longer.

Add the potatoes, tomatoes, bay leaf, thyme, and stock. Bring this mixture to a boil, reduce the heat to simmer, cover, and cook for 30 minutes or until the potatoes are tender. Cool slightly. Then run the entire mixture through a food mill or sieve to remove solids and purée it. Season with Tabasco, salt, and pepper.

To prepare the croutons, trim the crusts from the bread and cut the bread into small dice. Put the butter and garlic into a small saucepan and heat to boiling. Remove from the heat and let the butter sit for about 10 minutes to increase the garlic flavor.

Strain the pieces of garlic out of the butter and pour the butter into a skillet. Heat the skillet. When the butter is quite hot, toss the cubes of bread through the butter until they turn golden brown. Transfer them to a cooky sheet and keep them warm in a 300° oven.

The soup may be served hot with the croutons or cold with a dollop of sour cream or plain yogurt.

4 tablespoons butter
1 onion, chopped
2 cloves garlic, mashed
2 tablespoons curry powder
2 Idaho potatoes, peeled and diced
5 pounds very ripe tomatoes, chopped
1 bay leaf
½ teaspoon dried thyme
2 to 3 cups chicken stock (homemade or canned)
A dash of Tabasco
Salt and freshly ground black pepper to taste
1 loaf French or Italian bread
8 tablespoons butter
3 cloves garlic, peeled and cut in half

Seafood Florentine

Florentine invariably indicates spinach, and fresh is best. In French cooking any mixture of fresh seafood is called *fruits de mer*, or fruits of the sea. You might not use all the seafood suggested here, but be sure to use a combination of at least two kinds. The greater the variety, the more interesting the dish.

Unique to this entrée is the finishing touch — a combination of two sauces basic to French cooking, béchamel and hollandaise.

1 pound bay or sea scallops
1 pound fresh shrimp
1 pound fresh lump crab meat
1 pound freshly cooked lobster meat
4 tablespoons sweet butter
4 shallots, finely minced
½ pound white mushrooms, thinly sliced
¼ cup cognac or sherry
Salt and pepper to taste
1 tablespoon sweet butter
1 tablespoon flour
1 cup warm milk
½ pound sweet butter
4 egg yolks
2 tablespoons fresh lemon juice
Salt, white pepper, and a dash of cayenne pepper
1 pound fresh spinach
2 tablespoons sweet butter
Salt, pepper, and a dash of nutmeg
½ cup freshly grated Parmesan cheese

Rinse the scallops, drain, and pat them dry with paper towels. If you are using sea scallops, slice them into thin slices. Peel and devein the shrimp, rinse, and dry with paper towels. Pick over the crab meat to remove any cartilage. Cut the lobster meat into small dice. (If freshly cooked lobster meat is unavailable, use frozen lobster tails, cooked according to the package directions, cooled, and removed from the shell.)

Heat the butter in a skillet and gently sauté the shallots and mushrooms for a few minutes until golden brown. Remove them from the pan and drain them in a colander.

Add more butter to the skillet if necessary and gently sauté the scallops for a minute or two. Transfer them with a slotted spoon to the colander containing the mushrooms.

Add the shrimp to the skillet and sauté for a few minutes until they turn bright red. Transfer to the colander. Add the crab meat and the cooked lobster meat to the colander.

Pour the cognac or sherry into the skillet and let it come to a rolling boil and reduce slightly. Add the ingredients in the colander to the skillet, stir in the salt and pepper, and heat for a few minutes.

To make the béchamel sauce, heat the tablespoon of butter in a small saucepan and when it is hot and foamy, whisk in the flour, stirring to form a *roux*. Stir in the warm milk and bring the mixture to a boil. Cook for another minute or two and remove from the heat.

To make the hollandaise sauce, melt the ½ pound of butter in a small saucepan until hot and foamy. Put the egg yolks into the container of an electric blender or a food processor fitted with the steel blade. Add the lemon juice and salt, white pepper, and cayenne pepper. Blend for a few seconds. Begin adding the hot butter, a drop at a time, until the mixture begins to thicken. Then increase the butter to a slow, steady stream until it is all incorporated.

Mix the béchamel sauce into the hollandaise sauce.

To cook the spinach, wash it well and remove the thick stems. Put the washed leaves into a deep kettle but do not add additional water; the spinach will steam in the water clinging to the leaves. Cover the pot and steam the spinach over low heat for 5 minutes or until it collapses and looks soft. Remove it from the kettle, drain well, and chop fine. Heat the 2 tablespoons of butter in a small skillet and gently cook the spinach in the hot butter for a minute or two. Season with salt, pepper, and a dash of nutmeg. The spinach can be prepared up to this point a day in advance.

To assemble the dish, spread the spinach over the bottom of a shallow gratin dish. Spoon the seafood mixture evenly over it and spoon the mixed sauces over all. Sprinkle the grated cheese over the top. The dish can be prepared up to this point early in the day.

If the ingredients in the dish are still quite hot, it will only be necessary to run the dish under the broiler for a few minutes to heat and glaze the top. If the dish has been prepared ahead and/or refrigerated, heat it for about 15 minutes in a 350° oven before broiling it. Serve with plain white rice.

Chocolate Velvet

This is a chocoholic's dream. A frosted thin layer of cake is completely filled with a rich, dense, and full-flavored chocolate mousse.

The use of the thin cake to enclose the mousse filling allows you to unmold, frost, and garnish this dessert for a fabulous presentation.

Fresh praline paste is a rather rare delicacy, but it is also available canned, imported from France, in specialty food shops. If you can't track it down, proceed without it.

6 eggs
10 tablespoons sugar
6 tablespoons unsweetened Dutch cocoa
1 teaspoon vanilla extract
3 eggs
1 tablespoon fine-grind instant coffee
¼ cup kirsch
¼ cup dark crème de cacao
¼ cup dark rum
⅓ cup praline paste
24 ounces semisweet chocolate
6 tablespoons sweet butter
2 cups heavy cream
¼ cup confectioners' sugar
A dash of salt
6 ounces semisweet chocolate
3 tablespoons boiling water
1 cup heavy cream

Butter an 11-by-16-inch jelly-roll pan and line it with wax paper. Butter the wax paper and trim off the edges. Set the pan aside.

Separate the six eggs and put the whites into a clean, dry bowl. Set aside. Begin to beat the yolks and gradually pour in the sugar. Continue to beat until the mixture turns a pale creamy color and thickens. Add the cocoa and vanilla and mix well.

Beat the egg whites until stiff, firm peaks form. Gently fold them into the chocolate mixture and spoon the batter into the prepared pan. Bake the cake in a preheated 350° oven for 30 minutes or until the top springs back lightly when you touch it.

Loosen the cake from the sides of the pan and invert it onto a sheet of wax paper. Gently pull the bottom piece of wax paper away from the cake and let the cake cool completely.

When it is cool, cut it into pieces that will fit the bottom and sides of an 8-cup bowl or mold. Line the mold with the cake, reserving any unused cake to cover the top after the filling is in. Chill the prepared bowl.

To prepare the mousse filling, separate the three eggs and put the whites into a clean, dry bowl. Set aside.

Add the coffee, kirsch, crème de cacao, rum, and praline paste to the egg yolks and beat until well blended. Melt the 24 ounces of chocolate and butter in the top of a double boiler and when the mixture is smooth whisk it into the egg yolk mixture.

Beat the heavy cream until thick and stiff. Beat the egg

whites until soft peaks form, add the confectioners' sugar and salt, and continue to beat until stiff peaks form.

Whisk the whipped cream and the egg whites into the chocolate mixture and pour this mousse into the cake-lined bowl. Chill thoroughly, at least overnight. The dessert may be made up to two days ahead to this point.

Melt the 6 ounces of chocolate in the top of a double boiler and when it is melted stir in the boiling water until a smooth spreading consistency is achieved. You may need more boiling water. Unmold the cake onto a serving platter and spread the melted chocolate over the entire outside of the cake. Return it to the refrigerator and chill until the frosting is firm.

To serve, whip the cup of heavy cream and put it into a pastry bag fitted with a rosette nozzle. Pipe out attractive rosettes around the sides and top of the cake. Slice and serve.

October

LESSON 39

Onion Soup Gratinée
Sautéed Steak with Three Colored Peppercorns
Soufflé Normandy

LESSON 40

Escabèche
Roast Loin of Pork with Prunes and Mustard Sauce
Fresh Kiwi Tart

LESSON 41

Deep-Fried Shrimp with Plum Sauce
Chicken and Artichoke Hearts Gratinée
Frozen Hazelnut Cream with Hot Chocolate Sauce

LESSON 42

Sausage in Brioche with Potato Salad Lyonnaise
Chicken in Red Wine
Chocolate-Dipped Pears

LESSON 43

Scallops Provençale
Roast Duckling with Apples
Chocolate Mousse Cake

39

Onion Soup Gratinée

Sautéed Steak with Three Colored
Peppercorns

Soufflé Normandy

Steak *au poivre* is a classic French-restaurant offering. The
pink peppercorns are the latest thing in *nouvelle cuisine* condiments. They are softer, milder, and sweeter, but at the same
time complement the vinegar-steeped green and the spicier
black peppercorns.

This menu requires some last-minute cooking for the
steaks, but the onion soup can be prepared well ahead and
the soufflé bakes while the steaks are being enjoyed.

Onion Soup Gratinée

A recipe for homemade beef stock is included as the basis for this traditional French onion soup. It is also the basic stock for many vegetable and meat soups and the start of the entire family of brown sauces. Though the simmering of the stock takes time, it is not a complicated procedure, and the stock can be stored in the freezer for months. The best substitute for the homemade variety is canned beef broth. Since it is considerably stronger and not as mellow as homemade stock, you might want to dilute it with water or chicken stock.

The soup can be made a day or more ahead of time. Add the garlic croutons and cheese just before serving.

3 large Bermuda or Spanish onions
3 tablespoons sweet butter
2 cloves garlic, mashed
Salt and freshly ground black pepper to taste
1 tablespoon flour
8 cups brown beef stock (see page 215)
1 cup dry white wine
1 bay leaf
¼ teaspoon dried thyme
1 long loaf French or Italian bread, sliced 1 inch thick
4 cloves garlic, peeled and cut in half
8 tablespoons salted butter
1 pound Gruyère cheese
¼ cup freshly grated Parmesan cheese

Peel the onions, cut them in half lengthwise, and slice them thin. Heat the sweet butter in a deep soup kettle and sauté the onions over low heat for about 5 minutes, until they are very soft and golden. Don't let them get too brown. Stir in the mashed garlic, salt and pepper, and flour. Mix well to incorporate the flour.

Add the stock, wine, bay leaf, and thyme. Bring the soup to a rolling boil, reduce the heat to simmer, cover the kettle, and cook for about 30 minutes.

While the soup is simmering, slice the bread. Put the peeled garlic pieces into a small saucepan and add the salted butter. Heat to boiling, remove from heat, and let the butter stand for a few minutes to increase the garlic flavor. Discard the pieces of garlic. Using a small pastry brush, brush the pieces of bread liberally with the garlic-flavored butter. Put the slices onto a cooky sheet and bake them in a 350° oven for about 20 minutes or until they are crisp and golden.

Slice the Gruyère cheese into thick slices large enough to cover the top of the soup bowls you plan to use. (You can buy bowls designed expressly for onion soup.)

To assemble the bowls for the oven, spoon the hot soup into each bowl, place a piece of garlic bread on the soup, and top the bread with sliced cheese, taking care to cover the surface of the bowl completely. The cheese may overhang the bowl. Sprinkle the Gruyère with grated Parmesan. Place the prepared bowls on a cooky sheet.

Preheat the oven to broil. When ready to serve the soup,

slide the prepared bowls under the broiler for a few minutes until the cheese melts and browns on the top. Serve at once.

Brown Beef Stock

A B O U T   2   Q U A R T S

Put the bones, meat, onions, carrots, parsnips, celery, and leeks into a large roasting pan. Place in a 400° oven and roast for about 1 hour or until everything is very brown. Stir the ingredients occasionally so they brown evenly. When everything is quite brown and crisp, transfer all the ingredients to a deep soup kettle or stockpot. Pour about 1 cup of hot water into the roasting pan, scrape up all the browned bits from the bottom, and pour this into the stockpot.

Add the remaining ingredients to the stockpot. Be sure the water is cold and just covers the ingredients in the pot.

Place a cover over the pot, slightly ajar to allow steam to escape, and turn the heat on low. Let the stock cook very slowly, never boiling, for at least 6 to 8 hours. Occasionally skim the surface of the liquid to remove the gray film that forms. Do not stir the stock with a spoon. Stirring or boiling the liquid will cause the stock to become cloudy.

After 6 to 8 hours, turn off the heat and let the stock cool. Either the cooking or cooling procedure can be done overnight. The skimming of the surface is only necessary during the first hour or two of cooking. After that time, the stock can be cooked without disturbing it.

When the stock is cool enough to handle, lift out all the solids with a slotted spoon and discard them. Then strain the liquid through very fine cheesecloth to remove all particles. After the stock has been strained, chill it overnight to let the excess fat rise to the surface. The solid fat can then be discarded easily.

The strained stock may be frozen in 1-cup containers for future use. It can be frozen for as long as 6 months.

5 pounds beef marrow bones, cut into small pieces
A 2-pound piece of boneless chuck, cut up
2 large onions, peeled and chopped
4 carrots, peeled and chopped
2 parsnips, peeled and chopped
4 stalks celery, chopped
2 large leeks, well washed and chopped
2 teaspoons salt
1 teaspoon dried thyme
2 bay leaves
Several sprigs of fresh parsley
3 cloves garlic, peeled and chopped
6 whole cloves
1 teaspoon whole black peppercorns
2 quarts cold water (or enough to cover ingredients in pot)

Sautéed Steak with Three Colored Peppercorns

SERVES 8

The French almost always serve their steaks sauced. In this recipe, steaks are first coated with crushed peppercorns for more flavor. A quick sauté in a hot skillet releases pan juices that are then merged with cognac, cream, and spicy mustard. This delicious combination gains piquancy with the addition of the three types of peppercorn: black, green, and pink.

8 boneless steaks, about 12 ounces each and ½ inch thick
Salt to taste
1 teaspoon each black, green, and pink peppercorns
4 tablespoons sweet butter
1 tablespoon corn or safflower oil
4 shallots, finely minced
2 tablespoons cognac
1 tablespoon Dijon mustard
1 cup heavy cream

Use filet mignon, boneless shell, or club steaks. Trim the excess fat and season the steaks on both sides with salt. Put the peppercorns into a paper or plastic bag and pound them with a mallet or hammer to crush and mix them. Using the heel of your hand, press the crushed peppercorns firmly into the steaks on both sides.

Have all the remaining ingredients handy at the stove. Heat the butter and oil in a large skillet and sauté the prepared steaks for a few minutes on each side, until they reach the desired internal doneness. As they are finished, remove them from the skillet and set aside while you prepare the sauce.

Add the shallots to the skillet and sauté them for 1 minute. Pour in the cognac and let it come to a rolling boil to burn off the alcohol and reduce slightly. Stir in the mustard and cream and mix well.

Return the steaks to the pan, spoon the sauce up and over the meat, and heat through. Serve immediately with Wild Rice au Chinois, page 19.

Soufflé Normandy

SERVES 8

A dish with *Normandy* in its title usually implies the use of apples or apple flavoring. This soufflé, like other dessert soufflés, starts with a thick white sauce and adds a flavored fruit. In this case the fruit is rolled in sugar and then sautéed in butter to achieve a slightly caramel flavor. The white sauce can be made hours ahead and the fruit can be prepared ahead, too. The only last-minute step is the beating of the egg whites. Bake the soufflé while you are eating the main course.

Spread the soft butter over the bottom and sides of a 6-cup soufflé dish. Sprinkle the buttered bottom and sides with the granulated sugar, coating well. Tear off a long strip of aluminum foil, fold it in half lengthwise, and butter one side. Tie this collar around the soufflé dish, and fasten it securely in place. Chill the dish.

Put the cornstarch into a small saucepan and pour in a few tablespoons of the milk. Stir well to dilute the cornstarch to a thin paste. Add the remaining milk and the ⅓ cup sugar. Place this mixture over medium heat and stir constantly until it thickens and comes to a boil. Remove from the heat and stir in the egg yolks, one at a time, mixing well after each addition. Add the apple brandy and 2 tablespoons of butter, cover with plastic wrap, and set aside. This soufflé base can be

▶ prepared several hours or even a day in advance.

Peel, core, and thinly slice the apple. Roll the apple slices in sugar. Heat the 2 tablespoons of butter in a small skillet and gently sauté the apple slices until the sugar melts and the apples begin to caramelize. Remove them from the skillet and set aside. This procedure can be done several hours ahead of

▶ time.

To finish the soufflé for the oven, put the egg whites into a clean, dry bowl for the electric mixer and beat with the salt until stiff peaks form. Gently fold the whites into the prepared base. (If the base of the soufflé has been refrigerated, be sure to bring it to room temperature before folding in the egg whites.) Spoon half of the soufflé mixture into the bottom of the prepared dish and spoon the sautéed apple slices and the crushed cookies on top. Spoon on the remaining soufflé mixture, filling the bowl just to its rim.

Bake the soufflé in a preheated 375° oven, taking care that the rack is in the exact center of the oven for even baking. Bake the soufflé for 40 minutes, remove it from the oven, and gently pull the collar away from the bowl. Sprinkle the top of the soufflé with confectioners' sugar and serve at once.

2 tablespoons soft sweet butter
2 tablespoons granulated sugar
3 tablespoons cornstarch
1 cup milk
⅓ cup sugar
4 egg yolks
2 tablespoons apple brandy (such as Calvados)
2 tablespoons sweet butter
1 large Golden Delicious apple
Several tablespoons granulated sugar
2 tablespoons sweet butter
6 egg whites
A dash of salt
3 *amaretti*, crushed (optional)

40

Escabèche

Roast Loin of Pork with Prunes and
Mustard Sauce

Fresh Kiwi Tart

Pork, one of the most tasty, juicy, and economical of meats, is
too often neglected in American kitchens. The contrast of
sweet prunes and spicy mustard complements this roast pork
loin and makes it a regal entrée.

Kiwi, similar in flavor to melon and appearing somewhat
like a banana at its center, is a newly popular fruit. Imported
from New Zealand, it seems to be available year-round. If it is
unavailable in your area, substitute seedless, halved green
grapes.

Escabèche

Escabèche is a Spanish seafood salad of sautéed and chilled shellfish in a cooked marinade. In this recipe scallops predominate. They should be prepared and marinated at least 8 hours before serving. The avocado, tomato, and green pepper garnish should be added just before this salad goes to the table.

Rinse the scallops well and drain them on paper towels. If you are using sea scallops, slice them. Put the drained and dried scallops into a colander and sprinkle them with flour, letting the excess strain off. It is important to rid the scallops of excess flour so the marinade will not be too thick.

Heat the oil in a skillet and gently sauté the scallops for just a minute or two. Do not overcrowd the pan. As the scallops are done, remove them to the colander again and let them drain while you prepare the marinade.

Add a bit more oil to the skillet if you need it and gently sauté the onions, carrots, and garlic for a few minutes, until the onions soften. Reduce the heat to very low and pour in the vinegar, wine, and lemon juice. Add the salt, sugar, pepper, red pepper flakes, and herbs. Cover the skillet and let the mixture cook for a few minutes until the onions and carrots are soft.

Transfer the drained scallops to a bowl and pour the hot marinade over them. Cool to room temperature and then refrigerate for 8 hours or overnight.

To serve, prepare the tomatoes, avocados, and peppers and stir them through the scallops. Serve on chilled salad plates with chopped parsley sprinkled on top.

2 pounds bay or sea scallops
½ cup flour
⅓ cup olive oil
2 large onions, peeled and thinly sliced
2 large carrots, peeled and thinly sliced
3 cloves garlic, peeled and mashed
¼ cup white wine vinegar
¼ cup dry white wine
3 tablespoons fresh lemon juice
1 teaspoon salt
1 teaspoon sugar
Freshly ground black pepper to taste
¼ teaspoon dried red pepper flakes
2 bay leaves
¼ teaspoon dried thyme
1 tablespoon chopped fresh parsley
2 large tomatoes, sliced into thin wedges
2 ripe avocados, peeled and thinly sliced or diced
1 green pepper, seeded and diced
1 red bell pepper, seeded and diced
Additional chopped fresh parsley

219

Roast Loin of Pork with Prunes and Mustard Sauce

A boned loin of pork has very little internal fat. Just be sure to trim the excess fat from the outside, leaving a thin covering to moisten the meat as it roasts.

Soaking the prunes in white wine plumps them, and the marinade itself adds flavor to the pan juices when you make the mustard sauce.

A meat thermometer inserted in the thickest part of the meat will help you determine when the meat is done. An internal temperature of 170° is ideal. Pork should be neither overcooked nor undercooked.

12 large pitted prunes
1 cup dry white wine
A 5-pound boneless loin of pork
Salt, pepper, and a dash of paprika
1 large onion, diced
1 large carrot, diced
1 stalk celery, diced
1 large leek, well washed and diced
1 cup dry white wine
1 cup chicken stock
1 tablespoon cornstarch
1 cup heavy cream
2 tablespoons Dijon mustard
Salt and freshly ground black pepper to taste

Pour the wine over the prunes and soak them for several hours or overnight to plump them. Drain and reserve the marinade.

Trim excess fat from the surface of the pork loin. Using a long thin knife, gently cut a pocket through the center of the loin. You may want to do this from both ends, then use your fingers to enlarge the pocket. When the pocket is wide enough, gently push the drained prunes into it, trying to line them up in a row so when the meat is sliced for serving, each slice will have a piece of prune in its center. Season the meat with salt, pepper, and paprika. Set aside.

Scatter the diced vegetables over the bottom of a shallow roasting pan and place the meat on top. Combine the 1 cup of wine and 1 cup of stock and pour half of this mixture into the roasting pan. Roast the meat in a preheated 400° oven for 45 minutes, turning once during this time. Then pour in the remaining liquid and roast for another 45 minutes or until a meat thermometer registers 170°.

When the meat is done and brown all over, remove it from the oven, transfer it to a slicing board, and cover it lightly with aluminum foil. Put the roasting pan across two burners on top of the stove. Put the cornstarch into a small bowl and dilute it with a bit of the cream, mixing until you have a thin paste. Pour the cream, cornstarch paste, and mustard into the roasting pan and bring the mixture to a boil. Add the reserved prune marinade. When the sauce has boiled and thickened, strain it through a fine sieve into a sauceboat and season with salt and pepper. Carve the meat into thin slices and serve with the mustard sauce passed separately.

Fresh Kiwi Tart

The procedure for this dessert is simplified if you make the pastry crust and filling a day ahead. Only the final assembly, fruit topping, and glazing remain for the day of service. Since the glaze finish helps keep the tart fresh for several hours while it is chilling, you can assemble the tart early in the day.

Sift the flour, salt, and sugar together onto wax paper and set aside. Cut the butter into small bits and put it into a bowl for the electric mixer. Add the egg and milk and mix for a few minutes until well blended. Then add the flour mixture and mix the dough on low speed until it forms a ball and leaves the sides of the bowl clean. Gather the dough together, wrap in wax paper, and chill for 30 minutes.

Lightly flour a pastry cloth or board and roll out the dough to fit a 10-inch tart pan with a removable bottom. Gently transfer the dough to the pan and fit it into the bottom and up the sides of the pan, pressing the dough to the edges to prevent shrinkage. Trim the dough. Line the pastry with wax paper and weight the paper down with raw rice, dried beans, or aluminum nuggets.

Bake the pastry in a preheated 400° oven for 10 minutes; then gently remove the wax paper and weights and continue to bake it for another 5 to 7 minutes or until golden and crisp. Remove it from the oven and set aside to cool. The pastry shell is now ready for filling. It can be baked a day ahead and kept at room temperature overnight.

To make the pastry-cream filling, put the egg yolks and sugar into a small saucepan and beat well with a whisk or hand-held mixer. Beat in the flour and slowly pour in the milk, whisking constantly to remove lumps. Put the pot over very low heat on the stove and, whisking constantly, cook the mixture until it just comes to the boiling point. It will be quite thick at this point. Do not overcook it. Remove from the heat and stir in the butter, vanilla, almond extract, and chopped almonds. Transfer the filling to a small bowl, cover it tightly with plastic wrap, and chill thoroughly.

To assemble the tart, press the apricot preserves through a fine sieve into a small saucepan and stir in the tablespoon of sugar. Heat thoroughly to form a smooth glaze.

Peel and thinly slice the kiwi fruit into rounds. Brush a

1⅓ cups flour
½ teaspoon salt
1 teaspoon sugar
8 tablespoons sweet butter
1 egg
3 teaspoons milk
3 egg yolks
¼ cup sugar
¼ cup flour
1 cup milk
1 tablespoon sweet butter
1 teaspoon vanilla extract
¼ teaspoon almond extract
¼ cup finely chopped blanched almonds
7 ounces apricot preserves
1 tablespoon sugar
6 ripe kiwi fruit
Sliced almonds (for garnish)

221

small amount of the apricot glaze over the bottom of the pastry shell. Spoon the chilled pastry cream over all, using a thin spatula to spread it evenly over the bottom. Arrange the slices of kiwi fruit over the custard in a spiral, covering the entire surface of the tart. Gently brush the remaining glaze over the kiwi, using a soft pastry brush or goose feather so as not to disturb the fruit. Scatter the sliced almonds over all and chill until ready to serve.

Deep-Fried Shrimp with Plum Sauce

Chicken and Artichoke Hearts Gratinée

Frozen Hazelnut Cream with Hot Chocolate Sauce

It takes only a few hours to prepare this menu, and the tasks can be spread over a couple of days. It works well for a buffet meal because only fingers are needed for the first course, forks for the second, and spoons for the third.

To round out the buffet variety, add a hot Ratatouille Niçoise, page 153.

Deep-Fried Shrimp with Plum Sauce

The yeast in the beer makes for a delicate, puffed, and crispy fried batter. Dusting the shrimp lightly with flour helps the batter to adhere during frying. Leaving the tails on the shrimp provides a handle for dipping and frying as well as eating.

The shrimp should be fried to a crisp golden brown and, if necessary, can be held in a 250° oven on a rack over a flat pan for up to an hour.

When frying, remember that the temperature of the fat is 375°, so lower the shrimp gently. Don't splash them into the hot fat and don't overcrowd the fryer, or the shrimp will stick together and cook unevenly.

The sauce demonstrates that a simple blend of the sweet, the pungent, and the salty can create an entirely new flavor.

1 cup flour
12 ounces beer
1 teaspoon salt
1 teaspoon paprika
Freshly ground black pepper to taste
24 large raw shrimp
A 3-pound can of solid vegetable shortening
½ cup flour (for dredging)
1 cup Damson plum jam
½ cup ginger marmalade
2 tablespoons cider vinegar
2 tablespoons soy sauce

Put the flour, beer, salt, paprika, and black pepper into the container for an electric blender or a food processor and blend well for a minute or two until you have a thin batter. Allow the batter to stand for about 30 minutes.

Peel and devein the shrimp, taking care to leave on the last joint of the shell and the tail. (Most fishmongers will do this for you if you ask.) Rinse the shrimp in cold water and pat them dry with paper towels.

Fill a deep electric fryer or a kettle with the solid vegetable shortening. Heat the fat to 375°. If frying on top of the stove, attach a deep-fry thermometer to the side of the kettle. Put the beer batter into a small bowl, the flour for dredging into another, and the shrimp into a third. Have ready a flat pan lined with paper towels for draining.

While the fat is heating, put the plum jam and ginger marmalade into a blender or food processor. Add the vinegar and soy sauce and blend. Remove the mixture to a small saucepan. Heat for serving.

To fry the shrimp, hold each shrimp by its tail and dip it first in flour, then in beer batter. Carefully drop it into the hot fat and fry it for about 3 minutes on each side until crisp and golden brown. As the shrimp are done, remove them from the fat with a slotted spoon and drain on the paper towels. When all the shrimp have been fried, arrange them on a serving platter with a bowl of the heated sauce in the middle.

Chicken and Artichoke Hearts Gratinée SERVES 8

For a buffet dish, use cubed boneless chicken breasts. For service at the table, whole boneless breasts or pieces of chicken on the bone are attractive.

This version of sautéed chicken takes on added character with artichoke hearts and a blanket of melted cheese. Mozzarella is used for its melting ability and mildness. If you prefer a stronger cheese flavor, use Swiss or Fontina, or other stronger flavored cheeses like Bel Paese or even gorgonzola. The stronger the cheese, the more it will predominate in the dish.

Cut each breast of chicken in half and then cut each half into small cubes. Season with salt and pepper and set aside.

Mince the shallots. Trim the mushrooms and thinly slice them. Put the *porcini* mushrooms into a small bowl and cover with hot water. Let them soak for about 10 minutes; then drain off the water and squeeze excess water from the mushrooms. Chop them and set aside. Defrost the artichoke hearts and cut each in half. Shred or chop the prosciutto.

Put the chicken cubes into a colander over a bowl and sprinkle the flour over them. Toss well with your hands to coat the pieces of chicken and let the excess flour fall away through the colander. Heat the butter and oil in a large skillet until hot. Gently sauté the pieces of chicken for a few minutes, stirring until they are golden brown. Remove them from the skillet and set aside.

Add more butter and oil to the skillet if necessary and sauté the shallots, mushrooms, artichoke hearts, and prosciutto for a few minutes until golden and soft. Pour in the wine and reduce over very high heat until no liquid remains. Combine this with the chicken and spread the mixture over a shallow gratin dish.

Spread the grated mozzarella evenly over the chicken mixture and sprinkle the top with grated Parmesan.

Bake the chicken in a preheated 350° oven for about 20 minutes or until the cheese is melted and golden brown. Serve right from the gratin dish.

8 whole boneless and skinless breasts of chicken
Salt and pepper to taste
8 shallots, finely minced
½ pound fresh white mushrooms
1 ounce dried Italian *porcini* mushrooms
1 package (9 ounces) frozen artichoke hearts
¼ pound prosciutto
1 cup flour
4 tablespoons olive oil
4 tablespoons butter
1 cup dry white wine
2 cups grated mozzarella
Grated Parmesan cheese

Frozen Hazelnut Cream with Hot Chocolate Sauce

½ cup shelled hazelnuts
4 eggs
¾ cup confectioners' sugar
2 cups heavy cream
2 tablespoons sweet Marsala
  wine
8 ounces semisweet chocolate
3 tablespoons strongly brewed
  coffee
4 tablespoons soft sweet butter
1 teaspoon vanilla extract

The hazelnuts in this simple frozen cream recipe offer a double benefit: nutty taste and crunchy texture. Toasting them heightens the flavor and makes them easier to skin.

Because the dessert is frozen, it can be made well ahead. Just be sure to cover it tightly to ensure fresh flavor. Since it is light and airy, it can easily be scooped into champagne glasses before freezing, or placed in an attractive glass bowl for scooping at the table. The sauce should be piping hot when served. There is an exciting taste contrast in a frozen dessert with a meltingly hot topping.

Spread the hazelnuts over a small cooky sheet and put them into a preheated 350° oven for about 20 minutes or until they are toasted and the skins are crisp and cracking. Remove the nuts from the oven; when they are cool enough to handle, gently rub them between the palms of your hands to remove the skins. Put the skinned nuts into a food processor or a nut grinder and chop fine. Set aside.

Separate the eggs and put the whites into a clean, dry bowl. Begin beating the egg yolks, gradually adding 4 tablespoons of the confectioners' sugar. Continue to beat the yolks and sugar until thick and creamy.

Beat the egg whites until soft peaks form; then gradually add 4 tablespoons of the confectioners' sugar. Continue beating until you have a stiff and shiny meringue.

Put the heavy cream into a chilled bowl and beat until soft peaks form. Gradually add the remaining 4 tablespoons of confectioners' sugar and the 2 tablespoons of Marsala. Continue to beat until the cream is thick and stiff.

Gently fold the whipped egg whites, whipped cream, and crushed nuts into the egg yolk base and mix well. Spoon the mixture into a glass serving bowl or individual champagne or sherbet glasses. Freeze until firmly set like ice cream.

To make the chocolate sauce, put the chocolate and coffee into the top of a double boiler and heat until melted and smooth. Remove from heat and whisk in the soft butter, a small bit at a time. Stir in the vanilla and keep the sauce warm in the double boiler until serving.

LESSON

42

Sausage in Brioche with Potato Salad
Lyonnaise

Chicken in Red Wine

Chocolate-Dipped Pears

One would be hard put to find a countryside restaurant in Burgundy that didn't offer *saucisson en croûte* as an appetizer and a *coq au vin* entrée. Sausage baked in a crust and chicken braised in red wine is what you would enjoy; hearty, splendid fare that is surprisingly easy to prepare.

If the brioche has been made ahead and frozen, it can be defrosted and wrapped around a cooked sausage and readied for baking as much as a day in advance. The chicken is a one-pot dish that can be prepared to a point a day ahead, then finished 20 minutes before service.

The pears can be poached one day, dipped in the chocolate the next, then chilled for several hours before serving.

Sausage in Brioche with Potato Salad Lyonnaise

If you have a food processor, making brioche is a simple task. Like an ordinary loaf of bread, brioche dough freezes well and can stay frozen indefinitely. Be sure to start the process early in the day, since the dough goes through two risings for a total of 4 to 5 hours.

Choice of sausage is pretty much dependent upon what is readily available. Any plump fresh garlic sausage is fine; *kielbasa* and *cotechino* are usually easy to come by.

Potato Salad Lyonnaise and Dijon mustard are perfect accompaniments for this first course, as well they should be. Dijon and Lyons are both major gastronomic centers of Burgundy.

¼ cup lukewarm milk
1 envelope active dry yeast
1 tablespoon superfine sugar
6 tablespoons softened sweet butter
2 large eggs
2 cups flour, sifted with ½ teaspoon salt
1 garlic sausage, about 12 inches long and 3 inches in diameter
1 egg
1 tablespoon cold water
2 pounds small red-skinned new potatoes
2 tablespoons tarragon vinegar
2 tablespoons olive oil
1 tablespoon dry white wine
1 teaspoon Dijon mustard
Salt and freshly ground black pepper to taste

To make the brioche dough, put the lukewarm milk into a small glass measuring cup and sprinkle the yeast and sugar over it. Proof this mixture in a warm, draft-free place (such as the turned-off oven) until the yeast activates and bubbles. This should take about 10 minutes.

Put the butter into a food processor fitted with the steel blade and blend for a few seconds. Add the two eggs and blend again. Add the dissolved yeast mixture and blend again. Add the sifted flour and salt and process for a minute or two, until the machine turns the mixture into a smooth ball of shiny dough that leaves the sides of the bowl clean. (If you do not have a food processor, put the flour mixture into a clean bowl, make a well in the center, and add the eggs and the yeast mixture. Stir well with a wooden spoon and mix in the butter. Knead the dough for a few minutes until it forms a ball.)

Transfer the finished dough to a lightly buttered large bowl and roll the dough around in the butter. Cover the bowl and put it in the same warm, draft-free place as the yeast. Allow the dough to rise for about 3 hours. Then punch the ball of dough down to remove the air, re-form it into a ball, and let it rise again for about 1½ hours. At this point the dough is done. Punch the air out of it, re-form it into a ball, and wrap it in wax paper or plastic wrap. Chill the dough at least an hour before rolling it out. The dough can be refrigerated for several days or frozen at this point.

◄

Prick the skin of the sausage in several places with a fork, put it into a kettle, and cover it with cold water. Cover the pot and cook the sausage over low heat for 15 minutes or until it seems very tender. Remove it from the kettle and let it drain and cool.

When the sausage is cool enough to handle, gently pull off the skin. Lightly flour a pastry cloth or marble slab and roll out the chilled or defrosted ball of brioche dough to a rectangle about 16 inches long by 8 inches wide. Lightly beat the egg with the cold water and brush this mixture over the entire surface of the dough, using a pastry brush. Place the skinned sausage in the center of the dough and completely wrap it in the brioche, using the egg wash to seal the seams. Turn the loaf over onto a lightly buttered cooky sheet.

If you like, a small amount of dough can be set aside to use as decoration. Roll out this piece of dough into a long, thin strip and cut it into three long strips. Braid the strips and attach the braid down the center of the loaf, using the egg wash to hold the braid firmly in place.

Brush the entire surface of the dough with egg wash and bake the loaf in a preheated 350° oven for 30 minutes or until the dough is golden brown and crisp.

While the loaf is baking, scrub the potatoes and put them into a pot with several inches of boiling, salted water. Cover the pot and steam the potatoes for 20 minutes or until tender. Remove from heat, drain, and cool the potatoes slightly. Slip the skins off and thinly slice the potatoes. Toss them immediately with the vinegar, olive oil, wine, mustard, salt, and pepper.

When the loaf is done, remove it from the oven and let it stand about 5 minutes at room temperature before slicing.

Serve the sliced loaf of sausage with the warm potato salad, additional Dijon mustard, and a bowl of French pickles called *cornichons*.

Chicken in Red Wine

A hearty Burgundy is a good choice and true to the classic French recipe, but any leftover red wine is fine. Save your vintage Burgundy for service with the meal.

The bacon imparts a subtle smoky flavor to the dish. If you prefer a milder but equally delicious taste, leave it out.

Try to find pearl onions and button mushrooms of uniform size, for both the sake of appearance and the fact that they will cook evenly.

8 whole boneless and skinless breasts of chicken (or 2 whole fryers)
Salt and black pepper to taste
1 cup flour
Olive oil for sautéing
1 large onion, finely minced
4 shallots, finely minced
2 cloves garlic, mashed
¼ cup cognac
1 cup hearty Burgundy
Approximately 1 cup beef stock (homemade or canned)
1 tablespoon tomato paste
¼ teaspoon dried thyme
2 bay leaves
24 small pearl onions
A 1-pound piece of slab bacon, cut into small cubes
4 tablespoons butter
1 pound fresh button mushrooms
2 tablespoons sugar
Chopped parsley

Cut each breast of chicken in half. (If you are using whole fryers, have the butcher cut them into eight pieces each.) Season the chicken pieces with salt and pepper. Put them into a colander fitted over a bowl and sprinkle the flour over them. Toss with your hands to coat each piece with flour, letting the excess fall through the colander.

Heat the oil in a deep kettle or Dutch oven and sauté the chicken pieces until they are golden brown on all sides, removing them from the kettle as they are done. When all the chicken has been browned, add more oil to the kettle if necessary and sauté the onion, shallots, and garlic for a few minutes until they are soft and golden. Return the chicken pieces to the kettle and pour in the cognac. Bring the liquid to a rolling boil and allow it to reduce to about 1 tablespoon.

Pour in the wine, enough stock to almost cover the chicken, the tomato paste, thyme, bay leaves, and additional salt and pepper to taste. Cover the pot.

Braise the chicken in a preheated 350° oven for 30 minutes. The dish can be prepared to this point the day before and refrigerated overnight (bring it to room temperature before finishing) or it can be prepared early in the day and held at room temperature.

Drop the pearl onions into a pot of boiling water and blanch them for about 2 minutes. Drain and rinse with cold water. Slip off the skin from each onion, slice off the root end, and cut a small *x* in it, leaving the pointed end intact. Sauté the cubed bacon in a skillet until it is crisp and the fat is completely rendered. Transfer the bacon to paper towels to drain. Pour off the fat and wipe out the skillet with a paper towel. Return it to the stove and add 2 tablespoons of the butter. Sauté the mushrooms for about 2 minutes, until they turn golden; then transfer them to the bowl with the bacon cubes. Add the remaining 2 tablespoons of butter to the skillet and sauté the onions for a few minutes, until golden. Sprinkle the sugar over the onions and continue to sauté them until the sugar melts and begins to caramelize. Transfer the onions and the caramel drippings in the skillet to the bowl of mushrooms and bacon. The preparation of this vegetable-and-bacon garnish can be done early in the day or while the chicken is braising.

To finish the dish, add the bacon, mushrooms, and onions to the braising pot after the chicken has cooked for 30 minutes. Continue to cook for another 20 minutes, until the chicken is tender.

Serve the dish right from the pot, if desired, or transfer the chicken to a serving platter and surround with the vegetable-and-bacon garnish. Spoon the sauce over all and sprinkle chopped fresh parsley on top. This dish is traditionally served with plain buttered noodles.

___

Chocolate-Dipped Pears

SERVES 8

Maurice Moore-Betty, the well-known cooking teacher and author, and an early mentor of mine, taught me this simple but ingenious recipe.

It is perhaps the simplest of dramatic desserts, but a few warnings are in order. First, find pears that have stems firmly attached. Second, make sure the pears are ripe but not too soft. Third, poach one or two extra pears in case you lose a stem along the way. Success should be guaranteed if you take these precautions.

1 quart cold water
1 tablespoon fresh lemon juice
8 ripe, but still firm, pears
 (preferably Comice, Bosc, or
 Bartlett)
2 cups sugar
8 cups cold water
The juice of 2 lemons
The rind of the lemons, cut off
 in long strips
2 cinnamon sticks
4 whole cloves
12 ounces semisweet chocolate
4 tablespoons sweet butter
2 tablespoons boiling water
Crystallized mint leaves (for
 decoration)

Fill a large bowl with 1 quart cold water and add a tablespoon of fresh lemon juice. Peel the pears with a vegetable peeler, leaving the stems intact. Slice a thin slice off the bottom of each pear so it will stand upright. As the pears are peeled, drop them into the basin of acidulated water to keep them from discoloring.

Put the sugar, 8 cups of cold water, lemon juice and rind, cinnamon sticks, and whole cloves into a deep kettle and bring this mixture to a boil. Reduce the heat and simmer for about 5 minutes. Drop the pears into the gently simmering poaching liquid and cover the pot. Return the liquid to the boil, reduce the heat to a slow simmer, and poach the pears for 10 minutes or until a toothpick slides in and out easily. When the pears are tender, remove the pot from the heat and let the pears cool to room temperature in the poaching liquid. Then chill the pears in the liquid overnight.

Put the chocolate and butter into the top of a double boiler and melt until smooth. Remove the chocolate from the heat, and if it is too thick, stir in the boiling water to thin it out. It should be thin enough to spoon up and over the pears and coat them with a smooth, shiny surface.

Remove the chilled pears from their poaching liquid and pat them dry with paper towels. (The poaching liquid can be frozen and used one more time.) The pears must be well chilled and thoroughly dried, or the chocolate will not stick.

When the pears are dry, hold each one firmly by its stem and dip in the melted chocolate, using a spoon to completely coat the pear. Allow excess chocolate to drip off into the pot and place each dipped pear on lightly buttered wax paper on a cooky sheet. Refrigerate the chilled pears for about 15 minutes. Then firmly attach a crystallized mint leaf (or a real leaf) near the stem by letting it stick to the chocolate. Continue to chill the pears until serving. The dipped pears can be held in the refrigerator for as long as 8 hours. Since the pears are not cored, remember to serve them with a knife and fork.

43

Scallops Provençale

Roast Duckling with Apples

Chocolate Mousse Cake

Whenever duck is served, it becomes the highlight of the meal. In this menu, it has stiff competition from the scallops and the glorious chocolate dessert.

In reading the duckling recipe, you will notice that it can be prepared in several steps over a period of two days.

Scallops Provençale

Tomatoes, green peppers, olive oil, and fresh herbs are all typical ingredients of a Provençal sauce. In this dish the sauce is prepared independently of the scallops and therefore can be readied a day ahead if you like. The baking shells can be assembled several hours ahead, but they should be broiled just before serving.

2 ripe tomatoes
4 shallots
2 cloves garlic
1 small green pepper, seeded and diced
1 tablespoon chopped fresh parsley
1 tablespoon chopped fresh tarragon (or 1 teaspoon dried tarragon)
1 tablespoon chopped fresh rosemary (or 1 teaspoon dried rosemary)
3 tablespoons butter
Salt and freshly ground black pepper to taste
3 tablespoons dry white wine
2 pounds fresh bay scallops (or sea scallops)
Salt and freshly ground black pepper to taste
½ cup flour
3 tablespoons olive oil
¼ cup freshly grated fine bread crumbs
2 tablespoons olive oil
Chopped fresh parsley

Drop the tomatoes into a pot of boiling water and let them sit for 1 minute; then remove them and rinse with cold water. Cut the stems out with the tip of a knife and carefully slip off the skins. Cut the tomatoes in half horizontally, and holding each half over the sink, squeeze gently to remove all seeds and juice. Finely dice the remaining pulp. Mince the shallots and mash the garlic. Combine the chopped herbs.

Heat the butter in a small skillet and gently sauté the shallots, garlic, and green pepper for a minute; then stir in the chopped tomatoes and herbs. Add the salt and pepper and pour in the white wine. Let the mixture cook, uncovered, over high heat until the liquid reduces and the sauce thickens. Remove it from the heat and set aside. This sauce can be made ahead.

Rinse the scallops well and pat them dry with paper towels. (If you are using sea scallops, cut them into small pieces.) Put the scallops into a colander fitted over a bowl and season them with salt and pepper. Sprinkle the flour over them and toss, allowing excess flour to fall through the colander.

Heat the 3 tablespoons of olive oil in a skillet and sauté the lightly floured scallops for about 3 minutes, turning to crisp on all sides. Don't overcrowd the skillet — if necessary, sauté the scallops in small batches. As they are done, remove them from the skillet and distribute them equally among eight scallop shells or ramekins.

Mix the bread crumbs with the 2 tablespoons of olive oil and set aside. Divide the sauce evenly over the scallops and top each dish with some of the bread-crumb mixture. Preheat the broiler to high. Place the filled scallop shells on a broiler pan or cooky sheet and slide them under the hot broiler. Broil for 2 or 3 minutes, watching carefully until the tops are quite crisp. Remove from broiler, top with chopped parsley, and serve at once.

Roast Duckling with Apples

Calvados is an apple brandy from Normandy. In this recipe it complements the apple garnish as well as the sauce for the duck.

Cutting up the ducks before roasting simplifies serving, because no carving is required. Trimming the pieces of duck, preparing the duck stock, poaching the apple halves, and making the applesauce mixture can all be accomplished a day ahead. The remaining work of an hour's roasting and a 5-minute sauce preparation is hardly an awesome task to complete before serving.

Cut each duck into quarters, trim away all visible fat, and cut each quarter into smaller pieces if you wish. Trim away all extra bones, such as the rib cage, and any pieces of meat or bone that may be unnecessary to the proper shape of each serving piece. Save all the trimmings except solid fat.

Put all the bones and trimmings, including the necks and gizzards, into a shallow roasting pan. Scatter the sliced leek, carrot, onion, and garlic in the pan and roast in a 400° oven for 1 hour or until everything is nicely browned. Stir occasionally. When done, scrape everything into a kettle. Pour about 1 cup of hot water into the roasting pan and scrape up all the browned bits clinging to the bottom. Pour this into the kettle and add the chicken stock. Add salt and pepper to taste and bring this mixture to a boil on top of the stove. Reduce the heat to simmer, cover the pot, and cook for 30 minutes or until you have a rich golden brown broth. Strain this stock and discard the solids. Pour the stock back into the kettle and place it over high heat. Reduce the liquid by half. Cool and set aside.

Peel, core, and dice two of the apples and put them into a saucepan with the lemon juice, sugar, Calvados, and raisins. Cover and cook this mixture over low heat for 20 minutes or until the apples are quite soft. Remove them from the heat and stir well with a fork, mashing slightly, until they are the consistency of applesauce. Set aside.

Peel the remaining four apples. Cut each one in half and carefully scoop out the core, creating a space in the apple for filling. Put the cold water, 1 cup of sugar, cinnamon sticks, cloves, and lemon juice and rind into a kettle and bring to a

Two 4- to 5-pound ducklings
1 leek, well washed and sliced
1 carrot, peeled and sliced
1 onion, peeled and sliced
1 clove garlic, peeled and sliced
4 cups chicken stock
  (homemade or canned)
Salt and pepper
6 Golden Delicious apples
1 tablespoon fresh lemon juice
1 tablespoon sugar
1 tablespoon Calvados
1 tablespoon raisins
4 cups cold water
1 cup sugar
2 cinnamon sticks
4 whole cloves
2 tablespoons fresh lemon juice
The rind of one lemon
2 tablespoons butter
2 carrots, peeled and finely
  minced
2 onions, peeled and finely
  minced
2 leeks, well washed and finely
  minced
2 cloves garlic, peeled and finely
  minced
1 tablespoon chopped fresh
  parsley
¼ teaspoon dried thyme

235

Salt and pepper
4 tablespoons sweet butter
4 tablespoons sugar
2 tablespoons Calvados
½ cup port wine
¼ cup red wine vinegar (or
  raspberry vinegar)
1 tablespoon *glace de viande* (or
  Bovril or Kitchen Bouquet)
¼ cup Calvados
2 tablespoons cornstarch
  diluted in 1 tablespoon water

boil. Reduce the heat to simmer, drop in the peeled apple halves, cover the pot, and poach the apples for 10 minutes or until they seem tender when pierced with a toothpick. Cool the apples in the poaching liquid and set aside. The recipe may be prepared ahead of time to this point.

To roast the ducks, melt the butter in a roasting pan and add the minced carrots, onions, leeks, and garlic. Cook on top of the stove, stirring, for a minute or two until the onion softens and turns golden. Stir in the parsley and thyme. Place a rack over the vegetables in the roasting pan and put the pieces of duck on the rack, skin side down. Season lightly with salt and pepper and roast the ducklings in a preheated 450° oven for 30 minutes. Turn the pieces over, season, and continue to roast for another 30 minutes or until the ducks are tender and crisp.

While the ducks are roasting, remove the apple halves from their poaching liquid and dry them with paper towels. Melt the sweet butter in a skillet and sauté the apples, turning them carefully, until both sides are pale golden. Sprinkle the sugar and Calvados over them in the skillet and continue to sauté until the sugar melts and glazes the apples. Set aside.

When the ducklings are done, remove them from the oven, place them on a platter, and cover lightly with aluminum foil. Turn the oven off and return the duck to the oven to keep warm while you make the sauce. Put the roasting pan across two burners on top of the stove and pour in the port, vinegar, *glace de viande*, and Calvados. Bring this mixture to a rolling boil, scraping the bottom of the pan to get up all the browned bits. Pour in the reduced duck stock and the diluted cornstarch. Continue to cook, stirring constantly, until the liquid thickens and boils. Strain this liquid through a fine sieve.

To serve the duckling, fill each sautéed apple half with a spoonful of the cooked applesauce. (If you have cooked the applesauce ahead of time, be sure to heat it through before filling the apple halves.) Place the pieces of duckling down the center of a large platter and surround with the filled apples. Skim the fat from the surface of the sauce, and pour the sauce into a sauceboat to be passed separately. The dish is best served with Wild Rice au Chinois, page 19.

Chocolate Mousse Cake

You will find no flour in this cake because it is really a chocolate mousse that, when baked, turns into a rich, fudgey cake. If you bake the cake the day before and chill it thoroughly, it will be easier to unmold and slice.

Put the eggs and sugar into a bowl for the electric mixer and begin to beat on high speed. Continue to beat for at least 5 minutes, until the mixture is thick and creamy.

Meanwhile, put the chocolate in the top of a double boiler. Add the coffee and Grand Marnier or rum and melt until smooth. Remove from heat, add the vanilla, and set aside.

Whip 1 cup of the cream until thick and stiff. Fold the chocolate into the beaten egg mixture and gently fold in the whipped cream. Make sure the batter is well mixed and then pour it into a 9-inch springform.

Set the springform into a larger pan and fill the larger pan with about 2 inches of hot water. Bake the cake in a preheated 350° oven for 1 hour until the center of the cake seems firm to the touch.

When the cake is done, remove it from the oven and carefully lift it out of the water bath. Set it on a rack to cool completely. Cover it and chill at least 8 hours or overnight.

To serve the cake, whip the other two cups of heavy cream with the sugar and Grand Marnier or rum until it is thick and stiff. Remove the cake from refrigerator, run a knife around the sides, and gently release the sides of the springform. Invert the cake onto a serving platter and carefully lift off the bottom of the springform. Frost the top and sides of the cake with the whipped cream and scatter shaved chocolate curls over the top. Surround the cake with fresh berries and serve.

6 eggs
½ cup sugar
16 ounces semisweet chocolate
¼ cup strong brewed coffee
¼ cup Grand Marnier or dark rum
2 teaspoons vanilla extract
3 cups heavy cream
2 teaspoons sugar
1 tablespoon Grand Marnier or dark rum
Shaved chocolate
Fresh raspberries or strawberries (optional)

237

November

LESSON **44**

Linguini with Clam Sauce
Roast Rack of Lamb
Pear and Apple Flan

LESSON **45**

Chicken Liver Pâté in Aspic
Veal Chops with Apple Stuffing
Crème Brûlée

LESSON **46**

Smoked Salmon and Leek Quiche
Chicken Demi-Deuil
Monte Cristo Soufflé

LESSON **47**

Pâté Maison
Brook Trout Véronique
Chocolate Marquise

240

Linguini with Clam Sauce

Roast Rack of Lamb

Pear and Apple Flan

Except for the dessert, most of the work in this menu must be done just before serving. Although the flan may be baked several hours ahead and cooled to room temperature, it should not be refrigerated.

Linguini with Clam Sauce

3 dozen littleneck or
  cherrystone clams
½ cup clam juice
4 flat anchovy fillets
3 cloves garlic
4 shallots
1 tablespoon chopped fresh
  parsley
1 tablespoon chopped fresh
  basil (or 1 teaspoon dried basil)
1 tablespoon fresh chopped
  rosemary (or 1 teaspoon dried
  rosemary)
1 pound linguini, fresh or dried
A dash of olive oil
Several tablespoons melted
  butter
2 tablespoons butter
2 tablespoons olive oil
½ cup dry white wine
Freshly ground black pepper to
  taste
¼ teaspoon dried red pepper
  flakes (optional)

Use fresh clams if you possibly can; they make for a tastier sauce than canned ones. If you're opening clams yourself, putting them in the freezer for 10 minutes will relax them and make them easier to open.

Add other seafood if you like — or substitute squid, scallops, or shrimp for a different but equally delicious result.

Have the fishmonger open the clams or open them yourself. Remove the clams from their shells and pour any liquid from the shells into a measuring cup. If you don't have ½ cup, add bottled clam juice. Chop the clams into small dice and set them aside.

Mince the anchovies, garlic, and shallots. Combine them with the chopped herbs in a small bowl and set aside.

Before you begin the sauce, bring a large pot of lightly salted water to a rolling boil and add a dash of olive oil. Drop the pasta in and cook it for 4 to 6 minutes if it is fresh, 8 to 10 minutes if it is dry. Drain it through a colander and toss the melted butter through it.

While the pasta is cooking, start the sauce. Heat the butter and oil in a saucepan and add the anchovies, garlic, shallots, and herbs to the pan. Cook for a minute or two. Then add the wine and reserved clam juice. Add the clams, pepper, and pepper flakes; cover the pot and let the mixture come to a boil over medium heat. Reduce the heat to simmer and cook about 3 minutes.

To serve, heap the pasta in the center of individual plates or bowls and spoon the sauce over it. Serve with hot Italian bread to soak up the sauce.

Roast Rack of Lamb

Thirty minutes may seem a surprisingly short roasting time for this dish, but lamb has an entirely different and more delicate flavor when served pink at the center. In most lamb recipes — this one is no exception — the less that is done to the meat, the better.

Ask the butcher to "French" the bones of the racks. This is done by scraping all the meat down to clean the bones. It is done for appearance only and is not necessary to the success of the recipe. Season the meat with salt and pepper and set aside.

Dice the carrots, onion, and celery and scatter them over the bottom of a shallow roasting pan. Scatter the herbs over all and lay the lamb racks, curved side up, on the vegetables. Pour the stock and wine into the bottom of the pan.

Roast the lamb in a preheated 450° oven for 30 minutes. If you like the meat well done, roast it an additional 10 minutes.

Remove the lamb racks from the pan and place them on a carving board. Strain the pan juices through a fine sieve into a small saucepan and discard the vegetables. Keep the pan juices hot on top of the stove. Increase the oven temperature to 500°.

Combine the crumbs, shallots, parsley, and garlic in a small bowl and add enough olive oil to bind the mixture. Pat this crumb mixture over the entire curved side of the racks, pressing hard against the meat to make the crumbs adhere. Put the racks back in the roasting pan and return them to the hot oven for 5 minutes or until the crumbs are crisp and toasted.

To serve, carve the racks between each bone and pass a sauceboat of pan juices.

2 whole racks of lamb (8 chops per rack)
Salt and freshly ground black pepper to taste
2 carrots
1 onion
2 stalks celery
2 tablespoons chopped fresh parsley
1 teaspoon dried rosemary
½ teaspoon dried thyme
½ cup chicken stock
¼ cup dry white wine
½ cup finely grated unseasoned bread crumbs
4 shallots, finely minced
2 tablespoons chopped fresh parsley
1 clove garlic, mashed
Several tablespoons olive oil

Pear and Apple Flan

4 tablespoons sweet butter
½ cup peeled, sliced pears
½ cup peeled, sliced apples
2 tablespoons sugar
2 tablespoons apple or pear
  brandy, or kirsch
¼ cup golden raisins (optional)
A dash each of ground
  cinnamon and nutmeg
1 cup milk
⅓ cup sugar
3 eggs
2 teaspoons vanilla extract
A dash of salt
⅔ cup sifted flour
Confectioners' sugar

This flan and the Clafouti (page 116) are alike in that both have a custard filling. In this recipe, however, fresh pears and apples are sautéed and slightly caramelized before being incorporated into the custard for baking. The flan is best served freshly baked.

Heat the butter in a skillet and gently sauté the pear and apple slices for a few minutes until just pale golden. Sprinkle the 2 tablespoons sugar over all and add the brandy or kirsch. Continue to sauté the apples and pears until the sugar begins to caramelize and all the liquid in the pan is evaporated. Add the raisins and let them soften in the mixture. Sprinkle the cinnamon and nutmeg over all. When the slices are done, remove them from the skillet and spread them over the bottom of a 10-inch glass pie plate or any shallow, oven-proof 10-inch dish.

Mix the milk, sugar, eggs, vanilla, and salt in a blender or food processor for a few seconds and add the flour. Blend until the mixture is the consistency of thin pancake batter. Pour it over the fruit in the dish.

Bake in a preheated 350° oven about 1 hour or until the top is quite brown and puffy and a silver knife inserted in the center comes out clean.

Remove the flan from the oven and let it come to room temperature. Dust the top lightly with confectioners' sugar and cut into wedges to serve.

Chicken Liver Pâté in Aspic

Veal Chops with Apple Stuffing

Crème Brûlée

In this menu, the work on the appetizer and dessert should be started well ahead so you can cool and layer the aspic for the pâté and give the dessert time to chill. Even the entrée can be prepared in stages, stuffing the chops one day, then partially sautéing them on the day of service. Last-minute work then consists of a 20-minute finish for the chops in their cream sauce, and a quick sugar-crust broiling for the Crème Brûlée.

Chicken Liver Pâté in Aspic

Although this pâté is based on chicken livers rather than goose livers, the end result is a rich smooth dish more reminiscent of *pâté de foie gras* than hearty chopped chicken livers. Another time, serve it without the aspic on crackers, toast, or French bread.

The aspic is created in several stages, and the first is the most magical. As you cook the aspic, the crushed egg shells and beaten egg whites will attract and hold all the solids so the strained liquid is clear and golden.

2 cups chicken stock
  (homemade or canned)
1 cup tomato juice
3 tablespoons unflavored gelatin
1 teaspoon salt
Freshly ground black pepper to
  taste
1 teaspoon sugar
½ teaspoon dried tarragon (or
  4 sprigs of fresh tarragon)
2 egg whites, lightly beaten
2 crushed egg shells
2 tablespoons Madeira
Vegetables for garnish (such as
  scallions, fresh tarragon,
  stuffed green olives, carrots,
  black olives, and pimiento)
2 pounds fresh chicken livers
4 tablespoons sweet butter
4 shallots, finely minced
½ cup Madeira
1 tablespoon cognac
½ cup heavy cream
Salt and pepper to taste
A dash of ground allspice
¼ teaspoon dried thyme
4 tablespoons sweet butter,
  melted

Put the stock, tomato juice, gelatin, salt, pepper, sugar, tarragon, egg whites, and shells into a deep kettle and bring the mixture to a boil, stirring constantly. When the mixture is boiling, remove it from the heat and stir in the 2 tablespoons of Madeira. Cool slightly; then strain the liquid through very fine cheesecloth. Discard the solids. Cool the liquid; then chill until it becomes syrupy but still liquid.

Pour ½ cup of the syrupy aspic over the bottom of a pretty 8-cup mold (if you prefer, use eight 1-cup molds). Put the mold in the refrigerator and chill until the aspic is firmly set. While it is setting, prepare the vegetable for the garnish by cutting rounds of carrot or stuffed green olive, strips of pimiento, black olive, and the green of scallion, tarragon leaves, or any other vegetable decorations. Arrange these in flower patterns (or any pattern you choose) over the firmly set aspic in the bottom of the mold. Spoon a very thin layer of more syrupy aspic over these vegetables, taking care that they do not float around in the liquid aspic. Return to the refrigerator to set firmly. Then spoon a ½-inch layer of aspic over the set vegetable garnish and chill again until firm. Repeat this ½-inch layer about two more times, chilling well after each addition. Watch the unchilled aspic to make sure it is not getting too firm. If it is, reheat it slightly to melt it so you can continue to work with it in a syrupy consistency. When you have added as much aspic as you desire, pour the remaining aspic over a shallow cooky sheet to chill in a solid block.

To prepare the pâté, pick over the livers, removing any green bile that might be attached, and cut them into small pieces. Heat the butter in a skillet and sauté the livers until they are firm, but still pink inside. Add the shallots while the livers are cooking. Scrape this mixture into a blender or a food processor fitted with the steel blade. Return the skillet to the stove and pour in the ½ cup of Madeira and cognac. Allow the liquids to come to a rolling boil and reduce them to about 4 tablespoons. Scrape this into the processor with the livers. Purée the mixture until it is quite smooth. Add the cream, salt and pepper, allspice, and thyme while the mixture is blending. Taste for additional salt and pepper; then add the melted butter and blend until the mixture is very smooth.

When the aspic is firmly set, pack the liver mixture into the mold, spreading it evenly over the top. Cover tightly with plastic wrap to prevent discoloration, and chill the mold overnight.

To unmold, dip the mold in hot water for 10 seconds, run a knife around the edge, and invert the mold onto a serving tray. (If you are using individual molds, do the same to unmold them onto individual plates.) Garnish the mold with sprigs of parsley or watercress and serve with crackers or French bread.

Veal Chops with Apple Stuffing

1 tart apple
1 small onion
2 tablespoons chopped nuts
  (such as walnuts, pecans,
  pistachios, or a combination)
3 slices day-old white bread
1 tablespoon chopped fresh
  parsley
2 tablespoons butter
Salt and pepper to taste
2 tablespoons Calvados or any
  apple brandy (optional)
2 egg yolks
8 rib veal chops, 1½ to 2 inches
  thick
Salt and pepper to taste
½ cup flour
4 tablespoons butter
4 shallots, finely minced
½ pound firm white
  mushrooms, thinly sliced
¼ cup Calvados or any apple
  brandy
½ cup dry white wine
1 cup heavy cream
2 Golden Delicious apples
A few tablespoons sweet butter
1 tablespoon sugar

Rib veal chops are more economical than loin chops and work well for stuffing. Be careful when butterflying the meat, and try not to cut any holes in it. Once the meat is stuffed and sautéed, it will adhere to its filling. Be gentle when turning the chops in the sauté pan.

In this recipe, as is true with so many veal dishes, chicken can be substituted. Cut a pocket in boneless chicken breasts and then proceed exactly as you would for veal.

Chop the apple and onion. Set aside with the chopped nuts. Cut the crusts off the bread and cut into small dice. Set aside the chopped parsley. Melt the 2 tablespoons of butter in a small skillet and sauté the apples, onions, nuts, and bread cubes for a few minutes. Then add the remaining ingredients up to the egg yolks. Transfer the mixture from the skillet to a small bowl and stir in the egg yolks to bind it and create a stuffing. Let this mixture cool completely.

Scrape the meat off the long bone of the chops to "French" them, or have the butcher do this for you. If possible, have him cut and shorten this bone. This makes for a more attractive presentation. Using a long, sharp knife, cut through the round eye of the rib chop to the bone, creating a butterfly effect. Spoon a tablespoon or two of the cooled stuffing onto the bottom half of the butterfly; then press the top half down over the stuffing. Press around the ends to seal the meat.

Season the meat on both sides with salt and pepper and dredge the chops lightly in flour, holding them carefully so as not to let the stuffing fall out. Shake off excess flour.

Heat the 4 tablespoons of butter in a large skillet and sauté the chops a few minutes on each side, turning carefully, until they are golden brown. Remove them from the skillet as they brown. Add more butter if needed and sauté the shallots and mushrooms for a few minutes until firm and golden. Pour in the Calvados, wine, and cream and bring the mixture to a boil. Return the chops to the skillet, spoon some of the liquid up and over them, and reduce the heat to simmer. Cover the skillet and cook for 20 minutes or until the chops are fork-tender.

Serve the chops with the mushrooms scattered over the tops and spoon the pan juices over all.

For the garnish, peel, core, and slice the apples into rings. Sauté the slices in the sweet butter, turning carefully, until golden brown all over. Sprinkle the sugar over them and serve these glazed apple rings around the chops.

Crème Brûlée

This recipe is a very French and very elegant version of baked custard. The chilling process before the final sugar-crust broiling is important, because you don't want to soften the custard while broiling the top. The dish should have a cold-to-hot feel in the mouth. Also, give the broiling time your close attention so as not to burn the sugar. It just takes a few minutes to achieve the glazed, crusty finish.

Put the cream in a small saucepan and heat just to the boiling point. Add the sugar, remove from heat, and stir until the sugar is dissolved.

4 cups heavy cream
¼ cup sugar
8 egg yolks
¼ teaspoon salt
2 teaspoons vanilla extract
1 cup dark brown sugar

Beat the egg yolks with a whisk and add the salt and vanilla. Pour in the hot cream in a slow, steady stream, whisking constantly. Pour this custard mixture into a 6-cup custard dish, or a shallow square baking dish. The custard should come to within 1 inch of the top of the dish.

Place the custard dish in a larger pan and fill the pan with several inches of boiling water. This is a *bain-marie*; it prevents the custard from getting brown around the edges while baking. Bake in a preheated 300° oven for 1 hour or until a clean silver knife inserted in the center of the custard comes out clean. Remove the dish from the *bain-marie* and set it aside to cool. Then refrigerate for several hours or overnight until thoroughly chilled.

Sprinkle the brown sugar evenly over the entire top of the chilled custard. Preheat the broiler to hot and slide the dish under the broiler. Broil for 3 to 4 minutes or until the sugar topping becomes glazed and crusty. Watch it carefully so it does not burn.

Remove from the broiler and allow to cool for a minute or two. As it cools, the sugar will harden. To serve, crack through the sugar and spoon up portions of custard and topping.

If desired, this dessert can be made in eight 1-cup dishes. The individual custards will require only about 40 minutes' baking time.

Smoked Salmon and Leek Quiche

Chicken Demi-Deuil

Monte Cristo Soufflé

The odd French phrase *demi-deuil* literally means "half-mourning" and refers to the black truffle in the recipe. Though no one would dress a bird completely in black, there should be enough truffle slices inserted to be visible between the skin and the breast meat.

It is surprising that poaching is such a rarely used cooking procedure, considering the splendid results achieved. Here the poaching broth forms the rich base for the accompanying creamy sauce.

This menu is designed so the appetizer and dessert are made a day ahead. The quiche can be fully baked, and frozen if necessary, then reheated for service. The soufflé should be chilled thoroughly before serving.

Smoked Salmon and Leek Quiche

If leeks aren't available, substitute a large thinly sliced Spanish onion. It is the salmon and dill that give the most flavor to this quiche.

Put the butter and softened cream cheese into a bowl for the electric mixer and blend. Add the sifted flour and salt and mix on low speed until you have a soft ball of dough. Gather the dough together, wrap it in wax paper, and chill at least 30 minutes.

Lightly flour a pastry cloth or board and roll out the ball of dough to fit a 10-inch, fluted-side quiche pan with a removable bottom. Fit the dough into the pan and trim off the excess at the edges.

Line the dough with wax paper and weight the paper down with raw rice, dried beans, or aluminum nuggets. Bake the crust in a preheated 400° oven for 10 minutes, carefully lift off the paper and weights, and set the partially baked crust aside to cool.

Trim off the roots from the leeks and cut off all but about ½ inch of the green tops. Split the leeks and rinse them well under cold running water to remove all trace of sand. Chop them fine and put them into a small saucepan. Pour in the chicken broth, cover the pan, and let the leeks simmer for about 10 minutes to soften. Drain the broth and reserve it for another use. Set the leeks aside.

Heat the butter in a small skillet and gently sauté the drained leeks and the chopped salmon for about 3 minutes. Stir in the chopped parsley and dill and distribute this mixture evenly over the bottom of the cooled pie shell.

Mix the eggs, cream, salt, peppers, and nutmeg in a small bowl and pour over the salmon in the crust. Bake the quiche in a preheated 375° oven for 30 minutes or until the top is quite brown and puffy and a clean silver knife inserted in the center comes out clean. Slice and serve.

8 tablespoons sweet butter
3 ounces cream cheese, softened
1¼ cups flour, sifted with a dash of salt
4 large leeks
2 cups chicken broth (homemade or canned)
3 tablespoons sweet butter
½ pound Nova Scotia or Scotch salmon, chopped
1 tablespoon chopped fresh parsley
1 tablespoon chopped fresh dill
4 eggs
2 cups heavy cream
¼ teaspoon salt
¼ teaspoon white pepper
A dash of cayenne pepper
A dash of nutmeg

Chicken Demi-Deuil

Truffles are culinary black diamonds and hardly on everyone's "must buy" list. So it's okay to do without them. Call your dish Chicken with Creamy White Sauce and serve it with equal pride.

The stuffing has a mousselike texture. Cooking it inside the chicken enhances its flavor and it will slide out easily, in one piece, for slicing and serving. The mixture can be prepared a day ahead along with the poaching stock.

1 small onion, finely minced
2 shallots, finely minced
1 clove garlic, mashed
½ pound fresh white
  mushrooms, finely minced
¼ teaspoon dried tarragon
2 tablespoons sweet butter
Salt and a dash of white pepper
  to taste
1 whole boneless and skinless
  breast of chicken
A ¼-pound piece of boiled ham
1 egg white
¼ cup heavy cream
Salt, white pepper, and a dash
  of nutmeg
1 small soup chicken or a few
  pounds of bones and
  trimmings
1 large onion, cut into chunks
2 carrots, cut into chunks
2 stalks celery, cut into chunks
Several sprigs of fresh parsley
1 large leek, trimmed, well
  washed, and chopped
1 large parsnip, cut into chunks
Salt and freshly ground black
  pepper to taste
Two 3-pound chickens, cleaned
  and left whole
1 small can (7 to 8 ounces)
  whole black truffles
4 tablespoons sweet butter

To prepare the stuffing, sauté the onion, shallots, garlic, mushrooms, and tarragon in the butter in a small skillet for about 5 minutes, until the vegetables are soft and golden. Season with salt and pepper and remove from heat.

Cut the breast of chicken and the ham into small pieces and purée them together in a food processor fitted with the steel blade, or in a blender, until smooth. Add the egg white and the cream and continue to blend. Season with salt, white pepper, and nutmeg. Remove the mixture from the machine and stir in the sautéed vegetables. Mix well and set aside.

To prepare the chicken broth, put the soup chicken (cut into quarters) or the bones into a deep soup kettle. Add the onion, carrots, celery, parsley, leek, parsnip, salt, and pepper. Cover everything in the pot with cold water. Cover the kettle, bring the liquid to a slow boil, reduce the heat to simmer, and cook for about an hour or until it has good flavor. Strain out all solids and discard them. (Use the meat from the chicken to make chicken salad, if you wish.) Set aside 3 cups of the strained broth; it will be used later in making the sauce.

To prepare the chickens for poaching, gently stuff each one with the puréed stuffing mixture and sew or skewer it closed. Gently slide your fingertips between the skin and the breast meat and loosen the skin away from the bird. Drain the truffles and thinly slice them. Insert truffle slices between the meat and the skin, pressing the skin down firmly over the truffles.

Place the prepared chickens in a deep kettle and cover them with the remaining strained chicken broth. Cover the pot, bring the liquid to a slow simmer, and cook — with the cover slightly ajar to allow steam to escape — for about an hour, or until the chickens are fork-tender and the juices run clear when pierced. When the chickens are done, remove them from the kettle and set them on a platter. Cover with foil and place them in a low oven to keep warm while you prepare the sauce.

Melt the 4 tablespoons of butter in a saucepan and when it is hot and foamy, whisk in the flour, stirring to form a *roux*. Slowly pour in the reserved 3 cups of broth and the heavy cream and bring this mixture to a boil, whisking constantly until it is smooth and creamy. Season with salt and white pepper.

To serve the dish, carve the chicken wings, legs, and thighs away from the bird. Carefully slice the white meat. Slide the stuffing out of the center of the bird in one piece and slice it. Be sure when carving the white meat of the breast that the top slice contains the truffle and skin. Arrange all of the carved meat, truffled slices, and slices of stuffing around a platter and nap some of the sauce over all. If you like, reserve a small piece of truffle and finely chop it; garnish the dish with it. Serve with plain white rice and a sauceboat of the sauce passed separately.

4 tablespoons flour
1 cup heavy cream
Salt and a dash of white pepper
  to taste

Monte Cristo Soufflé

SERVES 8

Two years of study with Maurice Moore-Betty, followed by a year as that culinary sorcerer's apprentice, were among the most valuable of all my training experiences. Here is one of his most clever and innovative desserts.

Constructing a soufflé that completely surrounds a column of ripe fresh berries is accomplished by chilling and setting the soufflé around an empty soda can. Punch holes in both ends of the can to eliminate a vacuum effect on removal and you have the central column ready to contain the berries. (If strawberries are unavailable, substitute a cup of finely diced mixed seasonal fresh fruit, such as oranges, pears, and pineapple.)

When spooning out portions, include soufflé, berries, and some of the surprise central layer of finely grated chocolate for triple treats of texture, taste, and color.

253

1 tablespoon unflavored gelatin
¼ cup water
6 eggs
½ cup sugar
4 tablespoons kirsch
1 cup heavy cream
2 additional egg whites
2 squares semisweet chocolate,
  finely grated
1 pint fresh strawberries

Lightly oil a 6-cup soufflé dish, wiping out the excess oil with a paper towel. Cut off a long strip of aluminum foil and fold it in half lengthwise. Oil it on one side and tie it, oiled side in, around the soufflé dish, affixing it with Scotch tape and string. Chill the bowl.

Sprinkle the gelatin over the water in a small heat-proof glass measuring cup or bowl. Place this in a saucepan and add about 1 inch of water to the pan. Put the pan on top of the stove and bring the water in the pan to a boil, thereby melting the gelatin mixture. When it is completely melted, remove the cup or dish from the saucepan and set it aside to cool.

Separate the eggs, putting the whites in a clean, dry bowl. Set them aside. Begin beating the yolks on high speed with an electric mixer until they thicken. Add the sugar gradually and continue to beat until the mixture is a pale vanilla color and quite thick. Remove the bowl from the mixer and stir in the kirsch and the melted and cooled gelatin mixture. Set aside.

Whip the heavy cream in a chilled bowl until it is thick and stiff. Gently fold it into the egg mixture.

Add the two additional egg whites to the six others and beat them until firm peaks form. Gently fold them into the soufflé mixture.

Lightly oil the outside of a standard-size soda can, and holding it firmly in the center of the prepared soufflé dish, spoon half of the mixture around the can in the bowl. Sprinkle the grated chocolate over all; then spoon on the remaining soufflé mixture. It should rise above the sides of the bowl into the collar. Chill the soufflé for at least 6 hours or overnight.

When ready to serve, wash, dry, hull, and slice the berries, reserving about six whole berries for decoration. Run a silver knife around the soda can and gently pull it out, immediately packing this center column with the sliced berries. Run the knife around the collar and soufflé to loosen it. Cut the string and tape and gently peel the collar away from the soufflé. Arrange the whole berries decoratively over the top and serve at once.

47

Pâté Maison

Brook Trout Véronique

Chocolate Marquise

A fish dish as the main course should get all your last-minute care and attention. Therefore, it has been combined with an appetizer and dessert that can and should be made a day ahead. The pâté needs cooling and weighting down to make it slice well by resolidifying the juices. The Chocolate Marquise needs to be well chilled for easy slicing.

Pâté Maison

A properly made country pâté should have a coarse and grainy texture. It is a far cry from the Chicken Liver Pâté in Aspic on page 246. The taste is heartier, the texture rougher, and the appearance of the slices more varied.

Serve the pâté with a selection of mustards, including if possible a smooth and spicy Dijon and a grainy variety, as well as some *cornichons* and a crusty French or Italian bread.

2 pounds fresh pork fat
1 pound boneless shoulder of pork
1 pound boneless shoulder of veal
1 pound calf's or beef liver
3 tablespoons sweet butter
6 shallots, chopped
2 cloves garlic, mashed
¼ cup cognac or Armagnac
2 teaspoons fresh lemon juice
2 tablespoons flour
¼ cup heavy cream
1 egg, lightly beaten
½ teaspoon *quatre épice* or allspice
½ teaspoon dried thyme
1 tablespoon salt
Freshly ground black pepper to taste
½ pound boiled ham, cut into small cubes
¼ cup shelled pistachio nuts
2 large bay leaves

Cut off about ½-pound piece of the pork fat and set it aside. Cut the remaining fat into long, thin rectangular slices for lining the terrine. Set the slices aside.

Using a food processor fitted with the steel blade, or a meat grinder, grind together the reserved ½ pound of pork fat, the boneless pork and veal, and the liver until quite coarsely ground. Do not overgrind, or the mixture will not have the right texture. Transfer the mixture to a large bowl.

Melt the butter in a small skillet and gently sauté the chopped shallots and mashed garlic for about 2 minutes. Pour in the cognac or Armagnac and bring to a rolling boil, scraping up the browned bits until the liquid reduces to about 2 tablespoons. Scrape the mixture into the bowl with the ground meats.

Add the lemon juice, flour, cream, egg, spices, thyme, salt, and pepper to the bowl and mix well with a wooden spoon until the mixture is fairly light and fluffy. Gently fold in the cubes of ham and the nuts. Brown a teaspoon of the mixture in a small skillet until it is cooked through; then taste it. Add more salt and pepper or *quatre épice* if needed. If you want it spicier, add a dash of cayenne pepper.

Line the bottom and sides of an 8-cup loaf pan or terrine with the long slices of pork fat, allowing the side strips to hang over the edges. These will eventually be turned up and over the top of the mold. Save enough slices of pork fat to completely cover the top after filling the mold. Pack the meat mixture into the prepared mold, taking care not to disturb the lining of fat. After all of the mixture is in the mold, smooth the top and bring the side strips up and over the mold; arrange additional fat over the entire top. Place the bay leaves on top of the fat. The fat will act as an insulation layer to keep the pâté moist and juicy while it is baking.

256

Cover the prepared mold tightly with aluminum foil and place it in a larger pan or *bain-marie*. Add several inches of boiling water to the *bain-marie* and bake the pâté in a 350° oven for 2 hours or until the fat and juices are clear and yellow — no longer pink.

When the mold is done, remove it from the oven and lift it out of the *bain-marie*. Set it aside to come to room temperature. Place a heavy weight, such as a brick or several heavy tinned cans, on top of the mold to compress the juices while it is cooling. Then refrigerate the mold with its weights overnight.

To serve, lift off the weights and aluminum foil, run a knife around the edges of the mold, and invert the pâté onto a serving platter. Slice and serve. (The outside fat can be scraped away and discarded before slicing and serving the pâté.)

Brook Trout Véronique

Any firm white fish fillets can be substituted for the brook trout. You may also substitute salmon for sole in the mousse mixture. You will get equally good flavor and a nice color, too.

In cooking, the mousse layer will bind itself to the fillets, while the wine and juices in the pan will form a tasty base for the cream sauce.

1 pound fillet of sole
2 egg whites
1 cup well-chilled heavy cream
Salt, white pepper, and a dash
  of cayenne pepper
2 tablespoons soft sweet butter
3 shallots, finely minced
Several sprigs of fresh parsley
8 whole brook trout, filleted and
  skinned
1 cup dry white wine
2 tablespoons sweet butter
½ pound fresh white
  mushrooms, thinly sliced
½ pound small whole shrimp,
  shelled and deveined
1 tablespoon fresh lemon juice
1 pound fresh seedless green
  grapes (or an 8-ounce can)
4 tablespoons butter
4 tablespoons flour
1 cup heavy cream
Salt, white pepper, and dash of
  cayenne pepper
1 teaspoon fresh lemon juice

Cut the fillet of sole into small pieces and put them into a food processor fitted with the steel blade, or the jar of an electric blender. Purée the fish until very smooth. Add the egg whites, one at a time, and continue to blend. Add the chilled cream, a few tablespoons at a time, puréeing constantly until all of the cream has been incorporated. Season with the salt and peppers and scrape the mixture into a small bowl.

Lightly butter a shallow glass baking dish with the 2 tablespoons of soft butter and scatter the shallots, parsley, and a bit more salt and pepper over the bottom of the dish. Lay on eight pieces of trout and divide the mousse mixture evenly over the fillets, spreading evenly. Place the remaining eight fillets over the mousse mixture, creating small "sandwiches" of trout and mousse. Pour the wine into the dish. Butter a piece of wax paper cut to fit the inside of the dish, and place it over the fish. Cover the dish tightly with aluminum foil and bring the liquid to a boil on top of the stove. Transfer the dish to a preheated 350° oven and bake for 15 minutes or until the mousse in the fish seems well set and the fillets flake easily with a fork.

While the fish is baking, melt the 2 tablespoons of butter in a small skillet and gently sauté the sliced mushrooms for a few minutes until they are soft and golden but not too brown. Add the shrimp and sauté a few minutes more, until they turn bright pink and firm. Transfer these to a small colander and toss the lemon juice over all to prevent the mushrooms from darkening. Let drain.

Put the grapes into a small saucepan and cover them with cold water. Cover the pot and simmer the grapes for about 5 minutes, until they are tender. Drain and set aside. If you are using canned grapes, just drain them and set aside. It is not necessary to poach them.

When the fish is done, remove it from the oven and carefully lift the fillets to a serving platter. Cover the platter with aluminum foil and return it to the turned-off oven so the fish will stay warm while you make the sauce.

Strain the poaching liquid through a fine sieve and measure out 2 cups. If you do not have enough, add white wine to make 2 cups. Melt the 4 tablespoons of butter in a saucepan, and when it is hot and foamy, whisk in the flour, stirring to form a *roux*. Pour in the strained stock, whisking constantly, and bring the mixture to a boil. Add the cream and seasonings and cook the mixture for a few minutes. Remove it from the heat and stir in the lemon juice, mushrooms, shrimp, and grapes. Reheat the sauce thoroughly.

To serve, nap some of the sauce over the tops of the fish and surround the fish with the grapes, shrimp, and mushrooms. Pass additional sauce in a separate boat, if you like.

Chocolate Marquise

The way the British use ladyfingers in their desserts, and the French in this Chocolate Marquise, one wonders who would ever eat them plain!

This recipe contains no gelatin, yet on chilling it firms up and slices like a cake. The semisweet chocolate carries its intense flavor through the rather dense filling, while the outside layer of ladyfingers provides the required lightness.

16 ladyfingers, cut in half
  lengthwise
2 tablespoons Grand Marnier
8 ounces semisweet chocolate
1 cup (2 sticks) sweet butter
¼ cup superfine sugar
6 eggs
2 tablespoons Grand Marnier
1 cup heavy cream
1 tablespoon superfine sugar
1 tablespoon Grand Marnier
Shaved semisweet chocolate
  curls

Spread out the ladyfinger halves, flat side up, on a cooky sheet and sprinkle the 2 tablespoons of Grand Marnier over them. Let it soak in slightly; then arrange the ladyfinger halves, flat side toward the center of the pan, around the sides of a 9-inch springform. Form a daisy pattern of ladyfingers over the bottom of the pan, arranging them in a circle like spokes of a wheel. Cut a small round piece and place it in the center of the wheel. Chill the prepared mold.

Melt the chocolate, butter, and 3 tablespoons of the sugar in the top of a double boiler, over slowly simmering water, until smooth. Remove from the heat and set aside.

Separate the eggs and put the whites in a clean, dry bowl. Set them aside. Beat the yolks with an electric mixer, on high speed, until they thicken. Add the cooled chocolate mixture in a slow, steady stream, beating constantly. Then beat this mixture for 8 to 10 minutes, until it is very thick and stiff.

Beat the egg whites with the remaining tablespoon of sugar until stiff peaks form; then gently fold them into the chocolate mixture. Fold in the 2 tablespoons of Grand Marnier and mix well. Spoon this mixture into the prepared mold and refrigerate for several hours or overnight, until firmly set.

Whip the heavy cream with the tablespoon of sugar and the tablespoon of Grand Marnier until it is thick and stiff. Put the whipped cream into a pastry bag fitted with a rosette nozzle.

Run a knife around the sides of the mold, release the spring, and remove the sides from the cake. Invert the cake onto a serving platter, and using a wide spatula, lift the bottom of the springform away from the cake. Pipe out a decorative border of whipped cream around the bottom edge; then outline each petal of the "daisy" with whipped cream. Outline the side panels of ladyfingers with the remaining whipped cream, using up all in the pastry bag. Scatter the shaved chocolate over all and refrigerate until ready to serve.

December

Minestrone Casa Lingua

Veal Marsala

Crêpes Tivoli

The soup should be prepared well ahead of time, since it improves with reheating. The veal entrée is a simply sauced dish, best done quickly just before serving. The crêpe dessert is a three-part project that can be scheduled at your convenience.

Minestrone Casa Lingua

Probably no other soup is so identified with its country as minestrone is with Italy. This hearty dish is substantial enough to be the main course of a lighter meal, accompanied by a simple salad.

½ cup Great Northern white
  beans
4 tablespoons olive oil
2 potatoes, peeled and diced
½ pound fresh green beans, cut
  into ½-inch pieces
2 zucchini, diced but not peeled
1 large onion, chopped
3 stalks celery, sliced
2 carrots, diced
1 ounce dried Italian *porcini*
  mushrooms
A 2-pound can of Italian plum
  tomatoes
2 tablespoons chopped fresh
  parsley
1 teaspoon dried basil
1 teaspoon dried oregano
½ teaspoon dried thyme
½ teaspoon dried marjoram
Salt and freshly ground black
  pepper to taste
6 cups cold water
4 cups homemade beef stock
  (page 215), or canned beef
  stock
2 cups dry white wine
2 cups shredded fresh cabbage
1 pound fresh peas, shelled
¼ pound small pasta (such as
  shells, squares, or *penne*)
Fresh garlic toasts (page 133)
Freshly grated Parmesan cheese

Cover the dried beans with cold water and soak them overnight in the refrigerator. The next day, drain them and put them in a kettle. Cover them with fresh cold water and cook them, covered, for 45 minutes or until they are tender but not too soft. Drain them thoroughly and set them aside in a colander.

Heat the olive oil in a deep soup kettle and sauté the potatoes, green beans, zucchini, onion, celery, and carrots until they become golden and slightly soft, about 5 minutes in all. While the vegetables are sautéing, put the dried mushrooms in a small bowl and cover them with hot water. Let them soak for about 5 minutes; then drain them and squeeze out the excess liquid. Chop and add them to the soup kettle along with the drained beans.

Drain the liquid from the canned tomatoes and break them up into small pieces. Add to the kettle along with the herbs and salt and pepper. Pour in the water, beef stock, and wine. Cover the pot and simmer the soup for 30 minutes. Cool and refrigerate overnight if you wish.

To finish the soup, bring it to room temperature. Add the shredded cabbage, the peas, and the pasta. Cover the pot and cook for an additional 10 minutes.

Taste the soup for additional salt and pepper. Serve it with the hot garlic toasts and freshly grated Parmesan cheese.

Veal Marsala

This dish acquires its subtle sweetness from the Marsala wine. Madeira or sherry could also be used. Although scaloppini are supremely tender, they will toughen if you overcook them.

Lay each slice of veal out on a board and pound it with a mallet until it is thin and even. Season with salt and pepper on both sides. Heat the butter in a skillet and dredge each slice of meat in the flour. Shake off the excess.

When the butter is hot and foamy, reduce the heat slightly and add the veal. Sauté each slice for 2 minutes on one side, turn gently, and sauté for 2 minutes on the other side. Remove the meat from the skillet as it is done and set it aside.

Add the mushrooms to the skillet and more butter if necessary. Sauté for 3 minutes, until golden; then return the meat to the skillet. Pour in the Marsala and stock, cover the skillet, and cook for about 2 minutes, until all is heated through.

Serve the veal with very simple accompaniments such as lightly steamed green vegetables or a purée of vegetables and a broiled tomato. Garnish each serving of veal with chopped parsley.

3 pounds veal scaloppini
Salt and pepper to taste
½ cup flour
4 tablespoons sweet butter
½ pound fresh white mushrooms, thinly sliced
¼ cup Marsala wine
¼ cup chicken stock
Chopped fresh parsley

Crêpes Tivoli

A last-minute broiling of these filled crêpes is done to warm them quickly without melting the custard interior. The result is a cold custard wrapped in a warmed crêpe and covered with a hot, rich, ruby-red fruit sauce.

1 batch (24) dessert crêpes (from the Crêpes Suzette recipe, page 82)
3 egg yolks
¼ cup sugar
¼ cup flour
1 cup slightly scalded milk
1 tablespoon sweet butter
1 teaspoon vanilla extract
A 10-ounce package of frozen strawberries
A 10-ounce package of frozen raspberries
2 teaspoons cornstarch
1 tablespoon cold water
2 tablespoons kirsch, Grand Marnier, or framboise
¼ cup chopped pecans or hazelnuts
1 cup heavy cream, whipped
1 pint fresh strawberries, washed, dried, hulled, and sliced (optional)
¼ cup kirsch, Grand Marnier, or framboise (optional)

Prepare the dessert crêpes. Stack them and set them aside. They can be made ahead and frozen. ◀

Put the egg yolks, sugar, and flour into a small saucepan and beat well. Pour in the hot milk, whisking to form a smooth mixture. Cook this over low heat for about 5 minutes, whisking constantly until the mixture comes just to the boiling point. It will be quite thick. Remove it from the heat and stir in the butter and vanilla. Transfer the mixture to a bowl, cover it tightly with plastic wrap, and chill thoroughly. ◀

To make the fruit sauce, defrost the berries and put them, with their juices, into a blender or food processor and blend thoroughly. Run the mixture through a fine sieve to remove all seeds. Dilute the cornstarch with the cold water and stir it into the sieved fruit. Add the 2 tablespoons of liqueur. Put the mixture into a small saucepan and cook it over low heat until it comes to a boil and thickens and the cornstarch clears. Taste to see if additional sugar is needed. This sauce can be made ahead and kept in the refrigerator to be reheated before serving. ◀

When the pastry cream is quite chilled, fold the chopped nuts and the whipped cream into it. Fill each crêpe with a small amount of this cream mixture and roll it up. Place each crêpe, seam side down, on a shallow glass baking dish. Sprinkle the tops of the crêpes with a bit of granulated sugar. Preheat the broiler and place the broiler rack on the top level. Have the strawberries sliced and ready, and the fruit sauce hot. Fold together before serving.

Run the crêpes under the hot broiler for just a minute or two, watching them carefully so the tops don't burn. Bring them to the table with a sauceboat of hot fruit sauce. If you wish, the ¼ cup of liqueur can be poured over the crêpes and ignited at the table.

Roasted Red Pepper Salad

Fettucini with Four Cheeses

Glazed Pineapple and Bananas

Italians take their pasta many ways — hot in soup, cold in salads, *al dente* and sauced before a main course, and, as here, composed and baked with a variety of ingredients. This entrée, like most baked pasta dishes, can be fully assembled, ready for baking, a day ahead of time.

Roasted Red Pepper Salad

Broiling the peppers heightens the flavor by charring the skins, softens the flesh somewhat, and most important, allows for easy peeling. For variety, add anchovies, chopped olives, or a scattering of capers.

6 very ripe red bell peppers
1 small red onion, thinly sliced
2 cloves garlic, mashed
1 tablespoon chopped parsley
1 teaspoon dried basil
6 tablespoons olive oil
2 tablespoons wine vinegar
Salt and freshly ground black
  pepper to taste

Place the peppers on a shallow pan and slide them under a preheated broiler. Broil them, turning often, until the skins char and begin to split. Stab the peppers with a fork to see if they are somewhat tender. The whole procedure should take about 5 minutes. When the peppers seem tender and the skins are slightly blackened and crisp, remove them from the broiler and set aside to cool. When they are cool enough to handle, cut them in half and remove the seeds. Peel away the charred skins and cut off the stems. The skins should peel with your fingertips or with a small knife. If they are difficult to peel, wrap them in a damp towel for a few minutes to let them steam slightly.
  Slice the peeled peppers into strips and put them into a bowl. Add the remaining ingredients, mix well, and let them marinate in the refrigerator for several hours.

Fettucini with Four Cheeses

Four is the theme of this recipe: four cheeses, ranging from mild to mellow to strong to tangy, and four layers of ingredients — noodles followed by a savory prosciutto-mushroom mixture, covered with a creamy sauce, and topped with the mixture of cheeses.

½ pound prosciutto
1 pound fresh white mushrooms
2 ounces dried Italian *porcini*
  mushrooms
1 cup hot water
A 1-pound can of Italian plum
  tomatoes
4 tablespoons butter
8 tablespoons butter

Shred or chop the prosciutto and set it aside. Thinly slice the fresh mushrooms and set them aside. Pour the hot water over the dried mushrooms and let them soak for about 5 minutes to soften. Drain the soaking liquid and reserve it. Squeeze the excess liquid from the mushrooms and chop them. Strain the reserved liquid through fine cheesecloth to remove any grit and set it aside. Drain the tomatoes, discarding the liquid. Finely dice the tomatoes.

Heat the 4 tablespoons of butter in a deep skillet and add the prosciutto and fresh mushrooms. Sauté them for about 5 minutes; then add the dried mushrooms, tomatoes, and the reserved cup of mushroom liquid. Let this mixture come to a boil; then cook it over high heat, uncovered, until the liquid evaporates and the mixture becomes a thick sauce. Remove it from the heat and let it cool.

Heat the 8 tablespoons of butter in a deep kettle and sauté the chopped onions for about 5 minutes, until they are soft and golden. Scrape the onion-and-butter mixture into a blender or food processor and purée until smooth. Return the puréed onions to the kettle and add the flour. Mix well to form a *roux*. Pour in the milk, whisking constantly to remove lumps. Add the seasonings and bring this mixture to a boil, over low heat, stirring constantly to prevent the bottom from scorching. When the mixture has come to a boil and thickened, remove it from the heat.

Bring a large pot of lightly salted water to a rolling boil and add the tablespoon of oil. Drop the pasta in and cook it for 5 to 8 minutes, until it is very *al dente*. Remember, it will continue to cook while it bakes in the oven. (If you are using fresh, soft pasta, there is no need to cook it. Just pour boiling water over it in a colander to rinse away excess flour.) When the pasta has finished cooking, drain it and toss the melted butter through it to keep it from sticking together.

Combine all the grated cheeses. To assemble the dish for baking, spread a thin coating of the white sauce over the bottom of a 3-quart casserole or lasagne pan. Spread a layer of the cooked pasta over the white sauce and cover the pasta with a layer of the prosciutto-mushroom mixture. Spoon more white sauce over this and cover all with some of the grated cheeses. Continue layering in this fashion until all the ingredients are in the casserole. At this point the casserole may be covered well with foil or plastic wrap and refrigerated. Bring it to room temperature before baking.

Bake the casserole in a 350° oven for 40 to 50 minutes or until the top is brown and bubbly.

2 large onions, chopped
4 tablespoons flour
4 cups milk
Salt, white pepper, and a dash of nutmeg
1 tablespoon olive oil
2 pounds fettucini
2 tablespoons melted butter
½ cup grated mozzarella
½ cup grated Italian Fontina
½ cup grated Swiss, Gruyère, or Emmenthal cheese
½ cup grated Parmesan cheese

Glazed Pineapple and Bananas

8 slices fresh (or canned)
  pineapple
4 tablespoons sweet butter
4 whole bananas, split
  lengthwise or cut into 1-inch
  chunks
3 tablespoons sugar
3 tablespoons dark brown sugar
¼ cup fresh fruit juice (orange
  or pineapple)
4 tablespoons Myers's dark
  sweet rum
¼ cup shredded coconut

You will need only one skillet to make this light, sweet confection. Serve it with a simple cooky.

If you are using fresh pineapple, peel and core it and cut it into ½-inch-thick slices. If you are using canned, drain the rings and reserve the juice, which can be used in place of the fresh fruit juice.

Melt the butter in a skillet and add the slices of pineapple. Sauté for a minute or two on each side, then add the pieces of banana and sauté for a minute or two on each side. It might be necessary to remove the pineapple to make room for the banana. When all the fruit has been sautéed, return it to the skillet and sprinkle the white and brown sugars over all. Let the sugars melt and then pour in the juice.

Bring the mixture to a boil and let it reduce for about 5 minutes. Pour in the rum and either ignite it or continue to reduce the liquid to burn off the alcohol.

Spread the shredded coconut over the bottom of a small baking pan and toast it in a 350° oven for about 15 minutes, stirring occasionally with a fork, until it is golden brown and crisp. Serve the fruit with some of the pan juices spooned over and a sprinkling of toasted coconut over all.

50

Gnocchi with Mornay Sauce

Lamb Chops Italiana

Strawberry Cheesecake

The cuisine of northern Italy is represented in both the hearty appetizer and the entrée. The gnocchi, Italian dumplings that are first poached and then sauced, can be put together and then refrigerated overnight. The 20-minute baking is all that is necessary for completion. The cheesecake is a definite do-ahead, since it must firm up overnight before being removed from its springform.

Gnocchi with Mornay Sauce

The use of pâte à choux in these dumplings indicates the French influence on this Italian dish. These gnocchi expand and puff with air as they poach and are far lighter than their southern Italian cousins.

In forming the gnocchi into their classic oval shape, use two oval soup spoons, one to spoon up the dough and the other to shape and help slide the dumpling into the barely simmering water. If the water bubbles too fiercely, the gnocchi will not puff to the fullest and may break up.

8 tablespoons sweet butter
1 cup water
A dash of salt
A dash of nutmeg
1 cup flour
4 large eggs
1 cup grated Swiss cheese
½ cup grated Parmesan cheese
1 teaspoon butter
4 tablespoons sweet butter
3 tablespoons flour
2 cups milk
½ cup cream
Salt, white pepper, and a dash
 of cayenne pepper
½ cup grated Swiss cheese
½ cup plus 1 or 2 tablespoons
 grated Parmesan cheese
1 tablespoon soft butter

Put the butter, water, salt, and nutmeg into a small saucepan and bring to a rolling boil. Boil until the butter is completely melted; then remove the pan from the heat and add the flour all at once, stirring hard with a wooden spoon until the mixture forms a soft ball of dough and leaves the sides of the pan clean. Transfer this ball of dough to a small bowl or a food processor and beat in the eggs, one at a time, until they are all incorporated. Stir in the grated cheeses and set aside.

To poach the dumplings, fill a large deep skillet or shallow pot with several inches of water. Add salt and the teaspoon of butter and bring the water to a boil. Reduce the heat to low, so the water is barely simmering, and using two oval soup spoons, form the dough into small ovals. Slide them gently into the simmering water and poach for about 2 minutes on one side. Gently turn the dumplings over with a large spoon and poach for 2 minutes on the other side.

Using a slotted spoon, lift the finished dumplings out of the water and place them on a tray. Continue in this fashion until all the dough has been poached. Cover the poached dumplings lightly with plastic wrap or a towel to prevent them from drying out while you make the sauce.

Melt the 4 tablespoons of butter in a saucepan, and when it is hot and foamy, whisk in the flour, stirring to form a *roux*. Pour in the milk and allow the mixture to come to a boil. Pour in the cream, seasonings, and grated cheeses (except the extra 1 or 2 tablespoons of Parmesan) and cook a few minutes longer, until the cheeses are thoroughly melted.

Butter a flat gratin or baking dish with the tablespoon of soft butter and place the poached dumplings in one layer in the dish. Spoon the sauce over all and sprinkle the additional tablespoon or two of grated Parmesan cheese over the top. Bake the dish in a preheated 350° oven for about 20 minutes or until the top is lightly browned.

Lamb Chops Italiana

This dish is best prepared with fresh artichokes, although frozen hearts or canned bottoms will do. Fresh artichokes will involve you in some time-consuming work — steaming, dissecting, and trimming away the chokes to get to the bottoms used in the dish. But you could prepare the artichokes a day in advance and eat the leaves as a cold hors d'oeuvre served with a dipping sauce.

Slice off the stems of the artichokes and rub the bottoms with the cut lemon. Arrange the artichokes snugly next to each other in one layer in a wide pot, or deep skillet, with a tight-fitting lid. Add several inches of boiling water and a dash of salt, and squeeze the juice of the cut lemon into the water. Be sure the water comes only halfway up the artichokes; do not submerge them, or they will become waterlogged and lose flavor and color. Cover the pot and steam for 20 minutes or until a leaf pulls out easily and seems tender.

When the artichokes are done, drain them upside-down on a rack until they are cool enough to handle. Then gently pull off all the leaves, saving those you might want to serve with a dip. Scrape all the fuzz away from the bottom of each artichoke. Cut each bottom piece into quarters and set them aside. (Both the leaves and the bottoms can be stored, tightly covered with plastic wrap, in the refrigerator.) These are the artichoke pieces that will be used to garnish the lamb chops.

Trim away excess fat from the lamb chops. Heat 2 tablespoons of the butter in a large skillet and sauté the chops for a few minutes on each side, depending upon how rare you like the meat. Remove the chops as they are done, adding more chops to the skillet and the remaining butter as needed, until all the chops have been sautéed. They should be quite brown on the outside but still very pink inside.

When all the chops are out of the skillet, add the prosciutto, mushrooms, shallots, and garlic and sauté for about 5 min-

8 medium-sized artichokes
1 lemon, cut in half
16 loin or rib lamb chops, about 1 inch thick
4 tablespoons sweet butter, or more if needed
¼ pound prosciutto, shredded (optional)
1 pound fresh mushrooms, thinly sliced
4 shallots, finely minced
2 cloves garlic, mashed
½ cup Madeira
½ teaspoon dried marjoram or rosemary
2 tablespoons chopped fresh parsley
Salt and freshly ground black pepper to taste
1 cup Sauce Espagnole (page 120)

utes, until the mushrooms are golden. Pour the Madeira into the skillet and let it cook down to about ¼ cup. Stir in the herbs, salt, pepper, and Sauce Espagnole. Mix well and return the chops to the skillet. Stir in the pieces of artichoke, cover the skillet, and heat through for about 10 minutes.

Place the chops on a platter and spoon the mushrooms, artichoke pieces, and sauce over all. Serve at once.

Strawberry Cheesecake

SERVES 8

It seems everyone has his or her own special recipe for cheesecake. This one has some new twists. The cake is virtually crustless and the top is beautifully glazed with strawberry peaks and currant jelly. If fresh strawberries are unavailable, you could make the cheesecake without the topping. Serve it instead with the fruit sauce from the Crêpes Tivoli recipe (page 266), chilled. Incorporating stiffly beaten egg whites into the cheese base adds an airy, soufflé-like texture.

2 tablespoons soft sweet butter
½ cup finely crushed graham cracker crumbs
4 eggs
2 cups half-and-half or light cream
12 ounces softened cream cheese
¾ cup sugar
2 tablespoons flour
2 teaspoons vanilla extract
¼ teaspoon salt
1 pint fresh strawberries
½ cup red currant jelly

Spread the soft butter over the bottom and sides of a 9-inch springform. Scatter the graham cracker crumbs over the buttered bottom and sides, rotating the pan to completely coat the sides. They will stick to the butter and form a thin crust. Shake out excess crumbs and put the prepared pan in the freezer to firm up the butter while you are making the filling.

Separate the eggs and put the whites in a clean, dry bowl. Set them aside. Put the half-and-half or light cream into a small saucepan and heat it to the boiling point. Remove it from the heat and cool slightly.

Put the cream cheese, sugar, egg yolks, flour, vanilla, and salt into a bowl for the electric mixer and beat well. Slowly pour in the heated milk and continue to mix on low speed until smooth. Remove the bowl from the mixer and set aside.

Whip the egg whites until stiff peaks form; then gently fold them into the cheese base, using a whisk if necessary to incorporate them and remove lumps of egg white. Pour this filling into the chilled pan.

Set the springform into a larger pan filled with several

inches of boiling water. Place this *bain-marie*, with the springform in it, into a preheated 350° oven and bake for 1 hour and 15 minutes or until the top of the cake has risen, turned golden brown, and cracked slightly.

When the cake is done, remove it from the oven and lift it out of the *bain-marie*. Set it aside to come to room temperature. As the cake cools, it will deflate. When it has cooled sufficiently, cover it with plastic wrap and chill overnight.

To finish the cake, wash, dry, and hull the strawberries. Put the currant jelly into a small pot and melt it over low heat until smooth. Loosen the cake from the sides of the pan, open the spring, and lift off the sides. Run a spatula between the bottom of the cake and the bottom of the springform and lift the cake up and onto a serving platter. Dip each berry in the hot jelly and place them in circles around the top of the cake, working from the outside in. Place a final berry in the center of the cake. Using a small pastry brush, cover the berries completely with the remaining liquid jelly until they are thoroughly glazed. Return the cake to the refrigerator to firm the jelly before slicing and serving.

51

Mussels in Saffron Cream

Stuffed Suprêmes of Chicken

Paris-Brest

This is the perfect menu for a sumptuous New Year's Eve dinner. Although the ingredients are inexpensive, each course bespeaks elegance, from the mussels baked with a rich sauce topping, to the Paris-Brest, a cake that should be shown off in all its uncut glory before serving.

The mussels can be cleaned and steamed, and the broth strained, early in the morning. Prepare the sauce and arrange the entire dish for the oven ahead of time. Hold it in the refrigerator and bring it to room temperature before broiling.

Cut the pockets in the chicken breasts and prepare their stuffing the day ahead. Stuff and sauté early in the day of your party, leaving the final saucing and finishing for the last minute.

The Paris-Brest can be baked in advance and its custard prepared a day ahead for proper chilling, though the final assembly should be no more than a couple of hours ahead of serving.

Mussels in Saffron Cream

Saffron has a great affinity for mussels. The rich golden colors are compatible and the flavor combination is a delight.

Pick over the mussels and discard any with broken shells or that are wide open. Rinse the mussels well under cold running water, pulling off the "beards" and attached seaweed. Scrub off the remaining mud and sand with a stiff brush and put the mussels in a deep basin or bowl filled with cold water. Add the cornmeal and let the mussels soak for about an hour. This will help to release internal sand.

Rinse the mussels well again under cold water and set them aside to drain in a colander.

Melt the 4 tablespoons of butter in a deep kettle and gently sauté the garlic, shallots, onion, and celery for about 3 minutes. Add the parsley, salt, pepper, saffron, and wine. Put the mussels on top of these ingredients and cover the pot. Bring to a boil, reduce the heat, and steam the mussels for at least 10 minutes, shaking the pot occasionally, until they are all wide open.

Remove the mussels with a slotted spoon and put them aside to cool. Strain the cooking broth several times through fine cheesecloth and discard all solids. Set aside 1 cup of the strained liquid and discard the rest (or freeze it for later use).

To prepare the sauce, melt the 2 tablespoons of butter in a small saucepan and whisk in the flour, stirring to form a *roux*. Pour in the reserved mussel broth and the heavy cream. Let the mixture come to a boil and thicken. It should be a pale golden color from the saffron. Season the sauce with a bit of salt and white pepper.

Pull off the top half of each mussel shell and leave the mussel in the bottom half. Place the mussels in their shells on a large baking dish and pour the sauce over all. Run the dish under the broiler for a minute or two to glaze the top and heat through. Sprinkle chopped fresh parsley over the mussels and serve with crisp French bread.

4 pounds fresh mussels
2 tablespoons cornmeal
4 tablespoons sweet butter
2 cloves garlic, mashed
4 shallots, chopped
1 large onion, chopped
1 stalk celery, chopped
Several sprigs of fresh parsley
½ teaspoon salt
Freshly ground black pepper to taste
1 teaspoon saffron threads, crumbled
½ cup dry white wine
2 tablespoons sweet butter
2 tablespoons flour
1 cup heavy cream
Salt and white pepper to taste

Stuffed Suprêmes of Chicken

The easiest way to create pockets in the chicken breasts is to rely on the talents of your butcher. Have the breasts boned to include all of the meat off the rib cage in one piece. The result will be two sides of the breast meat. Each is composed of a large outer fillet and a long, slender inner section of tender meat known as the *contre-filet*. Between these two fillets is a natural pocket, just the right size for stuffing. When the double breast is cut in half, each half is a suprême.

If you lack the life-smoothing amenity of an obliging butcher, carefully cut your own pockets in boneless breasts, using the tip of a thin sharp knife.

1 pound fresh leaf spinach (or 1 package chopped frozen spinach)
4 tablespoons sweet butter
¼ pound fresh white mushrooms, finely minced
1 small onion, finely minced
4 shallots, finely minced
1 clove garlic, mashed
Salt and freshly ground black pepper to taste
A dash of nutmeg
2 tablespoons ricotta cheese
1 tablespoon grated Parmesan cheese
2 tablespoons sour cream
8 whole boneless and skinless breasts of chicken
Salt and pepper to taste
½ cup flour
2 tablespoons butter
2 tablespoons olive oil
1 pound fresh white mushrooms, thinly sliced
¼ cup chicken broth (homemade or canned)
¼ cup Madeira wine

If you are using fresh spinach, pull off the thick stems, wash the leaves well, dry them, and chop fine. If you are using frozen spinach, defrost it and squeeze out all excess liquid.

Heat the 4 tablespoons of butter in a skillet and sauté the minced mushrooms, onion, shallots, garlic, and spinach for a few minutes until all the excess liquid from the spinach is evaporated. Season with salt, pepper, and nutmeg and remove from the heat. Stir in the cheeses and sour cream and mix well to bind. Set aside to cool completely. If the mixture seems too loose, add a tablespoon of finely grated bread crumbs.

Cut each chicken breast in half to give you sixteen suprêmes of chicken. Carefully cut a pocket for stuffing in each piece of breast (if the butcher has not done this for you). When the stuffing is cool, put a small amount into each pocket, pressing firmly to contain the stuffing. Season the stuffed breasts with salt and pepper and dredge them lightly in the flour. Shake off the excess flour.

Heat the butter and oil in a skillet and sauté the prepared breasts for a few minutes on each side, until golden brown. Remove them from the skillet. Add the sliced mushrooms, and more butter and oil, if necessary, and sauté for a few minutes until golden. Then return the pieces of chicken to the skillet, add the liquids, cover the skillet, and cook the chicken over low heat for about 20 minutes.

Serve the breasts with the sliced mushrooms scattered over the top and the pan juices spooned over all.

Paris-Brest

This dessert is probably the largest cream puff you will ever make. The crisp baked *pâte à choux* ring is split, filled with a rich praline cream, and glazed to create a beautiful sight.

The components can be made ahead. The crushed praline caramel can be stored on the shelf in an airtight container for several days. The custard cream will hold for a day or two in the refrigerator, well covered. And the baked ring will gain in crispness if it is baked the day before and airs overnight. But, to avoid softening the baked ring, assemble it with the custard shortly before service. For easy slicing, use a serrated knife.

This dessert can also be prepared as eight individual rings, each about 3 inches in diameter.

Put the water, butter, and salt into a small saucepan and bring to a boil. Boil until the butter is completely melted, remove from heat, and add the flour all at once, stirring hard with a wooden spoon until the mixture forms a soft ball of dough and leaves the sides of the pot clean. Transfer this mixture to a food processor or small bowl and beat in the four eggs one at a time, until they are all incorporated.

Put the mixture into a pastry bag fitted with a ½-inch plain nozzle and set aside. Lightly butter a cooky sheet, and dust it with flour. Shake off the excess. Using a 9-inch cake pan as a guide, draw a circle in the flour. Pipe out a ring of dough through the pastry bag, following the guide. Make the ring about 2 inches wide and at least 1 inch high.

Brush the egg-and-water mixture over the top of the ring of dough, using a soft pastry brush. Bake the ring in a preheated 450° oven for 15 minutes; then lower the temperature to 350° and bake for an additional 15 minutes. At this point, pierce the sides of the ring every few inches with the tip of a knife to allow internal steam to escape, and continue to bake the ring for another 30 minutes or until it is very brown and crisp. Turn off the oven and let the ring sit in the turned-off oven for about 15 minutes. Then remove it from the oven and set it aside to come to room temperature.

When the ring is completely cool, cut it in half horizontally with a serrated knife and pull out any soft dough from the inside of the ring, creating a hollow shell. Set it aside to continue to dry and crisp.

1 cup water
6 tablespoons sweet butter
A dash of salt
1 cup flour
4 whole eggs
1 egg, lightly beaten with 1 tablespoon cold water
6 egg yolks
½ cup sugar
½ cup flour
2 cups slightly scalded milk
2 tablespoons sweet butter
2 teaspoons vanilla extract
1 recipe crushed praline candy (page 105)
2 cups heavy cream
½ cup sugar
½ cup thinly sliced almonds
1 cup apricot jam
1 tablespoon sugar

Put the egg yolks into a small saucepan and add the sugar and flour. Beat well with a whisk and slowly pour in the scalded milk, stirring well. Put this mixture over low heat and cook it for a few minutes until it comes just to the boiling point, whisking constantly to prevent lumping. Remove it from the heat and stir in the butter and vanilla. Transfer the custard to a small bowl, cover it tightly with plastic wrap, and chill thoroughly.

Make the batch of praline candy and fold ½ cup of it into the chilled custard. Whip the heavy cream with the sugar until it is thick and stiff. Fold ½ cup of the whipped cream into the custard and fill the bottom half of the ring with the custard. Put the remaining whipped cream into a pastry bag fitted with a rosette nozzle, replace the top of the ring, and decoratively pipe out some whipped cream around the ring where the bottom and top meet. Pipe out more whipped cream around the bottom of the ring after you have placed it on a serving platter. Any remaining whipped cream can be piped into the center of the ring.

Spread the sliced almonds over the bottom of a small pan and put them in a 300° oven for about 15 minutes, until they are lightly toasted. Set aside. Press the apricot jam through a fine sieve into a small sauce pan and add the tablespoon of sugar. Melt the mixture over low heat until it is smooth and liquefied. Brush this glaze over the top of the ring and scatter the toasted almond slices over the glaze. Chill the Paris-Brest until ready to serve. It can be chilled for up to 2 or 3 hours before it becomes soggy.

LESSON

52

Hot and Cold Hors d'Oeuvres
for a Cocktail Party for Twenty-Four

Any number of the appetizers in this book can serve as cocktail fare. Possibilities include the various mousse and pâté recipes (adjusted to be served with assorted breads or crackers), any of the hot stuffed vegetable dishes such as the Mushrooms Stuffed with Crab Meat or the Stuffed Zucchini, and, with toothpicks, the Shrimp in Ravigote Sauce or the Marinated Mushrooms; see the index for recipe pages.

Even without extra help, you can be a guest at your own cocktail party if you select recipes that can be prepared in advance. This is the reason deep-fried morsels have been omitted from this lesson. Hovering over a deep-fryer is not conducive to enjoying one's guests, nor is it kindly to one's party attire.

Each of the four hot and four cold recipes for this party will provide you with up to forty-eight individual portions — enough for a party of twenty-four, with plenty to spare. Each recipe can be reduced or increased.

Individual hors d'oeuvres, whether hot or cold, should be created with visual impact in mind. Use your best service trays and garnish the trays with attractive and appropriate selections such as parsley or watercress sprigs; olives of all types; radish roses; slices of white turnip cut with a daisy-shaped cooky cutter and with a small carrot slice centered on each one, held in place with a bit of cold butter; cherry tomatoes; or cut lemon halves. Doilies are a nice touch under the hot items.

Cheese-Stuffed Shrimp

48 large raw shrimp
2 ounces soft cheese (Roquefort, Boursin, *chèvre,* or any flavored packaged cheese spread)
3 ounces softened cream cheese
½ teaspoon Dijon mustard
2 small scallions, finely minced
1 cup finely minced fresh parsley

Drop the shrimp into a deep pot filled with salted boiling water. Allow the water to come back to the boil and boil the shrimp for exactly 3 minutes. Drain immediately and rinse with cold water. When the shrimp are cool enough to handle, crack each shell and pull it away. Slit the back curve of the shrimp with the tip of a small knife, cutting deep, but not quite all the way through, to create an opening for stuffing. Be sure to clean away any veins you find while splitting the shrimp. Chill the shrimp while you prepare the stuffing.

Mix the softened cheeses and the mustard together in a small bowl, or in a blender or food processor, until they are smooth. Stir in the minced scallions. Chill the mixture for about 30 minutes.

Spread the finely minced parsley out on a plate.

To stuff the shrimp, spread about ½ teaspoon of the cheese mixture in the slit of each shrimp. Then, holding the shrimp by its tail, roll the cheese edge in the minced parsley. The parsley will stick to the cheese and create a lovely garnish.

Chill the prepared shrimp until ready to serve. They can be stuffed and held in the refrigerator, tightly covered with plastic wrap, overnight.

◀

Purée of Smoked Trout with Red Caviar

Put the trout fillets into a blender or food processor and purée; or mash them well with the back of a fork. (Smoked trout fillets are available from specialty food stores canned or in bulk.) Mix in the lemon juice, sour cream, horseradish, and black pepper. Whip the heavy cream until it is thick and stiff; fold it into the mixture. Chill the mixture for several hours. This spread can be made a day ahead.

▶ Cut the bread slices into forty-eight 2-inch triangles, squares, or circles. Spread each piece with the softened butter, then spread smoothly with some of the chilled trout mixture. Press a small indentation in the center of each canapé, using your fingertip, the back of a small spoon, or the tip of a knife. Drop a small amount of red caviar into each indentation.

These canapés can be prepared and held in the refrigerator for several hours before serving. Be sure to cover them tightly
▶ with plastic wrap.

4 pieces boneless and skinless smoked trout fillets (about 2 pounds altogether)
2 tablespoons fresh lemon juice
2 tablespoons sour cream
2 tablespoons white horseradish (or to taste)
Freshly ground black pepper to taste
1 cup heavy cream
A 2-ounce jar of red salmon caviar
1 thinly sliced black or light pumpernickel or seeded rye bread
Soft sweet butter (for spreading)

Smoked Salmon on Cucumber or Zucchini

2 medium-sized cucumbers or
 zucchini
8 ounces cream cheese
2 slices onion
1 pound Nova Scotia salmon
2 tablespoons chopped fresh dill
 (optional)
Capers (for garnish)

If you are using the cucumbers, peel them and score the sides with the tines of a fork. If you are using the zucchini, do not peel or score them. Cut each vegetable into ¼-inch slices and spread the slices out on a paper-towel-lined tray to drain.

Put the cream cheese, onion, and ¼ pound (about two slices) of the salmon into a blender or food processor and purée thoroughly. Transfer to a small bowl. Stir in the chopped dill.

Spread a small amount of the cheese mixture over each vegetable slice. Using the remainder of the salmon, cut each slice into long strips, about ½ inch wide. Roll these strips up into small pinwheels and place each one on a slice of spread vegetable. This will create a rosette effect. Place a caper in the center of each rosette of salmon and chill the prepared slices until serving.

These canapés can be spread, garnished with the rosettes, and held in the refrigerator overnight, covered tightly with plastic wrap. If you refrigerate them for any length of time, place each slice of cucumber or zucchini on a paper-towel-lined tray to continue to absorb excess moisture. This helps to keep the vegetables crisp.

Crab Meat in Endive Leaves

If you are using fresh crab meat, drain it of all liquid; then pick through it carefully with your fingertips to remove any bits of cartilage. If you are using frozen crab meat, defrost it and squeeze out all the liquid, then check carefully for cartilage. Put the crab meat into a small bowl and mix in the onion, parsley, salt, pepper, and juice. Stir in the mayonnaise, using just enough to bind the mixture. Do not make it too soft. Chill the mixture for several hours or overnight.

Cut the root ends off the endives and separate the leaves, using only the leaves large enough to contain the crab meat. The small center leaves can be used in a salad at another time.

To serve, place about 2 teaspoons of the crab-meat mixture in the center of each endive leaf. Arrange the stuffed leaves in a circle like spokes of a wheel on a round platter and place a bunch of parsley or an attractively cut lemon half in the center. The filled leaves should be served shortly after filling, or they will soften. They can be held for up to an hour in the refrigerator, covered tightly with plastic wrap.

1 pound (16 ounces) freshly cooked or frozen crab meat
1 small onion, finely minced
1 tablespoon chopped fresh parsley
Salt and pepper to taste
2 teaspoons fresh lemon or lime juice
3 tablespoons mayonnaise (or enough to bind the mixture)
6 Belgian endives

Lobster and Asparagus Croquettes

1 pound fresh, canned, or frozen
  lobster meat, finely minced
48 asparagus pieces, fresh,
  canned, or frozen
1 cup grated Swiss cheese
¼ cup grated Parmesan cheese
1 tablespoon butter
1 tablespoon flour
½ cup heavy cream
Salt, white pepper, and a dash
  of cayenne pepper
A dash of nutmeg
1 tablespoon sherry
1 loaf thinly sliced white bread
Softened sweet butter (for
  spreading)

If you are using a fresh lobster, drop it in an inch of boiling salted water, cover the kettle, and cook for about 15 minutes. Remove the lobster from the kettle and let it cool to room temperature. Then crack the shells and remove all the meat from the tail, claws, and body. Finely mince the meat. If using canned lobster, drain it well and mince. If using frozen, prepare it according to the directions on the package, drain well, and finely mince. Set the lobster aside.

Trim the pieces of asparagus so they measure about 3 inches from the tip. Discard the trimmed stems or save them for soup or stir-fried vegetables. If you are using fresh asparagus, steam the trimmed pieces about 3 minutes, drain, and cool to room temperature. If using canned, drain well and pat dry with paper towels. If using frozen, defrost and drain on paper towels.

Combine the grated cheeses in a small bowl. Heat the butter in a small saucepan until it is hot and foamy; then whisk in the flour, stirring to form a *roux*. Pour in the heavy cream and bring the mixture to a boil, seasoning with salt, peppers, and nutmeg. Allow it to cook for a minute, remove from the heat, and stir in the sherry. Stir the lobster into the mixture and allow it to cool. Then stir in the cheeses. This mixture can be made a day ahead.

To prepare the croquettes, trim the crusts from the bread and cut each slice of bread on the diagonal into two triangles. You should have forty-eight triangles. If you cannot find thinly sliced bread, use regular white bread and roll each slice flat with a rolling pin. Spread each triangle with some of the softened butter and place a small amount of the lobster mixture on each piece, spreading evenly. Place a piece of asparagus in the center, with the tip pointing toward the tip of the triangle. Roll the bread around the asparagus into cylinders and spread a bit more softened butter over the top of each cylinder. The cylinders can be held in the refrigerator overnight. Cover tightly with plastic wrap.

Bake the croquettes in a preheated 400° oven for 15 minutes or until the bread is lightly toasted and the cheese is melted. Serve at once.

If you like, the lobster can be omitted from the recipe. Increase the grated Swiss cheese to 1½ cups and the Parmesan to ½ cup, and omit the sherry from the white sauce.

Empanadas (South American Meat Pies)

Put the butter and cream cheese into a bowl for the electric mixer and blend. Add the sifted flour mixture and blend on low speed for a few minutes, until the mixture forms a soft ball of dough and leaves the sides of the bowl clean. Gather the dough together, wrap it in wax paper, and refrigerate for at least 30 minutes. The dough can be held in the refrigerator for two or three days, or frozen for several weeks.

To prepare the filling, heat the oil in a small skillet and sauté the ground meat for a few minutes, until it loses its pink color. Break up any large chunks of meat with the back of a wooden spoon. Add the mushrooms, onions, and garlic and sauté for another few minutes. Stir in the remaining ingredients up to the egg yolks, mix well, and remove from heat. Transfer to a small bowl and add the beaten egg yolks, stirring well to bind the mixture. Cool the mixture to room temperature. It can be held in the refrigerator for two or three days or frozen for several weeks.

To prepare the empanadas, break off a small piece of the chilled dough and roll it out on a lightly floured board or pastry cloth to a thickness of ¼ inch. Using a 3-inch cooky cutter, cut rounds of dough; lifting them off the board and set aside. Continue with the chilled dough in this fashion until all of it has been rolled and cut. Any leftover scraps of dough can be rerolled once. Discard any remaining dough after the second roll. You should have at least forty-eight rounds.

Brush the rounds with the beaten egg mixture and place ½ teaspoon of the filling in the center. Fold the top half of the round over the filling to create a crescent-shaped patty. Press the edges of the dough together with the tines of a small fork. Continue in this fashion until all of the rounds have been filled, folded, and tightly closed. The empanadas can be refrigerated overnight at this point or they can be frozen for several weeks. Be sure to wrap them well for refrigerating or freezing.

To bake, brush the tops of the empanadas with some of the egg wash and place them on a lightly buttered cooky sheet. Bake in a preheated 400° oven for 20 minutes or until they are lightly browned and crisp-looking. Serve at once.

8 tablespoons soft sweet butter
3 ounces cream cheese
1¼ cups flour, sifted with ½ teaspoon salt
2 tablespoons olive oil
½ pound ground lamb or beef
¼ pound fresh mushrooms, finely minced
1 small onion, finely minced
1 clove garlic, mashed
2 tablespoons dried currants
2 tablespoons raisins, chopped
2 tablespoons chopped pine nuts, pistachio nuts, or almonds
2 tablespoons tomato paste
2 tablespoons chopped fresh parsley
¼ teaspoon dried cumin
¼ teaspoon dried coriander
Salt and pepper to taste
1 hard-boiled egg, finely chopped
¼ cup stuffed green olives, finely chopped
2 egg yolks, lightly beaten
1 whole egg, lightly beaten with 1 tablespoon cold water

Artichoke-Filled Toast Cups

1 loaf thinly sliced white bread
Softened butter for spreading
1 can (14 ounces) unmarinated
  artichoke hearts
1 cup mayonnaise
1 tablespoon spicy brown
  mustard
1 teaspoon Worcestershire
  sauce
2 tablespoons grated Parmesan
  cheese
Salt and freshly ground black
  pepper to taste
Additional grated Parmesan
  cheese

Using a 2-inch cooky cutter, cut forty-eight rounds from the slices of bread. Spread the rounds lightly with the softened butter and press each round, buttered side up, into a miniature muffin tin. (These are available at shops selling special baking equipment. If you cannot find them, just place the buttered rounds on a cooky sheet.) Toast the cups in a preheated 350° oven for 10 to 15 minutes, until they are crisp but not too brown. Remove them from the oven and cool to room temperature. These cups can be stored, like crackers, in an airtight container for several weeks, or they can be frozen in plastic bags for several months.

Open the can of artichoke hearts and drain off all the liquid. Cut each heart into quarters if they are large, half if they are smaller. You should have at least forty-eight pieces. Spread the pieces on paper towels to drain thoroughly.

Combine the mayonnaise, mustard, Worcestershire sauce, Parmesan, salt, and pepper in a small bowl. Put a dab of the mayonnaise mixture in the bottom of each cup (or spread a small amount over each round of toast). Place a piece of artichoke heart in the center and cover the artichoke with another dab of mayonnaise. Sprinkle the top with grated Parmesan. Continue in this fashion until all the cups are assembled. The prepared canapés can be refrigerated overnight at this point, covered tightly with plastic wrap.

To bake, place the cups in a preheated 400° oven and bake for 15 to 20 minutes, until the tops are slightly browned. Serve at once.

Miniature Pissaladières (French Pizzas)

Put the butter and garlic in a small saucepan and melt the butter. Remove it from the heat and let it sit for about 10 minutes. Using a pastry brush, liberally spread the garlic-flavored butter over the bread slices and set them aside.

Heat the olive oil in a small skillet and sauté the onions for a minute or two until they soften. Stir in the tomato sauce, tomato paste, herbs, and pepper and heat through. Let the mixture come to a boil and cook it for about 3 minutes, until it is quite thick. Remove it from the heat and cool slightly.

To prepare the *pissaladières*, spread a small amount of the tomato mixture over each slice of buttered bread and scatter some of the mozzarella over each. Place a crisscross of anchovy slices in the center and place an olive half on the anchovies where the cross meets. Sprinkle the tops completely with the grated Parmesan cheese. The *pissaladières* can be prepared to this point and held in the refrigerator overnight. Cover tightly with plastic wrap.

Preheat the broiler to high and slide the prepared slices under it to crisp and brown. Watch them carefully so they do not burn. They should be under the broiler no longer than 3 or 4 minutes. Serve at once.

8 tablespoons butter
2 cloves garlic, peeled and cut in half
48 slices of French bread, about ¼ inch thick
1 tablespoon olive oil
1 small onion, finely minced
¼ cup canned tomato sauce
3 tablespoons tomato paste
1 tablespoon chopped fresh parsley
1 teaspoon dried oregano
1 teaspoon dried basil
Freshly ground black pepper to taste
½ cup grated mozzarella cheese
Two 2-ounce cans of flat anchovy fillets, drained
24 pitted black olives, cut in half vertically
¼ cup grated Parmesan cheese

Index

Index

294